Twentieth-Century American Fiction on Screen

D1289578

The essays in this collection analyze major film adaptations of twentieth-century American fiction, from F. Scott Fitzgerald's *The Last Tycoon* to Toni Morrison's *Beloved*. During the century, films based on American literature came to play a central role in the history of the American cinema. Combining cinematic and literary approaches, this volume explores the adaptation process from conception through production and reception. The contributors explore the ways in which political and historical contexts have shaped the transfer from book to screen, and the new perspectives that films bring to literary works. In particular, they examine how the twentieth-century literary modes of realism, modernism, and postmodernism have influenced the forms of modern cinema. Written in a lively and accessible style, the book includes production stills and a detailed filmography. With its companion volume on nineteenth-century fiction, this study offers a comprehensive account of the rich tradition of American literature on screen.

R. BARTON PALMER holds Ph.D. degrees from Yale University (medieval studies) and New York University (cinema studies) and has published widely in those two fields. He is Calhoun Lemon Professor of English at Clemson University, directs the Film Studies Program at Clemson, and is the Director of the South Carolina Film Institute.

Twentieth-Century American Fiction on Screen

Edited by

R. Barton Palmer

CAMBRIDGE
UNIVERSITY PRESS

CAMBRIDGE UNIVERSITY PRESS
Cambridge, New York, Melbourne, Madrid, Cape Town, Singapore, São Paulo

Cambridge University Press
The Edinburgh Building, Cambridge CB2 2RU, UK

Published in the United States of America by Cambridge University Press, New York

www.cambridge.org
Information on this title: www.cambridge.org/9780521542302

© Cambridge University Press 2007

First published 2007

Printed in the United Kingdom at the University Press, Cambridge

A catalogue record for this publication is available from the British Library

ISBN-13 978-0-521-83444-5 hardback
ISBN-10 0-521-83444-9 hardback

ISBN-13 978-0-521-54230-2 paperback
ISBN-10 0-521-54230-8 paperback

Contents

Illustrations

(All film production stills courtesy of the British Film Institute)

Notes on contributors

WILLIAM RODNEY ALLEN teaches at the Louisiana School for Math, Science, and the Arts. His special interests are modern American culture, film, and literature. Among his books are *Walker Percy: A Southern Wayfarer* (1988), *Conversations with Kurt Vonnegut* (1988), and *Understanding Kurt Vonnegut* (1991). His most recent project is a collected edition of the interviews given by the filmmakers Joel and Ethan Coen (forthcoming).

CHRISTOPHER AMES is Provost and Dean of the College at Washington College. He taught formerly at Agnes Scott College where he chaired the English department and was Charles A. Dana Professor of English. In addition to many scholarly articles and book chapters on various aspects of modern American culture, including film, Ames has published *The Life of the Party: Festive Vision in Modern Fiction* (1991) and *Movies about the Movies: Hollywood Reflected* (1998).

MATTHEW BERNSTEIN is Associate Professor and Director of Graduate Studies in the Film Studies department at Emory University. Among his many writings on the history of American film and world cinema are *Walter Wanger: Hollywood Independent* (1994), *Controlling Hollywood: Censorship and Regulation in the Studio Era* (1999), and (both with Gaylyn Studlar) *Visions of the East: Orientalism in Film* (1997) and *John Ford Made Westerns: Filming the Legend in the Studio Era* (2001).

ROBERT H. BRINKMEYER, JR. is Professor of English and chair of the department at the University of Arkansas. Widely published on all aspects of Southern literature and culture, Brinkmeyer has written *Remapping Southern Literature: Contemporary Southern Writers and the West* (2000), *Katherine Anne Porter's Artistic Development: Primitivism, Traditionalism, and Totalitarianism* (1997), and *The Art and Vision of Flannery O'Connor* (1993), among other books.

MARC C. CONNER is Associate Professor of English at Washington & Lee University. His research interests include twentieth-century

American fiction and African-American literature. He edited *Speaking the Unspeakable: The Aesthetic Dimensions of Toni Morrison* (2000), and his essays have appeared in such journals as *Studies in American Fiction* and *Critique*.

STEFFEN HANTKE teaches for the Cultural Studies Program in the English department of Sogang University in Seoul, South Korea. In addition to essays on contemporary literature and film that have appeared in such journals as *Paradoxa*, *College Literature*, and *Post Script*, he has published *Conspiracy and Paranoia in Contemporary Literature* (1994) and *Horror: Creating and Marketing Fear* (2004).

MCKAY JENKINS is Cornelius A. Tilghman Professor of English and Journalism at the University of Delaware, specializing in environmental studies, nonfiction writing, and the history and literature of race relations. He is the author of *The South in Black and White: Race, Sex and Literature in the 1940s* (1999), *The White Death: Tragedy and Heroism in an Avalanche Zone* (2000), and *Bloody Falls of the Coppermine: Madness, Murder and the Collision of Cultures in the Arctic, 1913* (2006).

ROBERT P. KOLKER is Emeritus Professor of English at the University of Maryland. He has also taught at the Georgia Institute of Technology and the University of Virginia. Among his many books on the cinema are *Film, Form, and Culture* (1998), *A Cinema of Loneliness: Penn, Stone, Kubrick, Scorsese, Spielberg, and Altman* (2000), *Landscapes of Dread in the Scapes of Modernity: Welles, Kubrick, and the Imagination of the Visible* (2006), and *"Psycho": A Casebook* (2006).

THOMAS M. LEITCH is Professor of English at the University of Delaware, specializing in film and literary and cultural theory. He has a special interest in such popular narrative modes as detective stories and Hollywood genre films (westerns, musicals, gangster films, and comedies of all sorts). Among his books are *Find the Director and Other Hitchcock Games* (1991), *The Encyclopedia of Alfred Hitchcock* (2002), *Crime Films* (Cambridge, 2002), and *What Stories are: Narrative Theory and Interpretation* (1986).

R. BARTON PALMER is Calhoun Professor of Literature at Clemson University, where he also directs the Film Study Graduate Program. Among his many books on film and literary topics are *Joel and Ethan Coen* (2004), (with David Boyd) *After Hitchcock* (2006), and (with Robert Bray) *Hollywood's Tennessee: Tennessee Williams on Screen* (2006). With Linda Badley, Palmer serves as General Editor of *Traditions in World Cinema*.

ROBERT SKLAR is Professor of Cinema Studies at New York University. Among his many books on film and literary subjects are *F. Scott Fitzgerald: The Last Laocoön* (1967), *City Boys* (1992), *A World History of Film* (2001), and *Movie-Made America: A Cultural History of American Movies* (1999).

ROBERT STAM is University Professor at New York University. His numerous books in film and media studies include *Reflexivity in Film and Literature* (1992), *Subversive Pleasures* (1992), *Literature Through Film: Realism, Magic, and the Art of Adaptation* (2004), and, with Alessandro Raengo, *A Companion to Literature and Film* (2005).

MARK R. WINCHELL is Professor of English at Clemson University. He also serves as the director of the League of the South Institute for Southern History and Culture. His publications include *Cleanth Brooks and the Rise of Modern Criticism* (1996), *Where No Flag Flies: Donald Davidson and the Southern Resistance* (2000), *Too Good to Be True: The Life and Work of Leslie Fiedler* (2002), and *Reinventing the South: Versions of a literary Region* (2006).

ALLEN L. WOLL is Professor of History at Rutgers University-Camden, where he also directs the Film Studies program. He has published *Ethnic and Racial Images in American Film and Literature* (1987), *Black Musical Theatre: From Coontown to Dreamgirls* (1991), and *The Hollywood Musical Goes to War* (1982).

Acknowledgments

The idea for this volume, and its companion, emerged from discussions with Dr. Linda Bree, senior editor at Cambridge University Press, that followed our serendipitous meeting at the Medieval Institute. I have benefited greatly not only from Linda's continuing interest and sound advice on sundry matters, but also from the comments of several anonymous readers, all of whom made very useful criticisms and suggestions. A larger, if more indirect, debt is owed to Jim Naremore of Indiana University and Bob Stam of New York University, whose stimulating work on film/literature adaptation has provided this volume with a theoretical program of sorts. The Calhoun Lemon foundation at Clemson University provided necessary research funds for completing this project, while graduate assistants John Longo and Kevin Manus ably assisted with copyediting the manuscript.

Introduction

R. Barton Palmer

Since the early days of the commercial cinema, many, perhaps most, important works of literary fiction have found a subsequent life on the screen, extending their reach and influence. Filmmakers, in turn, have enjoyed the economic and critical benefits of recycling what the industry knows as "pre-sold properties." No doubt, this complex intersection has deeply marked both arts. Keith Cohen, for example, has persuasively argued that cinematic narrative exerted a decisive influence on the shift in novelistic aesthetics from "telling" to "showing," providing new depth of meaning to the old maxim *ut pictura poiesis*.[1] Film theorists, in turn, most notably Sergei Eisenstein, have emphasized the formative influence on cinematic storytelling of the classic realist novel, whose techniques and themes, adapted by D. W. Griffith and others, made possible a filmic art of extended narrative. Modern fictional form has been shaped by filmic elements such as montage, shifting point of view, and close attention to visual texture. An enabling condition of this constant and mutually fruitful exchange has been the unconventional conventionality of both art forms, their generic receptivity to outside influence. As Robert Stam puts it, "both the novel and the fiction film are *summas* by their very nature. Their essence is to have no essence, to be open to all cultural forms."[2]

Screen adaptations provide ideal critical sites not only for examining in detail how literary fiction is accommodated to cinematic form, but also for tracing the history of the symbiotic relationship of the two arts and the multifarious and ever-shifting connections between the commercial institutions responsible for their production. Until recently, however, neoromantic assumptions about the preeminent value of the source text have discouraged a thorough analysis of the complex negotiations (financial, authorial, commercial, legal, formal, generic, etc.) that bring adaptations into being and deeply affect their reception. Traditionalist aesthetic considerations have also foreclosed discussion of the place of adaptations within the history of the cinema. For this latter is a critical task that requires the identification and analysis of contextual issues that have little,

1

if anything, to do with the source. In sum, the notion of "faithfulness" as the sole criterion of worth positions the adaptation disadvantageously, as only a secondary version of an honored work from another art form. An exclusive view of the adaptation as a replication closes off its discussion not only *per se*, but also *in se*. From the point of view of the source, an adaptation can only reflect value, for it does not result from the originary, creative process that produced its model. Traditional adaptation studies thus strive to estimate the value of what, by its nature, can possess no value of its own.

For this reason, it is not surprising that literary scholars have too often viewed adaptations as only more or less irrelevant, if occasionally interesting, copies, as mere supplements to the literary source. From this viewpoint, the importance of adaptations is quite limited to the fact that they make their sources more available, extending the influence of literary masterpieces. Film scholars, in turn, have often viewed with suspicion and distaste the dependence of the screen adaptation on a novelistic pretext, seeing "literary" cinema as a less than genuine form of film art. The "grand theory" developed during the past three decades has emphasized the description and analysis of various aspects of cinematic specificity; grand theory, however, has not for the most part concerned itself with the intersemiotic relationships that generate and define the formal features of film adaptations. A nascent discipline, eager to establish its independence, perhaps could not afford such tolerance and breadth of critical vision. An approach that postulated films as in some sense secondary, especially as derivative versions of valued literary texts, would enact in microcosmic form the institutional bondage of film to literature. It would also reinforce the notion that the cinema was a parasitic art form, dependent on prior literary creation. Providing popular abridgements of literary masterpieces (to make the obvious point) hardly argued for the cultural importance of what Gilbert Seldes terms the seventh of "the lively arts." Studying filmic adaptation ran counter to the new theorizing about the cinema in the 1970s – not to mention the academic respectability and independence for which such work implicitly campaigned. For literary and film scholars alike, adaptation studies encountered disfavor on both intellectual and institutional grounds.

During the past five years, however, the increasing popularity in cinema studies of what is usually termed "middle level theory" has turned the attention of scholars back toward the analysis of, and limited *in parvo* theorizing about, the material history of films and filmmaking, including the cinema's relationship with literature. A key role in this development has been the increasing institutional presence of cultural studies (or, in its more politically self-conscious British form, cultural materialism). Now recognized as a legitimate academic specialty, cultural studies ignores the formal and institutional boundaries between film and literature, even as it provides fertile ground for working on their interconnections. As Stam has recently remarked, "From a cultural studies perspective, adaptation forms part of a flattened out and newly egalitarian spectrum of cultural production. Within a comprehensively textualized world of images and simulations, adaptation becomes just another text, forming part of a broad discursive continuum."[3] From this point of view, treating a film as an "adaptation" is a matter of critical politics as well as of facts, the result of a decision to privilege one form of connection or influence over any number of others.

Other recent developments in postmodern theory have made it possible for literary and film scholars alike to take a more nuanced and positive look at film adaptations. There is no doubt, in fact, that the field has been thriving, with a number of important theoretical works published during the past decade. In particular, intertextuality theory and Bakhtinian dialogics now hold prominent positions in literary and film studies. Intertextuality contests the received notion of closed and self-sufficient "works," their borders impermeable to influence, their structures unwelcoming of alien forms. As an archly postmodernist critical form, intertextuality provides an ideal theoretical basis from which can proceed an account of the shared identity of the literary source and its cinematic reflex. More radically, intertextual theory can be used to challenge the very notion of a privileged source/adaptation relationship by identifying the potentially innumerable pressures that affect the shaping of the adaptation; these pressures can be considered "texts" and any distinction between such texts and the contexts of production is arguably no more than a matter of analytical preference or rhetoric. In any case, any consideration of filmic adaptation means speaking of one text while speaking of another. Adaptation is by definition transtextual, to use Gérard Genette's more precise and inclusive taxonomic concept of textual relations. A peculiar doubleness characterizes the adaptation. For it is a presence that stands for and signifies the absence of the source-text. An adaptation refers to two texts with the same identity that are not the same. Such forms of permeable and shared textuality can be accounted for only by critical approaches that focus on interrelations of different sorts, including the (dis)connections between literary and cinematic contexts.

In film studies the decline of grand theory has enabled the field to take the direction that theorist Dudley Andrew has long advocated: a "sociological turn" toward the consideration of the institutional and contextual pressures that condition the process of adaptation and define what role the adaptation comes to play in the history of the cinema. Critical studies of literary/film relations are beginning to focus on "how adaptation serves the cinema," as Andrew puts it; and this new direction of inquiry has the added advantage of shedding light on how the literary source is affected by becoming part of an intertextual, intersemiotic, interinstitutional series.[4] Robert Stam provides an anatomy of source/adaptation relationships; these are surprisingly varied: "One way to look at adaptation is to see it as a matter of a source novel's hypotext being transformed by a complex series of operations: selection, amplification, concretization, actualization, critique, extrapolation, analogization, popularization, and reculturalization."[5]

Comparing the source and adaptation draws attention to the specific negotiations of various kinds involved in the process of transformation. Consideration can then be given to the role the resulting film comes to play within the cinema. The foundational premise of the approaches taken by the contributors to this volume has been that adaptations possess a value in themselves, apart from the ways in which they might be judged as (in)accurate replications of literary originals. Because it is sometimes a goal that guides those responsible for the adaptation process, faithfulness has found a place in the analyses collected here more as an aspect of context rather than a criterion of value. The fact (more often, the promise) of fidelity in some sense can also figure rhetorically in the contextualization of the film, most notably as a feature promoted by the marketing campaign. But very often it plays no crucial role in the transformation process and merits less critical attention than more relevant issues.

Undeniably, adaptations constitute an important area of modern cultural production, making them worthy and appropriate objects of study. But how to organize that study? Seeing a text as an adaptation means invoking its relations to two distinct but interconnected cultural series and its insertion within two divergent institutional histories; adaptations thereby become the analytical objects of two separate but not dissimilar disciplines in which topical, author-oriented, genre, and period forms of organization predominate. Film/literature adaptation courses are becoming increasingly prominent in university curricula, and they are usually housed within English or literature departments, where they are often organized, following the most common disciplinary paradigm, in terms of literary period. That practice has been followed in this volume and its companion, *Nineteenth-Century American Fiction on Screen*. This is by no means the only interesting or pedagogically useful way in which adaptations might be studied. In fact, Thomas Leitch, one of the contributors to this volume, in his essay on the various versions of *The Killers* raises an interesting challenge to such a privileging of the literary text and of the literary series more generally. Even so, it is indisputable that organization of the source-texts by period has the not inconsiderable virtue of offering literature teachers a familiar body of fiction with which to work. Additionally, this approach focuses narrowly on a selected stretch of literary history, permitting the analysis of how movements, themes, and dominant formal features have undergone "cinematicization." In treating American fiction of the past century, this volume marshals a broad sweep of expert opinion, literary and cinematic, on an equally broad field of texts.

Twentieth-Century American Fiction on Screen has been conceived to fill the need for an up-to-date survey of the important films made from these texts, with the book's unity deriving in the first instance from the literary and cultural connections among the various sources. The fourteen essays collected here, written expressly for this volume, each address the adaptation (occasionally adaptations) of single literary texts, though discussion, where relevant, also ranges over screen versions of other works by the same author, other releases from the same director, or films that are otherwise relevant. This book has a focus that provides a ready organization for courses in adaptation, with readings and viewings easily coordinated with the essays. Despite their singular emphasis, the essays also open up discussion into broader areas of importance. Although the scheme adopted here is in the first instance literary, the different essays are also deeply cinematic, addressing specific aspects of the adaptation process, including details of production where relevant and usually seeking to define the role the film came to play within the history of the American cinema. Some contributors discuss the intersemiotic aspects of transferring a narrative from one medium to another, while others consider in depth the problems of authorship, an important question whenever the work of a valued author becomes part of the oeuvre of an important director or when the contributions of a screenwriter prove significant and defining.

Much thought has gone into the selection of novels and films. My starting point was to review all commercial American adaptations of twentieth-century American fiction from the sound era, roughly 1930 to the present. The extensive corpus of cinematic material has made it possible to exemplify the varied fictional traditions of the period, from traditional forms of realism (*The Color Purple, The Killers, The Last Tycoon, The Member of the Wedding, Ship of Fools, The Thin Red Line*), modernism (*The Day of the Locust, Intruder in the Dust, Lolita, Wise Blood*), and postmodernism (*Naked Lunch, Short Cuts, Slaughterhouse-Five*). It has also proved possible to offer a cross-section of authors, with five works written by women. I thought it appropriate as well to include two works, Nathanael West's *The Day of the Locust* and F. Scott Fitzgerald's *The Last Tycoon*, that engage interestingly with the American film industry and with Hollywood as a cultural phenomenon. In the silent era not many feature films were adapted from twentieth-century fictional texts, and the few that were, in any case, are often too difficult to obtain for classroom use. Only films that had been commercially released in either VHS or DVD format and remain readily obtainable in either of these two formats made the final list. Full filmographies are included as an appendix.

The writers represented here are all *major* in the sense that they have been and remain the subject of substantial critical work. They also continue to find a readership; their works, in other words, remain in print. While nearly all the writers on the list are what we would now term "high cultural," I have decided to include one writer, James Jones, who might be described as a popular writer with substantial historical, but also literary, importance. In the final analysis, of course, both the criteria used and the particular choices made are subjective, in the sense that they are based, first, on my knowledge of and experience with literary and film study and, second, on my appraisal of what material would appeal to scholarly and general readers, yet also prove useful in the classroom. I do not know, of course, any more than anyone else, how to decide *objectively* what works, literary or cinematic, should be thought *major*. Among other prominent rankings, the American Film Institute has compiled a list of the "100 Best American Films." A number of the films I have selected, but by no means all, are on this list. If there is a comparable list for twentieth-century American novels and short fiction, I am not familiar with it, but most of the literary texts chosen for this volume would likely be on it. But even if such a list did exist, its authoritative value would be dubious. The canon of literary study remains very much in dispute and can hardly be said to be fixed or stable, as scholars such as Paul Lauter have shown.[6]

In planning this book, the status of both authors and works was in fact a preliminary condition. That I considered them *major* was a necessary but not sufficient reason for inclusion. Another important purpose of this volume is to exemplify the *process* of adaptation and provide detailed discussion of how adaptations have served the cinema. In making the selections from among major works by major authors, I have picked formally and culturally interesting adaptations, by which I mean those that can be shown to have served the cinema in some significant or revealing fashion. For example, the fictional text might offer technical challenges (e.g., how do you film a novel with prominent antirealist elements such as *Naked Lunch*?) or the context of the adaptation might be interesting from the viewpoint of Hollywood history (e.g., in the case of *Intruder in the Dust*, Hollywood's renewed concern during the late 1940s with racism). The film might constitute an important part of a director's oeuvre, with the source thus inserted into two expressive series, one literary and the other cinematic. In fact, most of the films selected here belong to the oeuvres of respected old and new Hollywood *auteurs*, a roll of honor that includes Robert Altman, David Cronenberg, John Huston, Elia Kazan, Stanley Kramer, Stanley Kubrick, Terrence Malick, John Schlesinger, Steven Spielberg, and Fred Zinnemann. As the contributors to this volume demonstrate, the films discussed herein all hold an interest that, while determined to a large degree by their status as adaptations, also derives from their insertion within the history of Hollywood and the larger cultural role that the movies played in twentieth-century America.

NOTES

1. Keith Cohen, *Film and Fiction: The Dynamics of Exchange* (New Haven: Yale University Press, 1979). See also his *Writing in a Film Age: Essays by Contemporary Novelists* (Niwot, CO: University Press of Colorado, 1991).
2. Robert Stam, "Beyond Fidelity: The Dialogics of Adaptation," in James Naremore, ed., *Film Adaptation* (New Brunswick, NJ: Rutgers University Press, 2000), p. 61.
3. Robert Stam, "Introduction," in Robert Stam and Alessandra Raengo, eds., *Literature and Film: A Guide to the Theory and Practice of Film Adaptation* (Oxford: Blackwell, 2004), pp. 9–10.
4. Dudley J. Andrew, "Adaptation," in Naremore, ed., *Film Adaptation*, p. 35.
5. Stam, "Dialogics of Adaptation," p. 68.
6. See especially Paul Lauter, *Canons and Contexts* (Oxford: Oxford University Press, 1991).

1   Filming an unfinished novel:
The Last Tycoon

Robert Sklar

When F. Scott Fitzgerald (b. 1896) died of a heart attack at age forty-four, on December 21, 1940, in Hollywood, he left behind a novel-in-progress about the motion picture industry. A few weeks later, his companion, the Hollywood columnist Sheilah Graham, sent the author's draft materials to his editor, Maxwell Perkins, at Charles Scribner's Sons. After considering several options, including hiring another writer to complete the work following Fitzgerald's outlines and notes, Perkins enlisted the literary critic (and friend of Fitzgerald) Edmund Wilson – whom Graham had also contacted shortly after the author's death – to shape and edit the manuscript for publication. As titles, Fitzgerald had considered "Stahr: A Romance," after the novel's central character, Monroe Stahr, a Hollywood studio executive, and "The Love of the Last Tycoon: A Western," giving the work a different, perhaps more ironic, genre connotation. Wilson's version was published in October 1941 as *The Last Tycoon: An Unfinished Novel*, in a volume with *The Great Gatsby* and five of Fitzgerald's most important short stories.[1]

"Unfinished works by great writers form a category as haunting as it is unsatisfactory," the novelist Alan Hollinghurst has written. "In gratifying a curiosity about what might have been, they heighten the feeling of loss."[2] One certainly feels a sense of loss at Fitzgerald's early death, yet in the case of *The Last Tycoon* what exists in published form seems almost more of a benefaction than a cause for regret. Perkins puzzled over whether what Graham had sent him was publishable at all. Fitzgerald had drafted little more than half of the planned episodes, and expected to rewrite nearly everything that he had completed. The unwritten sections were to have involved a turn toward violence and murder plots, and might have drastically altered the tone of what appeared in print in 1941. "It would require some re-arrangement, and it would not be well proportioned, and would chiefly tell a secondary story, a love episode in the life of the hero," Perkins wrote to Wilson, and the critic, following the editor's lead, changed words, moved scenes, and created chapters,

Figure 1. Elia Kazan's *The Last Tycoon* is largely the story of a doomed romance between studio mogul Monroe Stahr (Robert De Niro) and Kathleen Moore (Ingrid Boulting), who resembles his dead wife. A 1976 Academy Productions/Paramount Pictures release.

forging the work that we know now out of the author's more-or-less raw material.[3]

Matthew J. Bruccoli, who edited a scholarly version of Fitzgerald's drafts more than half a century after the novel's original appearance, criticizes the "cosmeticized text" that Wilson produced.[4] "*The Last Tycoon* is not really an 'unfinished novel,'" Bruccoli has asserted, "if that term describes a work that is partly finished. The only way to regard it is as material toward a novel."[5] Nevertheless, what Wilson accomplished for Fitzgerald should not be underestimated. As Fitzgerald's first book publication since a short story collection in 1935, the 1941 *The Last Tycoon* once again brought before the reading public what Perkins called "those magical sentences and phrases and paragraphs that only Scott could write," and launched the revival of the author's reputation that catapulted him from neglect to preeminence as a twentieth-century American writer.[6]

As a facet of Fitzgerald's recuperation, the Philco Television Playhouse adapted *The Last Tycoon* for live dramatization on October 16, 1949, a few months after Paramount Pictures' *The Great Gatsby*, the first sound film based on a Fitzgerald work, appeared in cinemas. John Frankenheimer directed another live television version of *The Last Tycoon* for the Playhouse 90 series on March 14, 1957, with Jack Palance in the role of Monroe Stahr.[7] In 1965 the producer Lester Cowan (who in 1939 had hired Fitzgerald to write a screenplay of his short story "Babylon Revisited" as a potential, but unrealized, vehicle for Shirley Temple), announced plans to film *The Last Tycoon* for M-G-M release, with a script by the novelist and screenwriter Irwin Shaw.[8] Nothing came of this, either, and the producer Sam Spiegel acquired rights to the novel in the early 1970s. Spiegel engaged the British playwright Harold Pinter to write the screenplay, even though he had heavily criticized Pinter's script for Joseph Losey's *Accident* (1967) and dropped out of producing that film.[9] Eventually, Elia Kazan joined the project as director, and *The Last Tycoon*, with principal photography completed in January 1976, was released by Paramount on November 15, 1976. The relation between two collaborations – the Fitzgerald-Perkins-Wilson novel and the Spiegel-Pinter-Kazan film – is the subject of this essay.

2

"There is probably no more pathetic image in recent literary mythology," writes Mark Royden Winchell, "than that of F. Scott Fitzgerald in Hollywood."[10] The myth that Winchell interrogates is of Hollywood as corrupter and destroyer of literary talent. Yet Fitzgerald's image, as he describes it, adheres closely to the known facts: the author's literary and financial difficulties that led him in the mid-1930s to seek employment as a screenwriter; his contract with M-G-M beginning in July 1937; bitter squabbles with co-workers; limited success at his work; feelings of abjection and resentment at his status and treatment; renewed alcohol abuse. When M-G-M dropped him after eighteen months, there was fruitless freelance screen work and short story writing to pay the bills. Not to speak of his fatal heart attack and truncated novel-in-progress.

At the heart of his difficulties, claims Tom Dardis, lay "a certain snobbish contempt for, or perhaps fear of, the medium" of motion pictures.[11] In a 1936 *Esquire* essay that formed part of his "Crack-Up" self-reflections, Fitzgerald framed such attitudes within his characteristic concerns about cultural change and power. "I saw that the novel," he wrote in "Pasting It Together,"

> which at my maturity was the strongest and supplest medium for conveying thought and emotion from one human being to another, was becoming subordinated to a mechanical and communal art that, whether in the hands of Hollywood merchants or Russian idealists, was capable of reflecting only the tritest thought, the most obvious emotion. It was an art in which words were subordinated to images, where personality was worn down to the inevitable low gear of collaboration. As long past as 1930, I had a hunch that the talkies would make even the best selling novelist as archaic as silent pictures . . . there was a rankling indignity, that to me had become almost an obsession, in seeing the power of the written word subordinated to another power, a more glittering power, a grosser power.[12]

If these sentiments hampered his survival as a screenwriter, as he became more deeply familiar with the movie industry they also stimulated his thinking about its creative processes, its personnel and internal politics, and its cultural significance. *The Last Tycoon* is almost invariably, and necessarily, apprehended within the framework of Fitzgerald's biography and artistic goals – as is the case in my study of his career, *F. Scott Fitzgerald: The Last Laocoön*[13] – or within the genre of the Hollywood novel, alongside contemporaneous works such as Nathanael West's *The Day of the Locust* and Budd Schulberg's *What Makes Sammy Run?* Yet Fitzgerald's effort also deserves to be taken seriously as film history. His notes (Wilson's selection, covering thirty pages in the 1941 edition, and Bruccoli's more extensive publication of photocopied handwritten notes and typescripts) and the novel itself comprise one of the earliest and most elaborated attempts to analyze the studio system and its transformations at the height of its success.[14]

The relevant comparison in this context is to Leo C. Rosten, whose sociological study of the structure and values of the motion picture community, *Hollywood: The Movie Colony, The Movie Makers*, funded by foundation grants and involving more than four thousand questionnaires filled out by studio employees of all ranks, was completed in summer 1941 and published later that year, around the same time as *The Last Tycoon*.[15] It should be emphasized that Fitzgerald's manuscript and notes delve more deeply than does the sociologist into the role of unions and the Communist Party in 1930s Hollywood politics, and make a more concerted attempt to link motion pictures to overarching themes of American history. The subject of Jews in the movie industry, moreover, is of considerable interest to Fitzgerald, while Rosten, already becoming known as a popular writer on the Yiddish language and American religions, almost entirely elides it.[16]

Fitzgerald modeled his protagonist principally on Irving Thalberg, the "boy wonder" movie executive who had managed Universal Pictures at the age of twenty, became production head at the newly formed M-G-M at twenty-four, and died in 1936 age of thirty-seven from lifelong heart disease brought on by childhood rheumatic fever. Thalberg's peers regarded him as a figure who brought class and prestige to an industry that had sorely lacked both. With even its pioneers displaying a hearty longevity, his early death seemed all the more stark. A few months afterward, the Academy of Motion Picture Arts and Sciences enshrined his name by creating the Irving G. Thalberg Memorial Award, to be given to individuals who had attained "the most consistent high level of production achievement."[17] Thalberg's memory was still fresh when *The Last Tycoon* first appeared, and a few astute readers noted the unpublicized links between him and the fictional Stahr. As Fitzgerald's legend soared over the next generation, however, his fictional character surpassed in prominence its historical source. In a 1969 Thalberg biography, the Hollywood journalist Bob Thomas devoted the first chapter to disentangling his subject from Fitzgerald's creation.[18]

The word "tycoon" derives from Japanese and Chinese written characters signifying "great prince." It was applied in pre-1868 Japan to the shoguns who held virtually complete power over their domains while persons of higher rank – Japan's emperors – were nominally in charge. If the analogy between the shoguns and figures such as Thalberg and Stahr was not exactly precise, Thalberg's reputation rested on his effective control of the entire moviemaking process, even though he was technically subordinate to Lewis B. Mayer, M-G-M's first vice-president and general manager – who was in turn overseen by the studio's corporate owner, Loew's, Inc. Thalberg effectively made the day-to-day decisions involving all the company's projects: acquisition of properties, scriptwriting, casting, assignment of directors, reviewing the daily rushes, editing and postproduction. Producers like Thalberg supervised and evaluated the work of their creative talent. Whether they were themselves "creative," or authors in any conventional meaning of the term, has been a matter of debate. Yet one might choose to regard them as the true *auteurs* of the studio system, in the sense that their company's products bore the stamp of their personal taste (or commercial calculation) more than that of any other individual.[19]

But how could Thalberg or Stahr be construed as "last" tycoons? In Thalberg's case, because of his delicate health, in the early 1930s he began to doubt whether he could survive the demanding schedule that his responsibilities entailed. Linked to this calculation were mutual antipathies and resentments that were souring his relationship with Mayer. When Thalberg and his wife, the actress Norma Shearer, took an extended overseas vacation in spring 1933, Mayer seized the opportunity to remove him as head of production. On Thalberg's return to a restructured studio, he became one of several producers in charge of their own individual units. No longer would a shogun-like figure hold more actual power than the emperor at M-G-M. Nevertheless, tycoons did not disappear from Hollywood. One such figure, who never managed to build a legend comparable to Thalberg's, was Hal B. Wallis at Warner Brothers, nominally subordinate to Jack L. Warner, the brother whose title was vice-president in charge of production. Wallis won the Thalberg Award for 1938 (following first-time recipient Darryl F. Zanuck) and again for 1943, galling his boss.[20]

In Thalberg's image, Fitzgerald's "last" tycoon confronted a rival within his studio – Pat Brady was clearly drawn from Mayer, though his ethnic origins were Irish rather than Jewish – and also faced opposition from outside the movie industry. The final chapter in Wilson's edition involves Stahr's intellectual and finally physical confrontation with a Communist union organizer, Brimmer. The novelist replicated Thalberg's antipathy to the founding in 1933 of the Screen Writers Guild, which the executive tried to counter by forming a house union, the Screen Playwrights, and by threats to close down the studio if the writers went out on strike. At one point in their verbal sparring, Fitzgerald has the union man say to Stahr, "We'd like to take you over as a going concern" (125). The remark represents one strand in Fitzgerald's configuration of the industry's power struggles, and of the tycoon under siege. In a manuscript note Fitzgerald wrote, "Stahr didn't die of overwork – he died of a certain number of forces allied against him."[21]

3

Fitzgerald chose to tell Stahr's story through the narrative voice of Cecilia Brady, his antagonist's daughter. The author had used a similar strategy previously with Nick Carraway in *The Great Gatsby*, but in the new work the narrator's circumstances were markedly different – in age, in gender, and in her emotional attachment to the protagonist. Carraway takes a more mature and reserved perspective on his novel's central character, and one that is less judgmental (so far as this is an apt comparison between a finished and an unfinished work). As with *The Great Gatsby*, Cecilia is looking back on events that occurred years before her recounting of them – in Carraway's case two years, in hers, five. In 1935, the setting of the novel's action, she was nineteen years old, a college junior, and Stahr was thirty-four. Her status as a movie executive's daughter solicits the reader's credence that she has sufficient access and experience to be a trusted chronicler – in the novel's opening paragraph she notes ironically that Rudolph Valentino attended her fifth birthday party, "to indicate that even before the age of reason I was in a position to watch the wheels go round" (3).

Nevertheless, Fitzgerald may have felt the need to give further attention to Cecilia's narrative authority. Twice in Chapter 5 of Wilson's edition similar phrases occur – "This is Cecilia taking up the narrative in person" (77), "This is Cecilia taking up the story" (98), to indicate events in which she personally participates as opposed to those she imagines. The link between what she observes and what she invents is earlier elaborated at the beginning of several chapters that are intended, she tells us, to relate how Stahr functions at the studio. "It is drawn partly from a paper I wrote in college on *A Producer's Day* and partly from my imagination," she writes. "More often I have blocked in the ordinary events myself, while the stranger ones are true" (28–29). As the novel stands in its unfinished state, these paradoxical self-reflections add a tantalizing open-ended element to the reader's opinion of the narrator's reliability, in ways that further differentiate her from Carraway's role in *Gatsby*.

At the end of the day in Stahr's life that Cecilia describes, which comprises nearly a third of the published text, she returns to the question of how she knows what she tells. She cites several sources for her information about Stahr's activities: her father, a visiting European dignitary who was a guest at an important luncheon, and a writer friend. "As for me," she concludes, "I was head over heels in love with him then, and you can take what I say for what it's worth" (67). This confession – actually an intensified reiteration of feelings she has averred from the beginning – adds a further twist to the issue of her narrative credibility. It may also bring into focus Fitzgerald's thinking when he proposed as a tentative title, "Stahr: A Romance." With his roots in the Romantic poets and a continuing interest in literary modes, he may have been positioning his work within a genre whose contours were familiar to him. "The romancer," writes Northrop Frye, "does not attempt to create 'real people' so much as stylized figures which expand into psychological archetypes . . . That is why the romance so often radiates a glow of subjective intensity that the novel lacks."[22] Frye, to be sure, suggests that the forms of prose fiction are mixed, so that the archetypal and allegorical qualities of the romance are typically rooted in the novel's social world.

In its generic sense, and with its narrator speaking of her love for the hero, *The Last Tycoon* often builds Stahr into a figure of romantic imagination. "He had a long time ago run ahead through trackless wastes of perception into fields where very few men were able to follow him," (17–18) says Cecilia, and later, "He was a marker in industry like Edison and Lumière and Griffith and Chaplin. He led pictures way up past the range and power of the theatre, reaching a sort of golden age, before the censorship" (28). Yet even toward Stahr the narrator cannot repress the ironic tone that she establishes from the start about herself. For the writer Wylie White, after a script meeting, "the mixture of common sense, wise sensibility, theatrical ingenuity, and a certain half-naïve conception of the common weal which Stahr had just stated aloud, inspired him to do his part, to get his block of stone in place, even if the effort were fore-doomed, the result as dull as a pyramid" (43). Watching rushes in the screening room, "Stahr must be right always, not most of the time, but always – or the structure would melt down like gradual butter" (56).

To what extent is Stahr himself a romantic? As Perkins had noted to Wilson, the material that Fitzgerald had most extensively developed told chiefly "a secondary story, a love episode in the life of the hero." Like Thalberg, Stahr had married an actress, but (fiction veering from fact) she had died. When an earthquake strikes Southern California, causing a flood at the studio, Stahr sees, clinging to a floating head of the goddess Siva, a woman who is identical in appearance to his dead wife. His pursuit, conquest, and then loss of her indeed comprise a major focus of the existing work. What precisely is the significance of this element in the story? The arrival of this simulacrum seems to offer him a second chance. His marriage, says Cecilia, "had been the most appropriate and regal match imaginable" (96), but he had not been in love with his wife until just before she died, and then, curiously, with her and death together. "Like many brilliant men, he had grown up dead cold" (97) but he had learned emotions like lessons – how else could he have conceived the romantic ideas that suffused his movies? In the crucial moment, however, when he is ready to step forward into a new life with the dead wife's double, "something else said to sleep on it as an adult, *no romantic*" (115; italics added). The chance is lost.

"Monroe Stahr is a hero without a flaw," the novel's most assiduous scholar, Matthew Bruccoli, astonishingly asserts.[23] How is it possible to contemplate such a view in the light, for example, of an episode in which Stahr and his dead wife's lookalike, Kathleen Moore, after lovemaking, are walking on the beach during a grunion run. They meet a "negro man" (sic) who, in conversation, tells them that he never goes to movies. "There's no profit. I never let my children go," he says (92). The man leaves, "unaware that he had rocked an industry" (93). Stahr goes back to the studio and throws "four pictures out of his plans . . . he submitted the borderline pictures to the negro [sic] and found them trash" (95). One might say that this odd, brief interpolation in what is otherwise a love scene exposes a flaw so fundamental that it calls everything Stahr does in his work into question, exposing a gap between Hollywood's self-created legend of its world-historical significance, and the possibility of public indifference or inattention.

The Last Tycoon is filled with similar probing moments, insightful passages, striking turns of phrase. As an uncompleted fragment, its ambiguities and contradictions are apparent, and Fitzgerald's path to resolving them remains unclear. They stand as a legacy to anyone who undertakes the novel's adaptation to another medium.

4

The project to make a movie of *The Last Tycoon* rolled forward on waves of overlapping cycles in 1970s Hollywood filmmaking. The Fitzgerald boom was still ascending, highlighted by the Robert Redford-Mia Farrow *The Great Gatsby* (1974) – a fashion rather than a cinematic success – but also including two made-for-television biopics, *F. Scott Fitzgerald and "The Last of the Belles"* (1974) and *F. Scott Fitzgerald in Hollywood* (1976), both of which played in primetime on the ABC network. The 1930s era also held a fascination for the post-1960s generation, nostalgic in *The Sting* (1973), sociopolitical in *Chinatown* (1974), both nostalgic and sociopolitical in *Bound for Glory* (1976), among numerous other titles with Depression-era themes; *The Sting* won an Academy Award and the other two were Best Picture nominees. And the novel with which *The Last Tycoon* was often paired, West's *The Day of the Locust*, came to the screen in 1975 (see the chapter on this by Chris Ames in this volume).

Producer Spiegel wanted to adapt the novel, his friends joked, because he thought its title applied to him. This was not entirely a narcissistic delusion. Born in 1901, he was indeed among the last of Hollywood's old-style producers – and, to boot, as an independent his power was shogun-like in relation to the studio executives who financed and distributed his movies. He received the Thalberg Award for 1963, and over the next nine years it was either not given out (five years) or went to directors who produced their own films (William Wyler, Robert Wise, Alfred Hitchcock, Ingmar Bergman). He owned the record – and still does – for three Best

Picture Oscars won as a solo producer (*On the Waterfront* [1954]; *The Bridge on the River Kwai* [1957]; *Lawrence of Arabia* [1962]).

At first M-G-M backed the project, with Buck Henry slated to write and Mike Nichols to direct.[24] When Thalberg's old studio dropped out, Spiegel moved on to Paramount, whose production head, Robert Evans, had shown an affinity in developing *Gatsby*, *Chinatown*, and the West adaptation. Nichols stayed on after the shift but Henry did not, and it was at this point that Spiegel turned to Pinter for the screenplay. Calling this choice "both brilliant and bizarre," a Spiegel biographer, Andrew Sinclair, offers perhaps the most reasonable justification, that the producer wanted a writer with a detached perspective – with neither experience of Hollywood nor a style in any way similar to Fitzgerald's evocative, lyrical prose.[25] Pinter wrote, Spiegel and Nichols worked with him on rewrites, and then Nichols also opted out. With a final screenplay apparently set, Elia Kazan – whose greatest triumph, *On the Waterfront*, had been with Spiegel, but who earlier in the 1970s had declared himself finished with filmmaking – agreed to direct, and the last elements began to fall into place.

The Last Tycoon – to jump ahead – flopped critically and at the box office (though it has defenders and admirers), and such prominent failures inevitably produce a welter of anecdotal finger pointing, shoulder shrugging, and buck-passing. Who made the poor decisions? Whose heart was not in it? Was the whole idea not misbegotten from the start? The wily Spiegel, having spent $7.5 million of other people's money on a film that took in perhaps $1.5 million in rentals at the domestic box office, nevertheless made a profit, because his foreign investors were not to be paid back until the picture earned in overseas revenue a figure it never came close to attaining.[26]

Of the principals, Kazan was the most voluble, and the least forgiving. His major input at the preproduction stage was to campaign successfully for the casting of Robert De Niro as Stahr, though Dustin Hoffman had been the frontrunner, and had perhaps been offered the role. "He is young for us but he has something of mystery and magic," Kazan wrote to Pinter, "and something surprising and powerful that Hoffman doesn't have."[27] The director's assessment prevailed, and De Niro was the only figure involved in the film – other than the art direction-set decoration team, who received an Oscar nomination – to garner favorable notices. The casting of South African model Ingrid Boulting for her first significant screen role as Kathleen Moore was widely considered to be a mistake, not only in the reviews but also by some, Pinter specifically, prior to production. Kazan suggests that Spiegel promoted her because of his amorous intentions – and similarly with Theresa Russell, who made her film-acting debut as Cecilia Brady – yet managed to maneuver the director into the role of advocate, enabling the producer himself to take on an appearance of neutrality.[28]

A key phrase in Kazan's letter to Pinter is "[h]e is young for us." In his early thirties when the film went into production, De Niro would be several years younger than the character he was playing (Hoffman, born in the same year as Jack Nicholson, another contender mentioned for the role, would have been several years older). Yet Kazan's remark highlights an unacknowledged aspect of the film, its geriatric aura. Someone seems to have had the idea that peopling the supporting roles with recognizable veterans of the studio era would increase the nostalgic appeal, ignoring the fact that Hollywood in the 1930s was predominantly a young person's game. The film plays old: with the exception mainly of De Niro and Russell, who was in her late teens like Cecilia, most of the performers played characters whose historical antecedents would have been younger than they were.

Louis B. Mayer was fifty in 1935, Cecilia says in the novel that her father is forty-seven, while Robert Mitchum (Pat Brady) was ten years older. Aldous Huxley, Fitzgerald's model for Boxley the writer, was in his early forties at that time; Donald Pleasance (Boxley) was nearly sixty. M-G-M's leading female star, Greta Garbo, turned thirty in 1935; Jeanne Moreau, who plays the studio's female star, was approaching fifty. Dana Andrews (Red Ridingwood, the sacked director) was in his mid-sixties, but it is unlikely that anyone near that age was directing on the M-G-M lot. The studio's veteran directors were in their late forties; in 1935 D. W. Griffith, who started directing one-reel films back in 1908, was a mere sixty. Then there's Ray Milland (Fleishacker), John Carradine (Guide), and Jeff Corey (Doctor), each also in his sixties. One does not begrudge these mature actors a chance to work, or denigrate their skills, yet it is also not ageism to say that the film dissipates its energy in inaccurately imagining Old Hollywood as old. With this casting strategy, moreover, *The Last Tycoon* leaves unacknowledged the cultural and ideological connections between the 1930s and the late 1960s/ early 1970s era that films such as *Chinatown* exploited artistically and commercially.

5

During postproduction, discussing the music that Maurice Jarré was composing for the film, Kazan wrote to Spiegel, "Our story streams by, a series of incidents, obliquely joined, half seen. Harold once said to me, 'It all happened under water.' I have tried to carry this out in the way I've directed the film."[29] Later, as he refined his version of how the film got

made, first for publicity, then for posterity, Kazan claimed authorship of
the remark he attributed previously to Pinter. In a 1977 *Film Comment*
interview, describing working with Pinter on the script, he quotes himself
as saying, "It's like it's all happening underwater," and Pinter replying,
"Isn't that where things happen?"[30] In the interview the director more or
less defends the writer's viewpoint, as he has characterized it; but a decade
later, in his autobiography, he repeats this account of their exchange (with
a few words altered) and concludes, "What the hell could I say to that? I
shut off my objections, dived right in, and did the best I could."[31]

It is significant that this anecdote of a Kazan/Pinter exchange comes
up when the *Film Comment* interviewers raise a question about "a couple
of crucial scenes in the novel that are left out of the film."[32] The scenes
they mention are two that this essay has also emphasized. The first is
the encounter of Stahr and Kathleen with the "negro man" during the
grunion run; the other is Stahr's decision not to take Kathleen away with
him, and not to say anything to her, but, as the narrator Cecilia observes,
"to sleep on it as an adult, no romantic" (115). These, as discussed
earlier, are centrally ambiguous moments in the novel that reveal Stahr's
strengths or his limitations; his self-mastery or his vulnerability; or the
way these terms cannot be opposed to one another, but are in fact the
same.

Kazan's appropriation of the "under water" line marks one of the ways
in which he retrospectively ceded to Pinter the dominant role in setting the movie's tone. (At times, however, he claimed responsibility for
inventing elements, such as the final shot of Stahr disappearing into the
darkness of a sound stage, which were in Pinter's script before the director
joined the project.) Working with Nichols and Spiegel, Pinter limited his
screenplay almost entirely to the text of Wilson's edition. He did eliminate the opening chapter, the airplane trip, and also added, after the
Stahr-Brimmer meeting with which the written portion ends, scenes that
draw on Fitzgerald's notes (or Thalberg's life) to indicate Brady's coup
against him. Only one substantial scene in the published screenplay –
no. 37, Cecilia and Wylie driving down Sunset Boulevard – does not
appear in the film, which may demonstrate how carefully Kazan hewed
to the writer's version.[33] And yet, between the published screenplay and
the screen dialogue, there are a considerable number of small changes,
often involving the substitution of American cadences or idioms for Pinter's British usage.

Given Pinter's aesthetic predilections, it was probably inevitable that
Cecilia would be dropped as narrator, rendering inconsequential her role
in the film. In the *Film Comment* interview, Kazan makes the intriguing suggestion that Fitzgerald might have dispensed with her as narrative

voice as he revised the novel. Yet this was another occasion in which his public and his private views diverged. In an undated letter to Pinter, written, on internal evidence, after an early reading of the script, Kazan wrote, "It is no accident, as I told Sam, that Fitzgerald worked much of the time with Cecilia as the narrator. Her search for the answer for the obsessive quality of Stahr's love is full of emotion."[34] Put another way, it is Cecilia who supplies the novel's emotional intensity, while the other characters are often wary, calculating or withholding (another contrast with *Gatsby*, where the narrator is the calm, reflecting voice among overwrought principals). This is consistent with Kazan's other comments about the script's "great hole in the center," the "vague and skimpy" nature of the "love story."[35] To paraphrase, without Cecilia's passion and her perspicacious remarks on the movie industry's denizens, what exactly did you have – a story about how they made movies in the old days?

Working around what he saw as the script's deficiencies, it seems clear that Kazan hoped to replicate the force of Cecilia's romantic imagination through the power of De Niro's performance. As he was being cast, the actor was on the verge of winning a best Supporting Actor Oscar as the young Vito Corleone in *The Godfather Part II* (1974). But it was his disturbing, riveting portrayal of Johnny Boy in Martin Scorsese's *Mean Streets* (1974) – which Spiegel arranged for Pinter to see – that would have persuaded most people that he could make Stahr a compelling screen figure.[36] Kazan's notes and memos focus almost exclusively on defining Stahr's attraction. "Monroe Stahr has a sense of nobility and a sense of mission that promises us a tragedy," he wrote. "De Niro has to characterize Stahr this way. *He is a young king*, a prince with a moral mission, the chosen one, the one destined (as he saw it) to move films up to better things. And he is combating a mercenary and reactionary crowd."[37] The director's annotated working script has additional remarks along these lines on its cover page.[38] In the postproduction phase he sent several notes to film editor Richard Marks, analyzing Stahr's character and emphasizing how he wanted significant scenes to play, especially the studio luncheon and the final confrontation with Brady and Fleishaker.[39]

With De Niro, in short, Kazan aimed at putting on screen the book that Fitzgerald had been in the midst of writing, as much as, or more than, Pinter's screenplay adaptation. One might judge whether he accomplished this goal with reference to the two scenes about which he sent instructions to Marks. For the studio luncheon scene, Kazan wrote two memos, the first describing Stahr, the second the reaction of the other men to him. The first states in part, "He thinks of himself as a young prince regent . . . From his eminence he is kind, patient and patronizing.

He will seem arrogant *and should* from time to time . . . There is a constant play of humour around his lips. Every line is played with this quality in it." In the second memo, composed in capital letters, he emphasizes, "PLEASE NOTE: THE POINT OF THIS SCENE IS THAT ALL THE MEN ADMIRE STAHR AND THINK HE'S SMART, CAPABLE AND CREATIVE. THEY HANDLE HIM WITH *GREAT CARE*," and added, in lowercase, "Stress Fleishacker and Brady trying to understand Stahr's genius." For the scene at the end, where Stahr is deposed and then tells Brady, "This studio will fall without me," Kazan recommended a specific take that he described as "Best for 'studio will fall' line. GOOD FOR ARROGANT DEFENSIVE AMUSEMENT – *SECRET* DEFENSIVE AMUSEMENT IN STAHR. STRETCH MOMENTS ON STAHR."[40]

To this viewer, those scenes do not convey what Kazan wanted them to; they do not convey very much at all. De Niro at this stage of his career does not seem, after all, quite capable of creating a quality of mystery in Stahr, of utilizing a repressed style to portray a powerful figure who masks his dynamic force behind a genial, opaque surface. Only in the scenes with Jack Nicholson as Brimmer, when Stahr, drunk and despairing, loosens his restraints, does De Niro project a sense of danger, excitement, the unexpected, that was his compelling hallmark as a performer. Nicholson's quiet arrogance, meanwhile, builds a creative tension against an agitated De Niro that the latter's aloof authority in scenes with Mitchum, Milland, and others never quite attains.

In a sense, Pinter's idea that things "happened under water" shaped a story in which the spectator does not so much see things happen as see characters' reaction to those things. *The Last Tycoon* is a film composed predominantly through reaction shots. Some are indicated by the script, for example, the end of the luncheon scene with Brady (shot by Kazan in close-up) saying "Boy," and in the immediately following sequence in which Stahr criticizes Wylie White's screenplay, ending with Wylie, standing alone, saying "Gee." The Stahr-Kathleen relationship is dominated by reaction shots, which might be appropriate given that it is formed by his vision of a double, and one could describe their interaction as an exchange of "What I am seeing?" and "Who is he seeing?" But it makes for a lugubrious, inert pace, which is not helped by playing much of it in the dark.

Pinter's screenplay is not without its subtle moments, but the writer often turns the comic, ironic aspect of Cecilia's narrative in the novel in a more sour, even grotesque direction. One egregious example occurs with the dialogue he invented for the studio executives during their luncheon, and carried over into their conversation at the Writers' Ball – nothing in Fitzgerald remotely resembles the jejune diatribes in which

they casually equate Communists and homosexuals. Another is the projection room scene in which an editor, Eddie, is found dead, and no one
heard anything, as his assistant explains to Brady, "probably because he
didn't want to disturb the screening." Perhaps the most telling instance,
however, concerns the film's treatment of the British writer Boxley. In
the novel there are two scenes with Boxley getting lessons from Stahr
about making pictures. The second one ends with Boxley working at it
and Stahr "touching Boxley on the shoulder in passing – a deliberate
accolade" (107). The film's first scene closely resembles the novel's, but
in the second Boxley is drunk and shouting at Stahr, and, we learn later,
has left the studio. No doubt it would be too reductive to say that Pinter
identifies with his Boxley rather than Fitzgerald's.

If *The Last Tycoon* represents yet one more inadequate attempt to bring
Fitzgerald to the screen, however, its most basic problem is not its lack of
fidelity to the novelist but its failure to seize its own historical moment.
The film was made at the zenith of a new Hollywood youth movement,
when the "movie brats" appeared to have gained ascendancy in the industry. It was younger filmmakers like Scorsese and Francis Ford Coppola
who had brought fresh acting talent like De Niro to the fore. The film's
most poignant missed opportunity was its makers' inability to envision
the 1930s in comparable terms, when not just Stahr, but nearly everyone
making movies, was young.

There is a brief glimpse of what that different movie might have been
in the scenes of Stahr's encounter with Brimmer. The casting of the
communist labor organizer had been settled by the time Kazan annotated
his copy of the screenplay, and the director noted, with reference to the
first scene of the antagonists together, with Cecilia at the Brady house:

Jack Nicholson has an antic quality I want to use not lose. Perhaps, because of the
period we're in [the 1930s], the C.P. leading cadre has great confidence in their
purpose, goals and ultimate victory and for this quality we can use Jack's physical
energy and bounce. His ebullient cockiness = the mood of the C.P. leaders you
knew back in that era.[41]

Although their initial encounter is the most low-key of their scenes
together, before Stahr gets drunk at a restaurant, Nicholson delivered
precisely those performance traits, and De Niro clearly responds to the
challenge. It is also one of the few scenes in which Pinter's dialog improves
on Fitzgerald's. After Cecilia cleverly quotes *Antony and Cleopatra*, the talk
veers from Shakespeare to origins. Stahr asks Brimmer where he comes
from, Brimmer replies, "Tennessee. Baptist," and Stahr says, "I'm New
York. Jewish" – the single reference to his Jewish background in the film.
"I know," Brimmer says. "At least we're all Americans," Stahr responds.

Brimmer, with Nicholson's enigmatic inflection, says, "We *sure* are, Mr. Stahr" (italics added). For once in the film, the passions and artistry of its principals – screenwriter, director, performers, and, indeed, Fitzgerald – mesh.

NOTES

Thanks to Vicente Rodriguez Ortega for research assistance; to Leith G. Johnson, co-curator, and Joan Miller, archivist, for aiding my consultation of materials relating to *The Last Tycoon* in the Elia Kazan Papers, Wesleyan Cinema Archives; and to Adrienne Harris for comments and suggestions on earlier drafts.

1. The most detailed accounts of the work's composition and publishing history are in Matthew J. Bruccoli, *"The Last of the Novelists": F. Scott Fitzgerald and The Last Tycoon* (Carbondale: Southern Illinois University Press, 1977), and in Bruccoli, ed., *The Love of the Last Tycoon: A Western* (Cambridge: Cambridge University Press, 1994). In the latter, a volume in *The Cambridge Edition of the Works of F. Scott Fitzgerald*, Bruccoli argues for the amended title that he has given to his editorial version of the novel-in-progress.

2. Alan Hollinghurst, "On 'The Ivory Tower,'" *New York Review of Books* 51:4 (March 11, 2004), p. 28.

3. Maxwell Perkins to Edmund Wilson, January 28, 1941, in Bruccoli, ed., *The Love of the Last Tycoon: A Western*, p. lxix.

4. Bruccoli, ed., *The Love of the Last Tycoon: A Western*, p. xiii.

5. Bruccoli, *"The Last of the Novelists,"* p. 3.

6. Perkins to Zelda Fitzgerald, January 29, 1941, in Brucooli, ed., *The Love of the Last Tycoon: A Western*, p. lxx.

7. The Playhouse 90 production can be viewed at the Museum of Television and Radio, New York. The script, by Don M. Mankiewicz, updates the story to the 1950s and emphasizes Hollywood's financial crisis of that era, along with other changes. The cast includes Lee Remick as Cecilia Brady, Viveca Lindfors as Kathleen Moore, Reginald Denny as Boxley, and Peter Lorre and Keenan Wynn as new characters created for this version.

8. "'The Last Tycoon' Is Set With M-G-M," *Hollywood Reporter*, November 1, 1965; "Irwin Shaw Re-Visits 'The Factory' But Will Do 'Last Tycoon' Script In Creative Air of Switzerland," *Variety*, December 1, 1965, pp. 2, 16, in *The Last Tycoon* Clipping File, Academy of Motion Picture Arts and Sciences.

9. For differing versions of Spiegel's departure from *Accident*, see David Caute, *Joseph Losey: A Revenge on Life* (London: Faber and Faber; New York: Oxford University Press, 1994), p. 182, and Natasha Fraser-Cavassoni, *Sam Spiegel* (New York: Simon and Schuster, 2003), pp. 275–276.

10. Mark Royden Winchell, "Fantasy Seen: Hollywood Fiction Since West," in David Fine, ed., *Los Angeles in Fiction* (Albuquerque: University of New Mexico Press, 1984), p. 149.

11. Tom Dardis, "The Myth That Won't Go Away: Selling Out in Hollywood," *Journal of Popular Film and Television* 11:4 (Winter 1984), p. 169.

12. F. Scott Fitzgerald, "Pasting It Together," *Esquire* 5 (March 1936), pp. 35, 182–183; cited from Fitzgerald, *The Crack-Up*, ed. Edmund Wilson (New York: New Directions, 1945), p. 78, in which the title of "Pasting It Together" is transposed with that of "Handle With Care."

13. Robert Sklar, *F. Scott Fitzgerald: The Last Laocoön* (New York: Oxford University Press, 1967).

14. F. Scott Fitzgerald, *The Last Tycoon*, in Fitzgerald, *Three Novels of F. Scott Fitzgerald* (New York: Charles Scribner's Sons, 1953), pp. 134–163. Further questions from the published version of *The Last Tycoon* will be from this edition and will be cited parenthetically in the text; *The Love of the Last Tycoon: A Western*, pp. 131–199.

15. Leo C. Rosten, *Hollywood: The Movie Colony, The Movie Makers* (New York: Harcourt, Brace, 1941).

16. Rosten's single reference to the subject is as follows: "There is a widespread assumption that the movie men are 'foreigners,' and even those of old native stock are believed to have 'Jewish' names. Some of the most important people in the movie hierarchy – Darryl F. Zanuck, Y. Frank Freeman, Sidney Kent, George Schaefer, Eddie Mannix, Joseph I. Breen, William Le Baron, Hal Roach, Cecil B. DeMille – are erroneously believed by many to be of the same faith as the mother of Christ" (Rosten, *Hollywood: The Movie Colony, The Movie Makers*, p. 178). Before his work on Hollywood, Rosten had published what would become a hugely successful work on immigrant Jewish culture and the Yiddish language, *The Education of H*Y*M*A*N K*A*P*L*A*N* (New York: Harcourt, Brace, 1937).

17. Bob Thomas, *Thalberg: Life and Legend* (Garden City, NY: Doubleday, 1969), p. 391.

18. Ibid., pp. 19–31.

19. In *The Genius of the System: Hollywood Filmmaking in the Studio Era* (New York: Pantheon, 1988), Thomas Schatz supports Thalberg's significance with chapter titles such as "MGM: Dawn of the Thalberg Era," "MGM and Thalberg: Alone at the Top," and "MGM: Life After Thalberg." For his extensive discussions of Thalberg and the studio, see pp. 29–47, 98–124, and 159–175. In contrast, Douglas Gomery's chapter on M-G-M in *The Hollywood Studio System* (New York: St. Martin's Press, 1985), pp. 51–75, mentions Thalberg only in passing and emphasizes Mayer's leadership and ultimately that of Nicholas Schenck, president of Loew's.

20. As head of production at Twentieth Century-Fox, Zanuck answered to no one above him on the West Coast, so he was a tycoon in the sense of a wealthy and powerful businessman rather than, as in the case of Thalberg or Wallis, with a shogun-like connotation. Zanuck was voted the Thalberg Award three times (for 1937, 1944, and 1950) over the first ten years it was given; during that span of 14 years, there were four years in which no recipient was chosen. Jack L. Warner finally gained the honor for 1958.

21. Bruccoli, *The Love of the Last Tycoon: A Western*, p. 179.

22. Northrop Frye, *Anatomy of Criticism: Four Essays* (Princeton: Princeton University Press, 1957), p. 304.

23. Bruccoli, "*The Last of the Novelists*," p. 4. Wheeler Winston Dixon argues against this claim in *The Cinematic Vision of F. Scott Fitzgerald* (Ann Arbor: UMI Research Press, 1986), p. 84.

24. The most detailed account of the film's development appears in Fraser-Cavassoni, *Sam Spiegel*, pp. 314–326.

25. Andrew Sinclair, *Spiegel: The Man Behind the Pictures* (Boston: Little, Brown, 1987), p. 126.

26. For Spiegel's financing, see Fraser-Cavassoni, *Sam Spiegel*, p. 325; a Paramount document dated September 23, 1978, in the folder "Financial Statements," Kazan Papers, Wesleyan Cinema Archives, lists the domestic rental total as of that date at $1,485,580.69.

27. Elia Kazan, Letter to Harold Pinter, December 19, 1974, in the folder "Pinter, Harold," Kazan Papers.

28. Elia Kazan, *Elia Kazan: A Life* (New York: Alfred A. Knopf, 1988), p. 765.

29. Elia Kazan, Letter to Sam Spiegel, March 8, 1976, in the folder "Sam Spiegel – Correspondence," Kazan Papers.

30. Charles Silver and Mary Corliss, "Hollywood Under Water: Elia Kazan on *The Last Tycoon*," *Film Comment* 13:1 (January–February 1977), p. 43.

31. Kazan, *Elia Kazan: A Life*, p. 768.

32. Silver and Corliss, "Hollywood Under Water," p. 43.

33. Harold Pinter, The French Lieutenant's Woman *and Other Screenplays* (London: Methuen, 1982), pp. 204–205.

34. Elia, Kazan, Letter to Harold Pinter, n.d., in the folder "Pinter, Harold," Kazan Papers.

35. Kazan, *Elia Kazan: A Life*, p. 768.

36. Fraser–Cavassoni, *Sam Spiegel*, p. 319.

37. Michel Ciment, ed., *Elia Kazan: An American Odyssey* (London: Bloomsbury, 1988), p. 147; italics in orginal.

38. Elia Kazan's Annotated Script, dated August 11, 1975, Kazan Papers.

39. Memos from Karen Hale Wookey (conveying Kazan's notes) to Richard Marks, n.d., in the folder "Film Editing," Kazan Papers.

40. Ibid. The scenes involved are marked in the published screenplay as "42. Interior. Company directors' dining room," pp. 210–214, and "142. Interior. Brady's office," pp. 273–274.

41. Kazan's Annotated Script, Scene 129 (in the published screenplay, "128. Interior. Brady's House. Leather Room," p. 263).

2   The texts behind *The Killers*

Thomas Leitch

At the risk of sounding ungracious, I should like to begin my contribution to this volume by quarreling with what I take to be the volume's founding assumptions: that modern American literature, in the form of a body of canonical texts, offers a privileged vantage point from which to analyze the intertextual relations of a series of film adaptations; that there is essentially a one-to-one correspondence between the films and what adaptation studies has agreed to call their originals; and that the obvious way to organize a volume like this one is around the common ground that the original texts rather than their adaptations share. These assumptions operate, even for those who accept them, as procedural guidelines rather than immutable articles of faith,[1] and it is just as easy to imagine, for example, a collection of essays entitled *Great Films Noirs and Their Literary Sources* as one entitled *Twentieth-Century American Fiction on Screen*.

Since for the moment, however, imagining such a collection is all we can do, I take it that these assumptions continue in force, making adaptation study a subset of literary studies in ways that are unwisely and unnecessarily limiting. I hope to indicate some of these limits and some of the ways we might think outside them, and so expand the range of adaptation studies, by examining a few of the texts in addition to their long-acknowledged literary source, Ernest Hemingway's (1899–1961) 1927 short story "The Killers," that inform the two films released by Universal Pictures under the title *Ernest Hemingway's The Killers*, the first produced in 1946 by Mark Hellinger, directed by Robert Siodmak, and starring Burt Lancaster, Ava Gardner, and Edmond O'Brien, the second, starring Lee Marvin, Angie Dickinson, and John Cassavettes, produced and directed in 1964 by Don Siegel.[2]

The Siegel film in particular would seem an apt vehicle for such a challenge because its director maintained until his death its independence from its nominal source. On May 27, 1964, Siegel wrote "a note . . . of mutual commiseration" to Angie Dickinson, the leading lady in a film that must by then have seemed as star-crossed as its doomed hero. "I feel very strongly that the reason for the unfavorable reviews is the idiotic,

Figure 2. Robert Siodmak's *The Killers* features a femme fatale (played by Ava Gardner) who is not a character in the Hemingway story that is ostensibly the film's source. A 1946 Mark Hellinger/Universal Pictures release.

Figure 3. Although mortally wounded, hired killer Charlie Strom (Lee Marvin) exacts a final revenge in Don Siegel's *The Killers*, a 1964 Revue Studios/Universal Pictures release.

dishonest main title '*Ernest Hemingway's The Killers*,'" he told her. "You will remember all of us at our running felt very strongly against the main title." Marketing the film as a Hemingway adaptation, he felt, had raised exactly the wrong expectations:

The reviewers were prejudiced before seeing the picture and looked on it as a remake which hoped to benefit financially by hanging its coattails on the magic name of Hemingway . . . The picture has absolutely nothing to do with Hemingway, either in dialogue or in story content, with the exception of the catalyst – a man who knows that he is going to be killed and doesn't run away.[3]

The film's cool reception by reviewers was the third strike against it in Siegel's view. The first had come as far back as 1946, when Hellinger had invited Siegel to direct a version of the film he was producing for Universal, only to be rebuffed by Siegel's boss, Jack L. Warner, who refused to approve Siegel's loan-out from Warner Brothers. Hellinger's film, ultimately directed by Siodmak, had gone on to become a genre classic, making stars of Lancaster and Gardner, and sending Siodmak into the noir pantheon, while Siegel languished on such routine assignments as *The Verdict* (1946) and *The Big Steal* (1949). Eighteen years later, the new film, originally financed by Universal as a feature film made for television, had been rejected by NBC as too violent for general audiences and pulled from broadcast. And now critics were using Siodmak's film as a gold standard against which to measure Siegel's film. Howard Thompson's review in the *New York Times* was typical in calling the Siodmak film, to which it devoted its first three paragraphs, "a memorable movie" that was "probably the screen's most successful attempt to capture the Hemingway mood," before comparing "the cliché-ridden rewrite" to "one of those remakes of old Hollywood movies that television used to serve up in its early days – usually with Anita Ekberg in the old Ingrid Bergman roles, and the plots compressed into 60 minutes minus commercials" – before concluding, "Hemingway is the victim in all this. All that remains of his original story is the author's name, big and enticing in the advertisements, giving discredit where it is far from due."[4] In only nine paragraphs, Thompson registered Siegel's failure to equal either Hemingway's or Siodmak's achievements and got in a dig for good measure at his film's questionable made-for-television pedigree.

Of all Siegel's grievances, he was most exercised over the accusation that unlike Siodmak, whose first reel follows the dialogue of Hemingway's story almost verbatim, he and his screenwriter, Gene L. Coon, had had the temerity to rewrite the master. From the beginning, Siegel would later recall in his autobiography, he and Lew Wasserman, president of Universal, had agreed not to make "a xerox of the Mark Hellinger picture" and resolved that "not one word of Hemingway's dialogue would be used, nor would there be any scenes similar to those in the [1946] movie."[5] When Coon suggested that the film was to be called *Johnny North* after its hero, a race-car driver who is beguiled into a mail-truck heist and a series of double-crosses, Siegel replied that the title was "fine with me, particularly as it certainly wasn't Hemingway's 'The Killers.'"[6] Siegel was incensed and dismayed when Universal changed its release title to *Ernest Hemingway's The Killers*. Although the studio had purchased the title in 1946 and was therefore contractually entitled to recycle it without further payment, the director insisted that it "made no sense," since "there was not a word in the motion picture written by Hemingway."[7]

Siegel was almost equally aggrieved, however, that his film was widely perceived as a remake of Siodmak's. In his notes to Coon's *Johnny North* script of September 9, 1963, he pointed out that "we have to remember, of course, that we're not doing *The Killers*. The *big*, important, one thing about *The Killers* is the fact that two killers come into town with one purpose, to kill a man, and this man, an ex-con, has done something, we are told, very bad. Yet he makes no effort to escape – *that's* the crux of their story."[8] The focal character of Siegel's film, by contrast, is Charlie Strom (Lee Marvin), the older of the two killers, who shifts over the course of the film from wondering which anonymous contractor has hired the hit on Johnny North (John Cassavetes) for the suspiciously high price of $25,000 – presumably somebody who is well-heeled enough to make a substantial contribution to Charlie's retirement fund in return for continued anonymity – to wondering why their quarry made no attempt to escape. "It's not only the money," he tells his younger partner Lee (Clu Gulager) halfway through the film. "Maybe we get that and maybe we don't. But I got to find out what makes a man decide not to run – why all of a sudden he'd rather die."

Charlie's quest for knowledge thus reverses the trajectory of that of his counterpart, the insurance adjuster Jim Reardon (Edmond O'Brien) in the 1946 film. Reardon begins with something of an existential riddle – why the big Swede Pete Lunn, *né* Ole Andersen (Burt Lancaster), would name as the beneficiary of his modest life insurance policy a woman he hardly knew, Mary Ellen Daugherty (Queenie Smith), the hotel maid who saved him from committing suicide after he was double-crossed by Kitty Collins (Ava Gardner), Siodmak's femme fatale, the night after what he took to be his own preemptive double-cross of gang boss Big Jim Colfax (Albert Dekker) – but ends by chasing down the $250,000 that Colfax's gang stole from the Prentiss Hat Factory. Charlie begins by seeking to fatten his payoff for the hit by holding up his anonymous employer but ultimately submerges this interest in a mystery he, unlike Reardon, witnessed firsthand: the mystery of why his victim accepted his death so passively.[9] Ironically, Siegel's and Coon's decision to make this question the driving force behind the killers' investigation would seem to make their film more Hemingwayesque than Siodmak's.

Indeed, Siegel's plaintive insistence that his film be viewed as an independent work rather than an adaptation or a remake that owes nothing but its opening situation to Hemingway and departs decisively from the 1946 film will not stand up to close scrutiny. His film's similarities to the Siodmak film are far more extensive than he acknowledges. Both films open with the dramatic deaths of men who, formerly involved in quintessentially masculine activities (boxing, race-car driving), are unmanned and rendered utterly passive by their betrayal at the hands of femmes fatales who have enticed them into ambitious, ill-fated heists whose progress unfolds in a series of flashbacks. Each hero, assured by his treacherous lover that the gang's boss plans to run off with the proceeds, hijacks the pot preemptively and runs off with the woman, only to be betrayed by her and the boss, whom she eventually marries. Both films therefore invoke the formula of caper films – a genre remote from Hemingway's story – and end with the death of the killers and the head criminal, though Siodmak is content to pack the fatal heroine off to prison while Siegel has one of the killers execute her just before he dies. In the light of these similarities, it is easy to understand why Siegel, though he bridled at accusations that he had not followed a Hemingway model he had no intention of following, acknowledged that "we expect to be compared to the Hellinger film."[10]

For all its alleged independence from Hemingway's story, however, Siegel's film echoes Hemingway in several telling ways. Geoffrey O'Brien has observed that:

Our recollections of Robert Siodmak's 1946 movie . . . are apt to center on three primary elements: Ernest Hemingway's story, so literally brought to the screen in the film's opening scenes; Ava Gardner, carrying the full weight of that late-'40s sense of female sexuality as enveloping power, pervasively narcotic if not downright supernatural; and finally the impression of dreamy spectral density evoked by Siodmak's Germanic camera play and the luminosity of Woody Bredell's black-and-white cinematography. All these elements are notably missing from Don Siegel's remake.[11]

What O'Brien does not point out is that jettisoning the second and third of these elements – the narcoticizing power of Ava Gardner and the poetic suggestiveness of Siodmak's and Bredell's visuals – actually makes Siegel's film more, not less, like Hemingway's unremittingly hard-edged story. So does its violent yet elegiac ending, the collapse of Charlie the curious killer in front of the opulent house whose owners he has just shot to death. In the light of these similarities, perhaps we should call Siegel's film a Hemingway adaptation and Siodmak remake in spite of itself. Instead of excoriating it for its infidelity to Hemingway, we could praise it for its independence, reserving our criticisms for those rare moments when it slips up and echoes its models explicitly. In the opening scene, for instance, Siegel seems to invoke Siodmak's film gratuitously by casting Virginia Christine, who played the Swede's ineffectual good angel Lilly Harmon in Siodmak's film, as the blind receptionist Miss Watson.[12] Later, when Siegel's gang boss, Jack Browning (Ronald Reagan), is punched by Johnny North in retaliation for slapping Sheila Farr (Dickinson), the woman they both love, Browning tells him ominously, "After the job, we'll settle this, North," and Johnny replies, "Let's settle it now!" – closely and again gratuitously echoing an exchange in the corresponding Siodmak scene in which Big Jim Colfax says, "The job comes first. But afterwards, we'll have business together," and the Swede replies, "Anytime you say."

Just as it is unfair to condemn Siegel's film for its failure to follow a pair of models it disclaimed from the beginning, however, it would be equally unfair, and considerably more perverse, to condemn it for following them at all. But if, as Siegel claims, his film is neither, strictly speaking, an adaptation nor a remake – if neither Hemingway's story nor Siodmak's film should be taken as his film's uniquely informing texts – then what are the crucial texts behind Siegel's film?

The obvious answer to this question – that there are no such texts because Siegel's film is an original work – will not do. It is not just that nature abhors an intertextual vacuum, or that Siegel owes more to Siodmak and even to Hemingway than he acknowledges; his film is shaped in important ways by many other texts as well. To begin with an obvious example, Siegel's contract with Universal to produce a film intended to be shown on network television had a decisive impact on its style, length, and format. Because no film aimed at the television market would imitate Siodmak's expressionistic black-and-white visuals, the cinematographer Richard L. Rawlings lit Siegel's film brightly and evenly and shot it in color. The film was timed to run for ninety-four minutes, filling a two-hour television time slot less thirteen minutes of commercials per hour. Moreover, the need to allow for a large number of commercial interruptions required radical alterations to Coon's draft screenplay of September 9, 1963, which included twenty-two flashbacks, twice as many as the labyrinthine screenplay that an uncredited John Huston, working under the supervision of Anthony Veiller, had written for Siodmak's film, since, as Siegel pointed out, "It's a pretty dangerous style . . . for TV which is interrupted by commercials, to have 22 flashbacks."[13]

The venue of television imposed constraints on the production far more stringent than any demand for fidelity to a literary source. The NBC Broadcast Standards Department, responding to the script, handed down a long series of rules for the production: "Pg. 2. Caution on the handling of the blind receptionist. This must not be excessively brutal . . . Pg. 5. The shooting of Johnny North must not be excessively violent and, to this end, it would be better if the camera were on the killers at the time of the shooting rather than the victim."[14] The fact that Siegel's film does not, in the instance, follow this latter injunction does not disqualify the rule as a text; it simply means that, like Hemingway's story, it is a text that the filmmakers felt able to treat with a certain freedom.

In proposing rules for details of the production cautioning against excessive displays of sex, violence, or subliminal advertising for name-brand products, the network was in turn following its own master text: the Television Code, whose own rules, though broader, are equally strict, as in this section from "Principles Governing Program Content": "6. *Human relationships; sex; costume.* The presentation of marriage, the family and similarly important human relationships, and material with sexual connotations, shall not be treated exploitatively or irresponsibly, but with sensitivity. Costuming and movements of all performers shall be handled in a similar fashion."[15] Although such texts obviously stand in a different relation to Siegel's film than predecessors such as Hemingway's story and Siodmak's film, they are at least equally important – far more important, Siegel would claim – in shaping the finished product. And the Television Code's injunction against the exploitative handling of sexual relationships and costuming invokes the vital series of texts it was clearly formulated to restrain: imperatives to market the film by implying as openly as possible the sexual content of the film. NBC's injunction that "Sheila's clothing is not so 'tight' around her fanny that it is objectionable"[16] is balanced by the unwritten but equally urgent imperative to emphasize Sheila's sexual desirability and availability at every point. Hence the trailer for the film's theatrical release opens with the voiceover line, "Temptation never came in a more dangerous package," and the posters that Universal approved for the film's 1964 theatrical release are repeatedly dominated by the full-length figure of Angie Dickinson's body, appearing far more prominently than the smaller representations of Lee Marvin and Johnny North's heads, and the slugline, "There's more than one way to kill a man."

Similarly, NBC's reaction to page 104 of the script – "Browning's reaction to being shot must not be sensationalized" – is balanced by Siegel's equally explicit determination that "Sheila [should be] a wonderfully exciting girl, who gets her kicks (almost a feeling of an orgasm) via the speed and danger of racing cars"; that "the racing scenes . . . should cause a great deal of excitement"; and that "when they commit the crime, it should be as exciting as possible."[17] Once they are distributed, these publicity materials, broadly extending the implied promise of sexual and violent excitement, become the basis for still another textual contract with the audience quite as exigent in its way as the Television Code is in its own, since a studio whose films failed to deliver in however attenuated a way the elements promised by its advance publicity would be in trouble.

Angie Dickinson's outfits, which must be as sexually alluring as possible without being treated exploitatively, raise the question of why Dickinson was hired for the film in the first place. It might be argued, for example, that Dickinson is not a particularly talented actress or even that the prototype for her character, Ava Gardner's scheming Kitty Collins, is one of the most gratuitous additions the 1946 film makes to Hemingway's story in the first place. But it would be more even-handed to note that once a given role is created, whichever performer is cast in that role brings a new set of textual pressures to bear on the role and the film. As the wife of pop composer Burt Bacharach, Dickinson combines a Hollywood star persona with a celebrity persona as "very high-priced arm candy" remote from Gardner's understated, moody seductiveness.[18]

Nor is Dickinson alone in exerting this kind of pressure on the film. Universal considered Steve McQueen, Rod Taylor, Cliff Robertson, George Peppard, and Tony Franciosa for the role of Johnny North. Each of them would have reshaped the film by evoking a different persona and a different set of expectations. So would a Charlie Strom played by Neville Brand, Harry Guardino, Joseph Wiseman, Carroll O'Connor, Paul Stewart, Charles Bronson, James Coburn, Dan O'Herlihy, Ralph Meeker, or Barry Sullivan instead of Lee Marvin. Each of these star or character actor personas is another text that, like Hemingway's story, cannot help exerting pressure on the film, even if only because it feels wrong. Wasserman wanted Ronald Reagan, a former client of his talent agency, for the role of Jack Browning precisely because he had never played a heavy before, and Reagan, already more active in politics than moviemaking (*The Killers* would be his last film) resisted for that very reason. It was not until Siegel pointed out to Reagan that many of his own friends – "Jim Cagney, Clark Gable, Edward G. Robinson, and, of course, Humphrey Bogart"[19] – had increased the admiration of their audience by establishing their mastery of a wider range of roles that Reagan agreed. Once he had been cast in the role, Reagan's discomfort with the role became part of the character he played, making him one of the screen's most reluctant gangsters. Casting choices can leave their imprints even on roles they never played, as Reagan does for many viewers with the role of Richard Blaine in *Casablanca* (1942). It is impossible to watch Norman Fell's performance as Browning's sometime partner Mickey Farmer in the same way once you know that Don Rickles was considered for the role.

Star and character personas shaped by earlier performances or real-life developments (e.g., James Stewart's wartime service, Robert Mitchum's bad-boy brushes with the law, Lana Turner's involvement in her daughter's killing of her lover Johnny Stompanato), studio-authorized trailers and publicity releases, self-censoring regulations and memoranda, unwritten demands that studios provide the obligatory genre stimuli of sex and violence, imperatives of television broadcast that place restrictions on a picture's length and construction, and indeed on its representations of sex and violence (even if a film produced for television is ultimately deemed too violent to debut there) – all these texts exert far more pressure than Hemingway's story or Siodmak's film on Siegel's film. So do the stylistic signatures of such technicians as cinematographer Richard L. Rawlings, art directors Frank Arrigo and George Chan, composer Johnny Williams (better known as John Williams), and of course Siegel himself, whose reputation as a highly professional craftsman able to work successfully within tight constraints of time and money undoubtedly recommended him to Wasserman for the project. Given the power of all these shaping forces, why has the study of Siegel's film as an adaptation systematically neglected them in favor of comparisons to a story and a previous film whose influence he repeatedly disclaimed?

Two possible answers arise here. These forces, we might say, are not texts but contexts for Siegel's film, which in any event is an exceptional case in adaptation history, a film that, despite the title under which it was released and publicized, is not a true adaptation at all, but one that owes more to its contexts than to its nominal progenitor text. Since these two explanations are both so plausible, I should like to test them against an adaptation that clearly owes a great deal to a progenitor text it follows faithfully: the Siodmak version of *The Killers*, asking to what extent this earlier adaptation, universally hailed for its fidelity to Hemingway's story, is shaped by other texts.

Even a cursory examination of the earlier film indicates that it is equally exceptional a case in its own way. For although it follows Hemingway's story almost line by line, it does so for only 11 of its 102 minutes; the rest is sheer invention. Or not sheer invention, since it is informed by numerous prototexts that Hemingway's story barely hints at. Learning that he is being stalked by hired killers only a few minutes behind him, why does the former boxer refuse to run away or call the police? In Hemingway, Ole Andersen says only that "I got in wrong," leading George the counterman to speculate, "He must have got mixed up in something in Chicago . . . Double-crossed somebody. That's what they kill them for."[20] Presumably Hemingway, to the extent that he wished to specify any backstory for Andersen, had in mind something like the story of a prizefighter who takes money from a criminal mob to throw a fight and then bets heavily on himself, wins the fight, and has to flee retribution – a story that inspired the contemporaneous "Fifty Grand," in which Hemingway adds the additional twist that Jack Brennan, having accepted the bribe and determined to throw his fight, has to summon superhuman reserves of strength and courage to stay on his feet against an opponent who brutally fouls him in an attempt to throw the fight himself. Interestingly, the Siodmak film picks up part of this backstory – its big Swede, Ole Andersen, is a former prizefighter who did indeed double-cross somebody – but jettisons the rest, since Andersen's double-cross had nothing to do with boxing. Instead, the Hellinger/Siegel/Brooks/Huston/Siodmak screenplay turns Ole's backstory into a gangster film whose plot owes more to movies such as *High Sierra* (1941), also co-written by Huston and co-produced by Hellinger, than to "The Killers."

The influence of other movies on the film's structure and visual style has been widely noted. The multiple flashbacks through which the Swede's descent into crime and betrayal are presented are clearly a legacy of *Citizen Kane* (1940), and the chiaroscuro visuals designed by Jack Otterson and Martin Obzina and photographed by Woody Bredell, emphasizing cluttered interior spaces, seductively deep shadows, and dramatically high contrast, owe a great deal to such prototypical films noirs as *Double Indemnity* (1944), *Laura* (1944), *Murder, My Sweet* (1944), and especially *Phantom Lady* (1944), which Bredell had shot and Siodmak directed. For the earliest look at the Swede's life, the boxing sequence, Siodmak could look for inspiration to such recent films as *Kid Galahad* (1937), whose pug, Wayne Morris, had been Hellinger's first choice for the role.

Even the opening sequence, apparently lifted directly from Hemingway's pages, shows the influence of other texts, an influence made more obvious by comparing the sequence to the even more literal short film that Andrei Tarkovsky based on Hemingway's story in 1956, when he was a student at the All-Russian State Institute of Cinematography (VGIK). Unlike Siodmak, who begins the film with two shots that do not correspond to anything in Hemingway's story – an over-the-shoulder shot from the back seat of the killers' moving car as they approach Brentwood, New Jersey, and a long exterior shot of the killers advancing toward the camera before they turn right and enter the diner – Tarkovsky begins, like Hemingway, in the restaurant, with an interior track-in from the killers' point of view, from which they emerge on either side, their backs to the camera. Unlike Siodmak, Tarkovsky retains Hemingway's repeated use of the word "nigger," though he also cuts Max's remark to his partner Al, "You must have been in a kosher convent" (284). And unlike Siodmak, who prefers group shots of the two killers together, often placing them in the background behind the counterman George or his customer Nick Adams, Tarkovsky tends to frame his all-student cast in separate shots, and he forgoes Bredell's lushly menacing high-contrast lighting for an evenly lit but ominously drab look. Both sequences place special emphasis on the clock and the mirror with which Hemingway furnishes the diner, but Tarkovsky handles the clock more freely, favoring match cuts but jumping forward abruptly in time,[21] whereas Siodmak places his mirror more expressionistically, at a 45-degree angle above the counter, where it turns each character's reflection into an abstract pattern overhead.

Each of Siodmak's additions to or departures from Hemingway's story is predicated on fidelity to some more pressing set of textual rules or guidelines. He adds two opening shots to accommodate the credits while following the convention of plunging the audience immediately into his darkly glamorous world; the screenplay he is using eliminates the words "nigger" and "kosher" (pegging at least one of the killers as Jewish) as inflammatory through a studio-sanctioned act of self-censorship; the harshly poetic wash of darkness and bright light he uses for the scene owes much more to contemporaneous films noirs than to Hemingway's sparse if telling references to the arc lights outside the restaurant.[22] Like Tarkovsky, he ignores Hemingway's lighting directions – "Outside it was getting dark. The street-light came on outside the window" (279) – and bathes the exterior shot that he adds in a deep, night-for-night blackness whose metaphorical charge is very different from Hemingway's falling dusk. The killing itself, which Hemingway pointedly omits, is marked in the screenplay as a scene to be presented "a la Siodmak"[23] – a reference to the noir visual style the director had already, in films such as *Phantom Lady* (1944) and *The Spiral Staircase* (1945), done so much to author.

These additions and changes to Hemingway's story, based on the texts of industry self-censorship, genre conventions, studio grammars of lighting and editing, and the need to fill in visual detail, would be utterly unremarkable were it not for Hemingway's reputation as the cinematic writer *par excellence*, the man who wrote as if he were recording a scene for a movie camera. Although Hemingway's dialogue is eminently playable, a fact handsomely demonstrated by both Siodmak's and Tarkovsky's films, his visual detail is sparse and figurative rather than photographically explicit; if he is a cinematic writer, that is because his stories resemble screenplays rather than movies. In other words, Hemingway's text is necessarily an incomplete text even for filmmakers whose goal is to follow it as closely as possible. And that goal is apt for only the first eleven minutes of Siodmak's film, which follows Hemingway's story not until the end, but only as long as Hemingway suits the film's larger purposes. When Nick Adams runs to the Swede's rooming house to warn him about the killers – departing once more from Hemingway, who writes, "Nick walked up the street outside the car-tracks . . . Nick walked up the two steps and pushed the bell" (286) – the camera flies ahead of him, shooting him from above as he hurtles down an alley alongside the rooming house before craning back and panning right, moving in a transitional *tour de force* to pause briefly on a recumbent body shrouded in shadow before coming to rest on the inside of the door that Nick knocks on, and so abandoning Nick's point of view for something apparently omniscient yet remote and uncomprehending. It is not until after Nick departs, having played out something very close to Hemingway's dialogue – with the crucial change of the Hemingway line, "I got in wrong" (288), to the line, "I did something wrong – once" – that the Swede rubs his eyes and a new camera set-up shows his face, heavily but delicately shadowed, for the first time. At this moment, Hemingway's discourse yields to Burt Lancaster's star discourse and never returns, since Siodmak, unlike Tarkovsky, omits

Nick's brief return to the diner, which rounds off both Hemingway's story and Tarkovsky's in a way that would work against the momentum Siodmak needs to propel his feature.

The long moment that passes as the Swede sits up and waits in silence for his killers is crucial to the design of the film because his impending death carries the real risk of stopping the film equally dead in its tracks. Siodmak has no intention of following the lightweight Nick Adams or any of the killers' other survivors, and he has not yet introduced Jim Reardon (Edmond O'Brien), the insurance adjuster who will carry the burden of extracting the flashbacks narrating the Swede's life from the rest of the characters. For this long moment, the film's success rests on the audience's close identification with a character they hardly know, and one, moreover, played by a newcomer who has no reserves of the audience's goodwill or familiarity with his persona on which to draw. Lacking a specific Burt Lancaster discourse to draw on, the film draws instead on the conventions of a more generalized star discourse: the tight, anguished, atmospheric close-up of a character who, his face first unseen and his voice now unheard, must be heroically important because the camera dwells on his unrecognizable face while he is doing nothing and his expression is unreadable.[24] More than any other moment in the film, this shot bids to establish Lancaster as a star, a function that extravagantly exceeds the role Hemingway assigns him.

This apotheosis of star discourse, already superseding Hemingway's discourse, is quickly supplemented by a third conventional discourse: the retrospective investigation that will explain why the Swede made no attempt to escape his killers. This discourse, usually called a whodunit, is actually quite different, as its nearest model, *Citizen Kane*, suggests. The crucial question in both Kane's and the Swede's lives is not who but why, and the goal of both films is to indicate not only what is the reason for their heroes' mystifying behavior – Kane's cryptic dying word "Rosebud," the Swede's equally defining refusal to run from his killers – but to reassure the audience that there is a reason. In deciding to supplement Hemingway's story to feature length, Hellinger curtailed its suggestive power. The point of Hemingway's story, and indeed of Tarkovsky's film, is that no rational explanation could possibly motivate Andersen's preternatural passivity; the point of both Siodmak's and Siegel's films is precisely that there is such an explanation, involving seduction by a beautiful woman into a criminal orbit and an ultimate betrayal that leaves the hero, like his murdered accomplice Blinky Franklin (Jeff Corey), already "behind schedule" for death: "He's dead now, except he's breathing."

Despite Hemingway's approval of Siodmak's film, therefore, it might be described as betraying its source on a more fundamental level than mere infidelity to the dialogue could reach, since its epistemologically reassuring structure reverses the force of its source story.[25] But it is unlikely that Hemingway's sense of stoicism and despair had attracted Hellinger to the property in the first place. Far less important in the marketing of the film, and perhaps in its making, than Hemingway's short story were several other Hemingway and quasi-Hemingway texts, and indeed Hemingway's own star discourse as America's foremost literary celebrity.[26] The Hemingway work most directly responsible for the film's production was probably *For Whom the Bell Tolls* (1940), which confirmed his status, more than ten years after his last well-received novel, as America's most highly regarded novelist. Working for Paramount from a screenplay by Dudley Nichols that replaced Hemingway's political critique with romance, Sam Wood had made *For Whom the Bell Tolls* into a 1943 film that had been nominated for nine Academy Awards and won Katina Paxinou, who played Pilar, an Oscar for Best Supporting Actress. Five years after what Hollywood perceived to be Hemingway's imprudently radical involvement with *The Spanish Earth* (1937), whose highly partisan narration he co-wrote and delivered, *For Whom the Bell Tolls* proved that Hollywood could split Hemingway himself into two texts, adapting the commercial Hemingway without burdening itself with the political Hemingway.

Howard Hawks tested this premise triumphantly in his film version of *To Have and Have Not* (novel, 1937; film, 1945). Working for the only time in Hollywood history from a script that featured the names of two Nobel Prize winners – Hemingway as author of the original property and William Faulkner as co-scenarist with Jules Furthman – Hawks demonstrated that he could make a novel he referred to as "that goddam piece of junk"[27] into successful entertainment by virtually ignoring the storyline. Like Hawks's adaptation, which had invoked its nominal source directly only in its opening scene, Hellinger's version of *The Killers* is emboldened by Hawks's success to spend most of its time unfolding a backstory that it invents for Hemingway's hero. Even more completely than *For Whom the Bell Tolls*, *The Killers* separated the commercial Hemingway from the political Hemingway, sanitizing its source by relegating every threat to the Swede's present-day life to a mythical conspiracy of domestic crime in the far-off wilds of New Jersey whose climax was played out six years ago, in the innocent days before World War II ever darkened the American landscape.

It would seem, then, that even in a film widely praised for its fidelity to Hemingway's story, that particular story is no more foundational a text than the film adaptations of *To Have and Have Not* and *For Whom the Bell Tolls*; the self-censorship that eliminates words such as "nigger" and "kosher" and potentially disruptive political overtones; the genre constraints of the gangster film, the whodunit, and the boxing film; the Hollywood textbooks of dramatic construction, continuity editing, and film noir visuals, focused by the specific influence of *Citizen Kane*; the discourses of Hollywood stardom, even though Siodmak's film is cast without any established stars; and of course the celebrity discourse of Hemingway himself, as distinct from any particular Hemingway story, that would make a studio interested in purchasing the title *Ernest Hemingway's The Killers*. The question that remains, in that case, is why Hemingway's story has universally been assumed to be the informing text behind both Hollywood features and these other texts reduced to the status of contexts. What exactly is the difference between texts and contexts?

The obvious answer, that texts are written and contexts unwritten, is clearly inadequate, since any number of texts behind either or both of the films, from the NBC Broadcast Standards Department memo to the advertising posters that do their best to flout industry self-censorship without crossing the line to open defiance, are written as well. Nor can it plausibly be argued that texts are publicly acknowledged in ways that contexts are not, for many films acknowledge both kinds of texts, for example, in their opening credits. Finally, it is no use claiming that texts are exigent in ways that contexts are not, for Siegel's film is much less respectful to Hemingway's story than to all sorts of other texts, and Siodmak's allegiance to Hemingway lasts only until it collides with the greater imperatives of the genre film (Siodmak's audience, like Siegel's, gets to see the passive victim murdered) and the discourse of Hollywood stardom.

The difference between texts and contexts, then, seems to be less a difference in the nature of the texts themselves than a difference in their relation to their adaptations. Adaptations may be framed by dozens of contexts exerting different kinds of force, but their need to follow the dictates of these texts is qualitatively different from their decision to follow what are often called their source-texts. In this account the source-text provides the primary inspiration for a given adaptation, even though that inspiration may be inflected or deflected by any number of variously exigent contexts. The source-text is what the adaptation freely chooses to follow; the contexts provide economic or operational imperatives that it is merely obliged to follow. Neither film adaptation of *The Killers* makes any attempt to reproduce for its audience the experience of reading the NBC Broadcast Standards or the Production Code or even the studio advertising, but they do both make an attempt, however successful, to give their viewers an experience something like the experience of reading Hemingway's short story.

This last account of the status of texts versus contexts represents something like the prevailing view of adaptations' relations to their source-texts. Yet that view is challenged by both adaptations of *The Killers* as begging the very questions it should be addressing. From all the considerable evidence, Siegel's film makes no attempt to replicate the experience that either the characters or the readers of Hemingway's story have; in fact, it does everything it can to deny the affinity its title proclaims. Even Siodmak's film, which uses a virtual line-by-line transcription of the dialogue from Hemingway's story as the prologue to an investigation of the Swede's life, makes no attempt to replicate the experience of reading Hemingway's story; if anything, its systematic transformation of the Swede's life into a series of seductively glamorized riddles that all have answers, even if those answers lead to the conclusion that "nothing has had any significance,"[28] ultimately reverses the force of Hemingway's spare enigmas. Hemingway's story provides less a text than a pretext for Siodmak's film.

Given the difficulty of formulating a distinction between texts and contexts that will stand up to logical analysis and the experience that both versions of *The Killers* offer, it might seem that the distinction between texts and contexts is too problematic to be useful. In practice, however, it is one of the most common distinctions in textual studies. The final question these films raise, therefore, is why such a fallacious distinction has remained so ubiquitous. One possible reason is to protect the legal status of authorship by insuring that the authors of texts will be paid for adaptation rights and acknowledged in the adaptations' credits and publicity, whether or not the adaptations' generally anonymous contexts are similarly acknowledged. A more general reason is to establish an ad hoc hierarchy of textuality, with original literary source-texts as the most textually prestigious, film adaptations in second place, and contexts such as screenplays, publicity releases, industry self-censorship, and star discourses far behind. And a still more general reason is to regulate what would otherwise be an endless flow of intertextuality by imposing labels that give some intertexts procedural, perhaps even institutional, primacy over others. When Jack Shadoian calls Kitty Collins "a modern Circe," when Stuart M. Kaminsky notes the "streak of knightly valor" in noir heroes, or when Jonathan Lethem refers to the "King Lear stage-makeup" that the Swede's cellmate Charleston (Vince Barnett) seems to be wearing in Siodmak's film,[29] their references open a Pandora's box of endless possible contextual referents for the films. Distinguishing texts from contexts is simply a way of imposing order on this welter of intertextual references by indicating a hierarchy of relative weight that makes some of them more textual than others.

"The Killers" and *The Killers* remind us, however, that all these attempts to impose order on the endless web of intertextuality by institutionalizing some intertexts as texts and marginalizing others as contexts is itself institutional, ad hoc, and subject to ceaseless revision. What makes a context into a text is the act of being treated as a text by somebody; what demotes a text to a context, as Siegel attempted to demote Hemingway, is being rejected as a text. Since new critical occasions are always arising in which the interests of adaptors, audiences, and analysts will elevate new contexts or dethrone once-powerful texts, the distinction between the two, however it is formulated and defended, is always a nonce distinction. For all their demystification of Hemingway's enigmatic story, Siodmak's and Siegel's films show that the search for a privileged source-text that is not merely a favored context is as chimerical as the notion of the original text on which adaptations are based – or the ultimate meaning of the tableau of Ole Andersen lying motionless on his bed waiting for the killers.

NOTES

I have been materially assisted in the preparation of this essay by the 2003 Criterion Collection release (Criterion 176) of a double-DVD set that includes with both the 1946 and the 1964 versions of *The Killers* a wealth of other material. The essay draws on the following materials from the DVD: an interview with Stuart M. Kaminsky; an interview with Clu Gulager; the pressbook for the 1946 film; insert essays on the Siodmak film by Jonathan Lethem and on the Siegel film by Geoffrey O'Brien; excerpts from the NBC Production Standards Department memo on the Siegel film; a memo from Siegel on the draft screenplay dated September 9, 1963, and another memo from Siegel to Jennings Lang, Universal Pictures' vice-president in charge of television, dated September 24, 1963; a letter from Siegel to Angie Dickinson dated May 27, 1964; Siegel's essay "Pale Carbon Copy"; a list of performers considered for the principal roles in Siegel's film; trailers and advertising posters for both films; and a copy of Andrei Tarkovsky's nineteen-minute student film *The Killers* (1956).

1. These assumptions have recently come under more direct attack in Imelda Whelehan, "Adaptations: The Contemporary Dilemmas," which offers the anthology she has co-edited as "an extension of this debate [over the relation of cinematic adaptations to their literary sources], but one which further destabilizes the tendency to believe that the origin text is of primary importance." See Deborah Cartmell and Imelda Whelehan, eds., *Adaptations: From Text to Screen, Screen to Text* (London: Routledge, 1999), p. 3.

2. For essays that generally accept these assumptions in their analysis of the relations between the two films and the Hemingway story – that is, examples of what the present essay is not – see Gene D. Phillips, *Hemingway and Film* (New York: Ungar, 1980); Frank M. Laurence, *Hemingway and the Movies* (Jackson: University of Mississippi Press, 1981); and Stuart M. Kaminsky, *American Film Genres*, 2nd edn (Chicago: Nelson-Hall, 1985). A prototypical example of the kind of hybrid intertextual study I undertake here is

Robin Wood, "*To Have* (Written) *and Have Not* (Directed)," *Film Comment* 9:3 (May–June 1973), rpt. in Bill Nichols, ed., *Movies and Methods*, 2 vols. (Berkeley: University of California Press, 1976–85), I, pp. 298–305.

3. Don Siegel to Angie Dickinson, May 27, 1964, Criterion DVD, 2003.

4. *New York Times,* July 18, 1964, p. 10.

5. Don Siegel, *A Siegel Film: An Autobiography* (London: Faber and Faber, 1993), p. 235.

6. Ibid., p. 236.

7. Ibid., p. 257. In his interview on the Criterion DVD, Clu Gulager, who plays the junior killer, suggests that the title *Johnny North* was vetoed by the Universal publicity department because earlier films with the word "north" in the title had flopped. But in view of the success of recently released films such as *North by Northwest* (1959) and *North to Alaska* (1960), this theory is hard to credit.

8. Don Siegel, Notes to September 9, 1963, script of *Johnny North*, Criterion DVD.

9. Oliver Harris has recently pointed out that unlike Siodmak's film, which "signally fails to motivate Reardon's obsessive activity as a response to Swede's radical passivity," Siegel's film does use "the victim's inexplicable and shocking passivity" as "the explicit motor for the narrative." See Harris, "Film Noir Fascination: Outside History, but Historically So," *Cinema Journal* 43:1 (2003), pp. 11, 22.

10. Don Siegel, "Pale Carbon Copy," Criterion DVD, 2003. Siegel's acquiescence in his film's kinship to the 1946 film may depend on his own ambivalence toward that film if, as Deborah Lazaroff Alpi contends, "the initial storyline was outlined by Don Siegel" before Hellinger turned it over to "Richard Brooks . . . who was largely responsible for the plot construction," and ultimately to Anthony Veiller and an uncredited John Huston. See Alpi, *Robert Siodmak: A Biography, with Critical Analyses of His Films Noirs and a Filmography of All His Works* (Jefferson, NC: McFarland, 1998), p. 153.

11. Geoffrey O'Brien, "*The Killers* (1964)," Criterion DVD insert, unpaged [p. 1].

12. Siegel clearly knew Christine's background, since he had already cast her as Wilma Lentz in *Invasion of the Body Snatchers* (1956) and in an uncredited bit part in *Flaming Star* (1960).

13. Siegel, Notes to September 9, 1963, script of *Johnny North*.

14. Memo from National Broadcasting Company, Inc., Broadcast Standards Department, November 20, 1963, Criterion DVD, 2003.

15. "The Television Code: Preamble," *Broadcast Self-Regulation: Working Manual of the National Association of Broadcasters Code Authority* (n.p., 1977), unpaged [p. 4].

16. Memo from NBC Broadcast Standards Department.

17. Ibid., Siegel, Notes to September 9, 1963, script of *Johnny North*.

18. O'Brien, "*The Killers* (1964)," [p. 1].

19. Siegel, *A Siegel Film*, p. 241.

20. Ernest Hemingway, "The Killers," in Hemingway, *The Short Stories of Ernest Hemingway* (New York: Charles Scribner's Sons, 1953), pp. 288, 289. Further quotations will be cited parenthetically in the text.

21. This effect echoes Hemingway's own abrupt leaps forward in time, indicated most clearly when he shifts without warning from 6:15, when he has apparently been recording without elision the most trivial dialogue, to the sentence: "At six-fifty-five George said: 'He's not coming'" (p. 284).
22. In *American Film Genres* Kaminsky acknowledges the generic overdetermination of Siodmak's film by placing it in a chapter titled "Literary Adaptation" and a section of that chapter headed "The Film Noir."
23. Quoted in Kaminsky, *American Film Genres*, p. 86.
24. For a more extended analysis of "Swede's look and its mirroring" of the audience's own dread from an instructively different point of view, see Harris, "Film Noir Fascination," p. 10.
25. In *Ernest Hemingway: A Life Story* (New York: Charles Scribner's Sons, 1969), Carlos Baker calls Siodmak's film "the first film from any of his work that Ernest could genuinely admire" (p. 457). Some commentators on Siodmak's film consider its epistemology more problematic. In *Dreams and Dead Ends: The American Gangster/Crime Film* (Cambridge, MA: MIT Press, 1977), Jack Shadoian argues that "the unraveling is worked out in an atmosphere of deliberate confusion, partly to undermine any notion that things have been settled . . . Reardon's quest is ironic because nothing can ever be made to come out right in an absurd universe" (p. 88).
26. For a perceptive analysis of Hemingway's celebrity persona, see Leonard Leff, *Hemingway and His Conspirators: Hollywood, Scribners and the Making of American Celebrity Culture* (Lanham, MD: Rowman & Littlefield, 1997).
27. Quoted in William Rothman, "To Have and Have Not Adapted a Novel," in Gerald Peary and Roger Schatzkin, eds., *The Modern American Novel and the Movies* (New York: Ungar, 1978), p. 70.
28. Shadoian, *Dreams and Dead Ends*, p. 112.
29. Ibid., p. 101; Kaminsky, *American Film Genres*, p. 85; Jonathan Lethem, "*The Killers* (1946)," Criterion DVD insert, 2003, unpaged [p. 2].

3   *The Day of the Locust*: 1939 and 1975

Christopher Ames

When Nathanael West (1903–1940) completed the manuscript of *The Day of the Locust* in 1938, he would not have envisioned the novel being adapted into a Hollywood film. Indeed, he consciously maintained a great distance between his screenwriting for Republic and RKO and his Hollywood novel, which focused on disaffected outsiders and drifters. The novel was explicitly an opportunity for him to create the kind of art and express the kind of vision that he could not within the confines of studio employment. As Claude Estee says of one of Tod's cynical observations about love in the novel, "It's good, but it's not for pictures."[1]

The Production Code was one reason that *The Day of the Locust* was not suitable for adaptation. Consider its romantic plot, in which an attractive ingénue is desired by three men (a studio artist, a cowboy extra, and an emotionally damaged early retiree), flirts with all of them and then sleeps with an indigent Mexican after a drunken party featuring cock-fights. Consider as well her friendship with prostitutes and her selling her body to pay for her father's funeral. The stag film at the bordello, the main character's rape fantasies, the disturbing ending with an assault on a child and a riot at a Hollywood premiere: virtually all the key features of the story would likely run afoul of the Production Code standards.

But these problems are merely symptomatic of a larger, ideological difficulty. For it was not unusual for racy material in a novel to be muted in a film adaptation: for prostitution to be glossed over, for lascivious relationships to be sanitized, for grim endings to be rewritten. But *The Day of the Locust* lacks any kind of uplifting story: West's novel depicts the Hollywood dream as a desperate, morbid, and violent response to modern meaninglessness; its characters' quests for physical and spiritual health reveal the emptiness enveloping the so-called "seekers." The novel is based on a crucial and disturbing premise of Hollywood fiction: that characters of extreme desperation reveal truths about society in the main and that Hollywood eccentricities reveal truths about America as a whole. A dark future for America is prefigured through the absurd present of the West Coast.

Figure 4. Apocalyptic fantasy dominates the image of Hollywood presented in *The Day of the Locust*, a 1975 Long Road/Paramount Pictures
release.

So the whole idea of a Hollywood motion picture based on West's
novel would have seemed laughable to West. What, then, can we make of
such a film created thirty-five years later by John Schlesinger? Obviously,
Hollywood changed in that thirty-five years: the demise of the studio
system and the Production Code and the rise of independent cinema
in the 1970s altered Hollywood in ways that transformed the filming of
The Day of the Locust from an unimaginable impossibility into a virtual

likelihood. While the values and techniques that dominated the so-called Hollywood renaissance of the 1970s fitted the values implicit in West's novel, West's novel also changed over that thirty-five years. Of course, the words on the page did not change, but the disruptive force of the novel was muted by the passing of time, by the rise of West and *Locust* as canonical author and text, and by the fact that a disturbing novel about contemporary Hollywood (what West wrote) inevitably became a colorful novel about classical Hollywood, an era removed by two generations from the audience of Schlesinger's film. Over time, West's novel became *the* Hollywood novel. Hardly any Hollywood novel can be marketed today without a blurb comparing it to *The Day of the Locust*. While this canonical status is a fitting tribute to an insightful book, it can also, ironically, make us lose sense of its genuinely disruptive qualities.

The counterculture elements of 1970s Hollywood filmmaking helped to make *The Day of the Locust* filmable. The novel's bleak depiction of a California peopled by "seekers" whose hunger for meaning in their lives is not satisfied by climate, religion or movies fed into a 1970s sense of dissatisfaction with American materialism, and it resonated with Watergate-era cynicism about American institutions. The trends that transformed the filming of West's *The Day of the Locust* from impossible to inevitable include the rise of *auteur* cinema, particularly in inexpensively produced films aimed at a youth market; franker depiction of sexuality arising from social changes and the replacement of the Production Code with the MPAA ratings system; the popularity of films with disaffected and generally male heroes (such as *The Graduate* [1967], *Five Easy Pieces* [1970], *Billy Jack* [1971], *The King of Marvin Gardens* [1972], *Night Moves* [1975], and *Taxi Driver* [1976]); the revision of genres such as the once-patriotic western into the so-called Vietnam-westerns such as *Little Big Man* [1970] and *Soldier Blue* [1970]; the growth of post-Watergate films that expressed distrust of government and other institutional structures (*Joe* [1970], *The Conversation* [1974], *The Parallax View* [1974], *Three Days of the Condor* [1975]); and the rise of self-referential films about Hollywood that banked on audience sophistication about film history and nostalgia (such as *The Wild Party* [1974], *Hearts of the West* [1975], *Inserts* [1975], *Gable and Lombard* [1976], *The Last Tycoon* [1976], *Nickelodeon* [1976], *Silent Movie* [1976], *W. C. Fields and Me* [1976], and *Won Ton Ton, The Dog Who Saved Hollywood* [1976] – all of which were made within one year of *The Day of the Locust*).[2] Examining the films that came out in the years surrounding *The Day of the Locust* reveals both a clear interest in the subject of Old Hollywood and a willingness to create movies with disaffected, antiheroic characters in which sexuality and violence are depicted more frankly than in earlier Hollywood history. The obvious impediments to adapting a novel such as *The Day of the Locust* seem to have disappeared by 1970.[3]

The 1970s cinema supported a countercultural school of filmmaking in which many of the values implicit in classical Hollywood and explicit in the Production Code were turned on their head. While it saw the evolution of the modern blockbuster and the development of different genres of exploitation movie, the decade's cinema also supported films that, to quote Nathanael West's estimate of his own work, included "nothing to root for."[4] In this context Richard Keller Simon's summary of the ways in which West's novel reverses film clichés is instructive:

In the movies the cowboy hero is quiet but smart, and he gets the girl and wins his fights; but in the novel Earle is quiet and dumb, and he loses the girl and his fights, even the fight with the midget. In the movies the Mexican sidekick is dominated by the cowboy and helps him out when he gets in trouble; but in the novel the Mexican sidekick hurts the cowboy and steals his girl. In the movies the girl is sexy but good, going off with the cowboy hero at the end; but in the novel she is sexy and bad, disappearing at the end under morally ambiguous circumstances. In the movies the child star is adorable; in the novel Adore Loomis is irritating and unnatural.[5]

Simon extends this contrast, brilliantly enumerating the ways in which the stock figures of West's novel deliberately reverse their typical filmic destinies. Yet, in his brief closing consideration of Schlesinger's film, Simon fails to make the connection that such reversals would make the novel perfect material for a 1970s film, an era in which movies deliberately inverted genre clichés and elevated alienated characters to antihero status.[6] When we examine Schlesinger's film attuned to its place in the 1970s and its selective transformations of West's novel, we discover a movie that perceptively foregrounds West's radical critique of Hollywood, recognizing how that critique is grounded in sexual and racial tensions too explosive to be filmed in West's era.

"The final dumping ground": Schlesinger's movie about movies

Movies about movies are always self-referential, particularly in those moments in which the audience is made deliberately aware of watching a film about filmmaking. Backstage scenes that show movie cameras, sets, lighting and make-up technicians provide such self-referential moments, as do moments when the characters within a movie watch a movie themselves, images that I refer to as "the framed screen."[7] *The Day of the Locust* (1973) includes several important self-referential scenes and these reinforce the recurring imagery of looking, reflections and windows.[8]

The film opens with a self-referential gesture. After a brief shot of Tod Hackett renting an apartment at the San Berdoo complex, the film cuts to the giant door of a soundstage opening to reveal the whole complex mechanical apparatus of filmmaking, the very elements that are invisible in the finished product. As the credits roll, Schlesinger's editing invites the viewer backstage. Human figures entering the soundstage are dwarfed by the long shot of the opening door. A close tracking shot moves our perspective through a crowded room of extras donning costumes and make-up. The camera stops at Faye Greener and moves up the length of her body as she pulls a ballgown up over her underwear. In a typical mirror-shot technique, only a camera pullback reveals that the image we are watching is her mirror reflection, not her. A mix of high- and low-angle shots display the confusion of a packed set, a thriving industry noisily working. The camera tracks in on Tod as observer and then uses an eyeline match to cut to a point-of-view shot of Faye, reinforcing Tod as onlooker and voyeur.

This scene places the film of *The Day of the Locust* squarely in the tradition of movies about movies. From the earliest days of moviemaking, there have been films that reveal some of the "tricks" of filmmaking to an inquisitive audience, while still managing to maintain the so-called magic of the filmic illusion. In particular, *The Day of the Locust* will provide insight into the use of extras, set building and design, and costuming. More than most films about Hollywood, it focuses on minor employees who operate on the margins of Hollywood. This emphasis, consistent with West's novel, reduces the risk of glamorizing the subject interrogated by the film. The most important figures in the Hollywood hierarchy to appear in the film are Claude Estee, apparently head of the art department (he is a screenwriter in the novel) and a couple of producers who appear briefly in the studio barbershop. Despite the absence of stars and directors, the film remains wholly consistent with the Hollywood-on-Hollywood genre in its display of backstage techniques and operations.

Very early in the film, Tod and Faye take a tour in Tod's newly purchased car. This scene, which has no literal equivalent in the novel, allows Schlesinger to depict certain elements of Hollywood that West describes in the novel outside of dramatic scenes, particularly the fabulous array of architectural styles in Beverly Hills mansions.[9] The scene fittingly concludes with Tod and Faye lingering near the back of a guided tour of the Hollywoodland sign, a Hollywood icon nowhere alluded to in West's novel, but one wholly appropriate to his vision. Since West's era, the sign has become the dominant symbol of Hollywood itself, appropriate because it represents self-advertisement as public art and because the origin of the sign in denoting the housing development "Hollywoodland" underscores the growth of Los Angeles out of speculative land and oil booms.

The emphasis on newcomers or tourists looking at Hollywood with fresh eyes is reinforced by Tod's photography as he snaps shots of Faye posing eagerly in her new surroundings. In one key moment of this scene, Tod snaps Faye preening in the parked car. The two then approach the locked gate of a mansion and the camera tracks toward them then shifts to their view of the mansion; that is, the camera adopts their tourist gaze. This theme is heightened by a reverse-angle shot that reveals a pair of elderly tourists photographing Tod and Faye. Tod comically photographs the tourists who, in turn, photograph them. The scene calls attention to Hollywood as myth and Hollywood as tourist destination. Photographing the photographer emphasizes the importance of the visual image, while also demonstrating that Tod is more interested in the onlookers than in what they are looking at, just as West and Schlesinger are more interested in those who have "come to California to die" (184) than in the supposed healing or dream-fulfilling virtues of the destination. Faye's quest, on the other hand, is to become the object of the camera's gaze, to become a celluloid image, a star. She poses eagerly for the camera, but it is only Tod's or a camera wielded by a tourist couple. *The Day of the Locust* will show Faye as object of the lustful male gaze, but only briefly of the celebrity-conferring gaze of the official Hollywood movie camera she desires.

The ironic music ("Isn't It Romantic?") comes to an end as Tod and Faye arrive at the iconic Hollywoodland sign. Schlesinger cleverly cuts from a postcard representation of the sign to the thing itself: taking us from a representation of the sign to the sign – but not quite to the thing itself that is Hollywood. A tour guide tells in brief the familiar narrative of Hollywood dream and disappointment, speaking of the 1929 Clam Queen of Pismo Beach who came to Hollywood and found not fame but humiliation. In 1932 she ascends the "great H" of the "mammoth metal monument to this mecca of broken dreams" and kills herself.[10] This moment encapsulates, in a cartoonish way, the stories of Tod, Faye, and Homer. Schlesinger, in this invented scene, reminds us that West's story is a variation on a familiar, even clichéd theme.

While the tour guide expounds the cautionary tale, Tod and Faye step aside and Faye reveals her own penchant for inventing stories, a characteristic presented in a different context in the novel. By relocating this scene at the Hollywood sign and placing it in the context of the tour guide's gruesome narrative, Schlesinger acknowledges the already-said quality of Hollywood mythology: he embraces the triteness of the story. Similarly, screenwriter Waldo Salt chooses not to use either of the stories that West attributes to Faye, but rather invents a new story to illustrate her habit of dreaming up film scenarios. In this story Faye describes two beautiful female identical twins, identical except that one is good and one is bad. The good one is engaged to marry a rich, handsome man when the jealous bad one poisons her and puts her in hospital so that she can take her place at the wedding. At the last minute, the good one interrupts the wedding, shrieking that she is the real betrothed. Since no one can tell them apart, the rich groom must kiss them both to identify the one whose kiss he remembers.

Faye's twin natures are the Hollywood deadly combination of innocence and sexual allure – goodness and badness, purity and a mercenary quality. The story resonates with Leslie Fiedler's description of Faye Greener as the type of the Bad Good Girl.[11] The story also prefigures Faye's "double date" with Earle and Tod in which she pertly offers to kiss them both as she sits between them at a movie showing in which she briefly appears. Perhaps the screen image allows her to double herself, to become her own identical twin, and thus justify dating two men simultaneously.

This date is the first of the two framed films in *The Day of the Locust*. Faye invites Tod and Earle to see her play "this sexy harem girl" in a film in which she is given a speaking line. Schlesinger's adaptation of the novel allows him to tap into the rich reservoir of films-within-films and the developed filmic syntax of those scenes. His treatment emphasizes the movie theater as erotic space and presents Faye's encounter with her screen image as sexually arousing. As the scene approaches, Faye kisses Earle and then offers to kiss Tod, too (a scene that occurs in the novel, but not at a movie showing). We cut to a flying-carpet scene, and Faye becomes visibly excited as her one speaking line approaches. As is traditional in such scenes, the director uses reverse-angle shots to cut from the image on the screen to the flickering faces of the audience. At the climactic moment of Faye's scene, we are thus cutting between two images of Faye – both cinematic to us, but one designated as "real" within the diegesis. Faye's palpable excitement gives way to peevishness as she sees that her scene has been trimmed somewhat. All three leave the theater, ignoring a newsreel about Hitler that rolls ominously in the background.

In the lobby Faye encounters yet another twin or representation of herself: a publicity still that includes her. Excited, she asks her escorts to steal it for her. Earle breaks the glass with his cowboy boot and runs off with the photograph. Tod lingers behind and sneaks another copy under his shirt. Both men are thus shown in thrall to her image – as, indeed, is Faye herself. The scene carefully contextualizes sexual desire within the system of photographic reproduction, and it suggests multiple doublings: the twins in Faye's story, her double date, her screen image and her real self, the two photographs of her stolen (in different ways) by her two male admirers.

We see Faye watching herself on screen in the first framed movie; in the second, in a more symbolic way, we see Tod watching himself on screen. Tod's nervousness about a trip to a bordello with his new boss is understandable. Schlesinger first depicts that anxiety in an extended mirror scene in which Tod is brushing his hair and downing a stiff drink. Schlesinger uses the familiar filmic syntax that he used when introducing Faye: a camera pullback reveals that the image we have been watching is a mirror image; similarly the pullback broadens the scope of the image to show us two images of Tod, self and reflection, a visual counterpart to the self-referentiality of the scene and movie themselves.

The sophisticated Hollywood party that Tod joins acts bored and complacent at the screening of a black-and-white, silent pornographic film about a French maid hiding various lovers in her bedroom. Schlesinger uses shots that alternate between the framed screen and the audience along with shots that show a smaller image of the screen simultaneously with the audience. The film is viewed as a disappointment: "There's no real sensuality," offers one viewer; the effects of a spanking scene are faked, another comments; "Well, if you excuse me, I must pee," says Estee's drunken wife, blocking the screen as she stands; finally, the film breaks and the patrons comically demand a refund. In the midst of this predictable banter, a revealing remark is made: the party notes that one of the men on screen "looks like Tod." Tod is embarrassed and shortly after wanders outside, where an eyeline match shows him peering at Mary Dove and another of Mrs. Jenning's girls sharing a smoke.

Schlesinger's editing calls attention to voyeurism and Tod's role as an observer who is uncomfortable at having his watching watched. If Hollywood movies can be seen as giving cinematic life to people's longings, aspirations, and dreams, then pornography very obviously envisions sexual desire. Schlesinger presents both movies-within-the-movie as corrupted eroticism. That Tod uses this opportunity to see if he can bed Faye by paying Mrs. Jenning stresses the mixture of voyeurism and commercialism in the corrupt commodification of desire. Faye's brief role as a harem girl and Tod's experience watching the pornographic film at the bordello are of a piece in the critique of Hollywood as dream merchant or pimp.

"Love is like a vending machine" – sexuality in *The Day of the Locust*

Prostitution is the central trope of sexuality in *The Day of the Locust*. "Love is like a vending machine," Tod and Estee agree as Estee leads his Hollywood party to a bordello. Later, Faye briefly becomes a prostitute to cover the costs of her father's funeral. And, throughout the film, Abe Kusich repeatedly suggests adjourning to a bordello, as if that is the normal way to conclude an evening.

The prominence of literal prostitution forms a background for the more metaphoric uses of the term. Tod is frustrated because Faye will not respond romantically to him because she cannot love a poor man. This theme, so crucial to West's contemporary F. Scott Fitzgerald, bitterly associates a woman's desire to be well taken care of in marriage with the financial transactions of prostitution. That Tod sees Faye as essentially prostituting herself also underscores the casting-couch cautionary tale so common in early Hollywood novels. That the young starlet may literally be forced to trade sex for employment or financial support shadows the broader sense in which the artistic compromises of movie acting are seen as prostitution for serious dramatic talents, just as scriptwriting is viewed as prostitution by the established writers who moved west from American cultural centers in search of Depression employment.

Significantly, Estee's excursion to the house of prostitution is to see a pornographic movie. *The Day of the Locust* quickly associates prostitution with filmmaking. Indeed, prostitution is the most common metaphor the Hollywood writer used to describe his work for the studios.[12] In *The Day of the Locust*, the writer has been transformed into a painter, but the same tension exists between Tod's grand painting of "The Burning of Los Angeles" and his studio work sketching set and costume ideas for a movie about Waterloo. Similarly, Harry Greener is presented as a failed vaudevillian who prostitutes his acting talents to sell silver polish door to door. And Faye's big speaking role depicts her as a harem girl in a piece of Eastern exotica. Thus even in the idealized on-screen world, opportunity comes in the form of a cash transaction: the female image exchanged for a bit of money and promises of celluloid immortality. While we encounter no literal casting couch in novel or film, its presence lurks behind the movie in Faye's business arrangement with Homer and her flirtatious interest in Tod and Estee, captured very effectively in Karen Black's performance.

That Homer Simpson is a retired hotel bookkeeper underscores the attention paid by novel and film to the financial underpinnings of human interactions. Homer's backstory (spelled out more fully in the novel than in the film) reveals that the central crisis of his repressed life came when he encountered an alcoholic hotel guest who was sexually available to him because she believed he could cancel her past due rent. Unable to control or understand his intense emotions at this scene, Homer retires and heads west for the California cure. His "business relationship" with Faye develops because Faye recognizes that he poses no sexual threat: he will never try to collect on his investment. Homer's sexual repression is manifested in his unusual hand gestures, described in detail in the novel and central to Donald Sutherland's portrayal of the character in the film. As William Cohen suggests, "When hands take on a specifically sexual meaning . . . they speak of masturbation . . . The metonymic association of hands with autoeroticism functions as a conduit between representation and sexuality."[13] Cohen is speaking of Dickens, but his symbolic reading applies to Homer's "manual ballet" (161) in West's novel as well. West writes of his "fever eyes and unruly hands" (79) and tells us that his "only defense was chastity." That same passage provides the fullest example of the troubled dance of Homer's hands: "His hands kept his thoughts busy. They trembled and jerked, as though troubled by dreams. To hold them still, he clasped them together. Their fingers twined like a tangle of thighs in miniature. He snatched them apart and sat on them" (101). Sutherland's performance interprets this passage vividly as he places the unruly hands in front of his crotch, acting out the sexual suggestiveness of West's prose.

Voyeurism is the other manifestation of Homer's repressed masturbatory sexuality. Afraid to touch, Homer looks at Faye, often through windows. In the sexual climax of the film, when Miguel succeeds in bedding Faye, Homer walks into the room and looks on in dazed horror. Homer's voyeurism is of a piece with the "teasing" film at the bordello and Faye's double date with Earle and Tod to watch her in the filmed seraglio. Desire fuels West's Hollywood, but that desire is commodified in financial transactions, converted to visual imagery on screen, and transmuted ultimately into violence.

Eventually, Homer's repressed sexuality emerges in such violence – violence directed against the ambiguously sexual child actor, Adore Loomis. Schlesinger furthers West's description by casting and costuming Adore to look female, a sort of vulgar Shirley Temple. West and Schlesinger emphasize the perversity or incongruity of the child actor whose act involves singing suggestive, sexualized lyrics – the grotesquely miniaturized adult: "He seemed to know what the words meant, or at least his body and his voice seemed to know . . . his buttocks writhed and his voice carried a top-heavy load of sexual pain" (141). Adore represents the simultaneous sexualization of childhood and juvenilization of sexuality in Hollywood, a place where it was possible for Mae West and Shirley Temple to be among the top box-office draws in the same year (both stars are mentioned by name in the novel).[14]

Homer's assault on Adore Loomis at the Hollywood premiere-turned-riot is the culmination of a series of violent or near-violent episodes in the film: multiple brawls at parties, an industrial accident on the set, a cockfight, and a rape attempt. If prostitution is the central trope of sexuality in *The Day of the Locust*, rape may be the secondary metaphor. Rape lingers just below the surface of the novel and is made more explicit in the film. When the drunken party in the Hollywood hills turns violent, Tod chases Faye. West renders it thus: "If he caught her now, she wouldn't escape . . . Already he could feel how it would be when he pulled her to the ground" (117). But he never catches her and instead falls to the ground himself. In the film Schlesinger wisely illustrates Tod's violent thoughts by having him tackle Faye and begin to assault her. The teasing and frustration central to Faye's character have their counterpart in the male lust and will to overpower that manifests itself as rape.

Although West's novel has aged well and still reads as a sharp satire of the Hollywood dream, its representation of sexuality is likely to appear dated. The driving sexual force in the novel is Faye, the Hollywood ingénue who uses flirtation in attempts to advance her career. Her flirtation or teasing inspires lust, rage, and rape fantasies in the men who surround her (primarily in Tod, Homer and Earle, but also in Estee, Kusich and Miguel). What appears dated, I believe, is the symbolic weight that West and Schlesinger place on male sexual frustration: Faye (described by her father in the movie as "a real c.t." [i.e., cockteaser]) somehow must stand for the elusiveness of the Hollywood dream of sunshine, fame, health, and riches, while the unsatisfied male lust she inspires represents the desolation that West encapsulates in "the cheated" of the novel. The novel lacks the self-consciousness or even self-deprecation that has accompanied representations of male sexual desire since the 1960s.

Fiedler was the first critic to place Faye in the context of American literary heroines, calling her "the most memorable and terrible woman in an American novel of the '30s" (Fiedler, *Love and Death*, 325). Fiedler's hyperbole exceeds West's: "[Faye] cannot really be touched, for she is the dream dreamed by all of America, the dream of a love which is death . . . her realest existence on the screen" (326). If Faye is to be more than what Tod angrily labels her ("a whore" and, in the movie, "a dumb blonde"), she must achieve a symbolic meaning, a challenge that is perhaps tougher for the film than for the novel. Fiedler postulates a straight line linking Daisy Miller, Daisy Fay Buchanan, and Faye Greener. As with his contemporary Fitzgerald, West portrays the emasculating heroine as a figure enamored of riches: she "would only let a wealthy man love her" (67). Faye's last name even echoes the beckoning green light on Fitzgerald's Daisy's dock.

I would take Fiedler's view of American literary history farther and read *The Day of the Locust* as a dark rewriting of *The Great Gatsby*. In *Gatsby* a Midwestern man of moral character comes east and meets the larger-than-life figures of the distorted American dream: Jay Gatsby and Daisy Buchanan. Nick Carraway observes them from his literate and judgmentally moral stance and ultimately embraces the romantic aspiration of Gatsby (his greatness) and rejects the betrayal and class loyalties of Daisy. In *Locust* Tod Hackett travels west, where he becomes an arch observer of the Hollywood scene. He encounters Faye Greener, the destructive female, and Homer Simpson, the Midwestern *tabula rasa*, whose love for the unattainable Faye parodies Gatsby's romantic longing for Daisy. The point of the parallel is this: the westward turn to Hollywood coincides with a savage recasting of the characters and their longings. Fourteen years after *Gatsby*, West retells the story stripped of any hope of romance or redemption. Of the two stories depicting a failed search for fulfillment explicitly tied to the westward mythology of America, the Hollywood tale is the more bitter and deflating. As West writes, "It is hard to laugh at the need for beauty and romance, no matter how tasteless, even horrible, the results of that are. But it is easy to sigh. Few things are sadder than the truly monstrous" (61). The challenge for the Schlesinger film is to tap this bitter sentiment – and its embodiment in the misogynistically imagined monster, Faye Greener – in the making of a film in the 1970s.

At a crucial moment in the film, Tod vents his frustration at Homer by bitterly telling him that he is not the first to "be cold-decked by a dumb blonde"; he also tells him that Faye is "a whore – your business arrangement." The danger is that Tod's criticism ultimately becomes a criticism of the novel and film: they, too, put too much weight on Faye as a symbol of the corruption of the Californian Dream. Tod's frustration may give voice to the viewer's: the symbolic weight of Faye Greener seems inversely proportional to the depth and believability of her character.

"No one was ever less a Negro than Homer" – racial discourse in *The Day of the Locust*

"What am I – a nigger?" rasps angry dwarf Abe Kusich as he barks at the apartment handyman and runs past the lawn sprinkler at the San Berdoo just a few minutes into the film. The racial epithet is one of several in the film, and it may give us pause in a film virtually devoid of black people. On the one hand, we might see Kusich comment simply as part of the casual racism of the time, the way people talked. He consistently uses bluster, a sharp tongue, and outright pugnaciousness to compensate for the stereotypes that people bring to encounters with a dwarf. Perhaps the racist comments are merely part of his defensive swagger, along with his frequent calls to visit a bordello.

Race is a more complex issue in the novel and the film than might at
first appear, however. A comic moment in the novel that does not appear
in the film is revealing in this context. At Estee's party, the host shouts
to his butler in a mock Southern accent: "Here, you black rascal! A mint
julep." The narrator dryly follows this by describing how "A Chinese
servant came running with a Scotch and soda" (69). The comedy here
calls attention to the inadequacy of the black–white racial paradigm for
representing the history of California, where Asian and Mexican popula-
tions play crucial roles. Indeed, West's novel gives considerable attention
to Mexican immigrants camping in the canyons and living off the animals they trap near the comfortable middle-class homes of people such
as Homer Simpson. More than fifty years later, T. C. Boyle would use
that proximity between homeless Mexican immigrants and wealthy white
Californians as the basis for a powerful novel, *Tortilla Curtain*, set in the
1990s.

But while black characters are absent from West's novel, black culture is not, appearing in two popular jazz tunes of the 1930s that are
repeatedly quoted in book and film: "Jeepers Creepers," associated with
Louis Armstrong, and "Mama Don't Want No Peas an' Rice an' Coconut
Oil," associated with Count Basie, among others. Krin Gabbard, the
foremost critic on the role of jazz in motion pictures, has commented
on how the soundtrack in Hollywood films is often the only integrated
space, signaling a displacement of African-American culture in popular
representation.[15] Schlesinger follows West in prominently using Louis
Armstrong's recording of "Jeepers Creepers" and a period-appropriate
recording of "Mama Don't Want No Peas an' Rice an' Coconut Oil," and
he provides a full score of swing jazz, including traditional Tin Pan Alley
romantic tunes such as "I Wished on the Moon," "Isn't It Romantic?"
"Everything's in Rhythm With My Heart," and "Dancing on a Dime,"
along with novelty songs that comment comically on exotic vices such as
"Hot Voodoo," "I'm Feeling High," and "Who's Your Little Who-Zis."

The two songs that figure most noticeably in the novel and film were
very much in the air and on the airwaves when West was writing *The Day
of the Locust*. "Jeepers Creepers" appears in a 1938 film, *Going Places*,
one of Louis Armstrong's earliest and most developed acting roles. In
this farcical comedy Armstrong plays a groom for a racehorse named
Jeepers Creepers, who can be ridden only if he hears his eponymous
song. Eventually, the lead, Dick Powell, masquerading as a jockey, rides
the horse to victory while Armstrong and his band follow along the track
performing "Jeepers Creepers" to ensure that the horse behaves. The
song was a hit, nominated for the Oscar for Best Song, performed by
Armstrong with Jack Teagarden and Fats Waller on a radio broadcast in

October, 1938, and recorded in the studio by Armstrong with Waller in December of the same year. "Mama Don't Want No Peas an' Rice an' Coconut Oil" was also on the radio in 1938, a popular Caribbean novelty tune recorded by Cleo Brown in 1935, Benny Goodman in 1936, and Count Basie in 1937. The song is a comic response to tropical tourism, since Mama wants only gin, not native cuisine, after the coming of the colonist.

Schlesinger broadens "Jeepers Creepers" into the theme for the movie, using it in the opening scene to underscore the voyeurism of the California bungalow apartment. His opening echoes that of Hitchcock's *Rear Window* (1954) in showing the denizens of an apartment complex watching each other. In that context the reference to "Where'd ya git those eyes?," the remarkable "peepers" of the song, begins to make some sense. The verse of the song suggests that the look of the beloved's eyes can make rainy weather turn sunny: "I don't care how the weather vane points/When the weather vane points to gloomy,/It's gotta be sunny to me,/When your eyes look into mine." Still, the chorus suggests a more freakish appearance, as the peepers are so bright that the singer has to put his "cheaters" or sunglasses on, and any tenderness in the song gives way to comedy. The song underscores the film's emphasis on looking. Linked to Armstrong's voice and his problematic film career, the tune must also call attention to the bug-eyed look of surprise that Armstrong and other African-American performers used for comic, albeit stereotyped, effect. "Jeepers Creepers" sets the tone for the voyeurism and racism that characterizes the Hollywood depicted in the film.

Armstrong, the most famous of jazz entertainers to perform in movies, emerges as the central figure in discussing how black entertainers had to adopt stereotyped personas to succeed in white culture. To many, Armstrong's public persona signified a clown or an Uncle Tom, while others have seen his adoption of such minstrel poses and gestures as a trickster strategy "brilliantly solv[ing] the problem of how to be a man in a racist culture."[16] It is no accident that the villains in *Going Places* (1938) twice refer to Armstrong's character as "Uncle Tom." The presence of his song on Faye's lips as well as in the movie's soundtrack calls attention to Hollywood's exploitative role vis à vis black entertainers – and it keeps race on the margins of both the film and the viewer's consciousness.

Against this background, we have West's assertion that "No one was ever less a Negro than Homer," a characterization that is picked up in a particular scene in the movie and more generally by Donald Sutherland's performance. West's comment arises in the context of describing a colorful outfit that Homer wears: "Only a Negro could have worn it without looking ridiculous" (143). Behind West's description lies the idea that blacks carry or are expected to carry a certain stylistic elegance or bravado that makes outlandish outfits appropriate. The characterization indicates economically how conventional, Midwestern and timid Homer is by contrast. That these qualities are defined as somehow the apotheosis of whiteness – whiteness as blandness – is a crucial part of Homer's characterization, as well as an important entry point into the submerged racial discourse of the novel and film.

Whiteness has tended to be invisible in American culture and art, especially Hollywood movies. That is, one effect of presenting an all-white view of the world is to make race and whiteness disappear. West and Schlesinger use racial epithets and the jazz soundtrack to make whiteness visible, particularly in presenting Homer as the essence of whiteness. What are the consequences of viewing Homer as representing whiteness? Most directly, West is highlighting the Midwestern migration to California that affected the cultural flavor of Los Angeles in the first half of the twentieth century. Different states held reunion barbecues in Griffith Park, where Nebraskans or Iowans would mingle with their kind.[17] This demographic was particularly evident to Hollywood writers, who tended to be from the East Coast or England and who viewed the masses with snobbery and disdain ("How will it play in Peoria?" signified the leveling common denominator of film audiences).

Homer's whiteness parodies and underscores the cultural narrowness of Hollywood's products. The strong Eastern European and Jewish ethnic presence in Hollywood was muted and disguised in the films themselves as actors changed their names and accents and producers strove for assimilation, a process described in all its complexity by Neal Gabler in *An Empire of Their Own: How the Jews Invented Hollywood* (1988). In both novel and film, Harry Greener voices disgust with the predominantly Jewish management of the entertainment industry. Burgess Meredith deftly uses a hand gesture to suggest a stereotypically Jewish physiognomy (prominent nose and long beard) to punctuate his bitter attribution of his lack of success to a Jewish conspiracy.

West and Schlesinger both use Homer to epitomize the blandness and inadequacy of Hollywood's "dream factory," and doing so depends on a marginal black presence to illuminate the whiteness of Homer, whose screechy singing of "The Star-Spangled Banner" in the bath contrasts with the jazz score. This racially tinted contrast reaches its height in the nightclub scene where Homer wears the outfit that Tod muses "only a Negro could have worn . . . without looking ridiculous."[18] The vivid scene brings together a transvestite performer singing about African voodoo while Faye forcefeeds Homer with liquor. In a condensed tableau Homer's blandness is contrasted with various forms of transgression or otherness: gender-crossing, exotic religious practices, blackness, and intoxication. Schlesinger captures West's critique of the irony of the Midwestern colonization of Los Angeles, in which the guardians of middleclass morality staked out the reputed capital of vice as a place for healthful recuperation and the exercise of religious faith. Aided by the climate of the 1970s, Schlesinger also succeeds in explicating the connection between racial tension and urban violence implicit in the history of Los Angeles and hinted at in West's novel.

"Hollywood's a disaster area": *The Burning of Los Angeles*

In the heart of Los Angeles, beside the County Museum of Art, lie the La Brea Tar Pits, a superb source of Ice Age fossils. Among the fossils are the remains of the so-called "La Brea Woman," 9,000-year-old bones that provide evidence of not only human habitation but homicide (her skull is smashed in). Animals got trapped in the tar and became prey to carnivores, including this woman who is referred to as Los Angeles's first homicide. I prefer to think of her as the star of Hollywood's first cautionary tale. Like Faye Greener, the La Brea woman was drawn toward a world of apparent riches in which she became mired. Drawn by visions of plenty, the people whom West dubs "the seekers" come to Southern California but encounter disappointment and doom rather than paradise.

Los Angeles combines a sunny Mediterranean climate with the extremes of natural disaster – earthquake, fire, drought, mudslide, and flood. Throughout the twentieth century, the depiction of Southern Californian natural disasters has symbolized the mixture of hope and doom characteristic of the Hollywood story. The key analytical text studying Los Angeles and disaster is Mike Davis's *Ecology of Fear: Los Angeles and the Imagination of Disaster* (1998), which explores the real natural and manmade disasters that have befallen Southern California and provides an enlightening inventory of literary and filmic imaginations of Los Angeles disaster, identifying 138 books or movies in the twentieth century that depict the destruction of Los Angeles.

The Day of the Locust is typically considered one of the most famous of Hollywood apocalypse novels. But is it genuinely apocalyptic? After all, the shocking end is merely a film premiere turned into a riot, not an actual apocalypse. West's novel suggests a broader apocalyptic vision in three ways. First, the title of the work suggests a biblical plague (see Exodus 10:3–15).[19] Second, Tod's epic painting, *The Burning of Los Angeles*, translates the characters he meets into figures in his painting, which mixes a conflagration with an angry riot. Third, by ending the novel with the riot in progress and Tod screaming, West promotes the feeling that the disaster is ongoing and unresolved – still in progress.[20] In both movie and novel, the actual riot has overlaid upon it Tod's painterly vision of the destruction of the city: "a great bonfire of architectural styles . . . the mob carrying baseball bats and torches . . . the people who come to California to die . . . all those poor devils who can only be stirred by the promise of miracles and then only to violence. . . . No longer bored, they sang and danced joyously in the red light of the flames" (184).

West's novel, however, makes little reference to Los Angeles as a city of natural disasters; Schlesinger's film does, by beginning and ending with the image of a red carnation placed in the wall crack in Tod's apartment caused by the Long Beach earthquake. But, although earthquake figures prominently in Fitzgerald's contemporaneous Hollywood novel, *The Last Tycoon* (1941), it is fire that dominates the apocalyptic imagination of *The Day of the Locust*. As Joan Didion so concisely put it, West's novel recognizes that "the city burning is Los Angeles's deepest image of itself."[21] While West was completing the book, a wildfire in Topanga canyon consumed 16,500 acres and 350 homes (in November 1938).[22]

The ambiguous apocalypse of *The Day of the Locust* combines two different disasters, riot and fire, disasters that can, of course, go hand in hand, as they did in spectacular Los Angeles riots in 1965 and 1992. Writing in 1939, West might be seen as prescient, his novel foreshadowing the Zoot Suit Riots of 1943. To a filmgoer watching Schlesinger's film, the concluding images of the burning of Los Angeles would doubtless suggest the Watts riots of recent memory, just as a contemporary viewer could be forgiven for thinking of Rodney King. These echoes lend support to Davis's assertion that "the abiding hysteria of Los Angeles disaster fiction . . . is rooted in racial anxiety."[23] Certainly, Los Angeles's actual riots – from the Chinese massacre of 1871 to the Zoot Suit Riots during World War II, Watts in the 1960s, and the Rodney King riots of 1992 – bear this out.

In West's *The Day of the Locust*, racial hatred and white fear lie near the surface, but the apocalyptic vision seems to grow more directly out of repressed sexuality. Literally, the riot grows out of overcrowding combined with Homer's violent response to being teased by Adore Loomis, the sexually ambivalent child actor. Earlier in the novel, West describes Homer's chastity as a defense against immolation: "In Homer's case, [lust] would be like dropping a spark into a barn full of hay" (102). In Tod's painting Faye stands naked in "the left foreground being chased by the group of men and women . . . One of the women is about to hurl a rock at her to bring her down" (108). But in the novel, it is Tod, Homer, Miguel, and Earle who are chasing Faye, not a nameless mob. Faye's "cockteasing" appears to stimulate an apocalypse.

The interpretative problem is not unknown to apocalyptic literature. When profound disaster is not prophesied genuinely as part of a religious vision, it tends to function as a satirical scourge by which the writer purifies the society he or she is examining. In *The Day of the Locust*, Faye's sexual allure symbolizes the recurrent frustration of desire built into the hyperbole of the Californian Dream. The violence arising from this frustration manifests itself in Tod's rape attempt, Earle's brawls with Kusich and Miguel, Homer's attack on Adore, and, finally, the unleashed and senseless mass hysteria of the premiere mob. To Schlesinger's audience, the parallel with Watts would seem plausible, as the riots were correctly seen as growing out of the frustration of the poor and marginalized living in the shadow of the city's opulence. That connection, intertwining the intimations of religious, racial, and sexual tension in West's novel with the different but related tensions of the American 1970s, expresses Schlesinger's success in translating West's unfilmable novel to the screen.

NOTES

1. Nathanael West, *Miss Lonelyhearts and The Day of the Locust* (New York: New Directions, 1962), p. 72. Further quotations will be cited parenthetically in the text.
2. This list of self-referential Hollywood films comes from David A. Cook, *Lost Illusions: American Cinema in the Shadow of Watergate and Vietnam, 1970–1979, Volume IX, History of the American Cinema*, vols., gen. ed. Charles Harpole (New York: p. 289).
3. Examining the social changes behind the transformation of 1970s cinema is beyond the scope of this essay. See Cook, *Lost Illusions*, and Robert Kolker, *A Cinema of Loneliness: Penn, Stone, Kubrick, Scorsese, Spielberg, and Altman* (New York: Oxford University Press, 2000) on films of the 1970s.
4. Jay Martin, *Nathanael West: The Art of His Life* (New York: Hayden, 1970), p. 334.
5. Richard Keller Simon, "Between Capra and Adorno: West's *The Day of the Locust* and the Movies of the 1930s," *Modern Language Quarterly* 54:4 (1993), p. 524.
6. Schlesinger's earlier collaboration with screenwriter Waldo Salt, *Midnight Cowboy*, provides an excellent illustration of the inverted values of counter-cultural 1970s cinema.
7. See my *Movies About the Movies: Hollywood Reflected* (Lexington: University of Kentucky Press, 1997), pp. 15–17.
8. Nancy Pogel and William Chamberlain discuss self-referentiality in Schlesinger's *The Day of the Locust* in "Self-Reflections in Adaptations of

Black Comic Novels," in Alan R. Pratt, ed., *Black Humor: Critical Essays* (New York: Garland, 1993), pp. 269–281. They stress how the self-consciousness that emerges from the depiction of "the whole apparatus of the film industry" works parodically to attune the audience to mock cinematic effects (such as dramatically lighting Faye with the car headlights in the cockfight scene). Pogel and Chamberlain also note Schlesinger's frequent use of window and mirror shots, and note the importance of the two film-within-a-film scenes.

9. Scenes invented in film adaptations offer an important opportunity to analyze the adaptive process. Schlesinger's film includes several powerful scenes taken quite faithfully from the novel (the cockfight, the drunken brawl that follows it, the crash of the Waterloo set). While crucial to the film, these scenes prove less useful in analyzing the process of adaptation.

10. Peg Entwistle, a starlet who leaped from the "H" of the Hollywoodland sign in 1932, is the only suicide documented in that location. See Ken Schessler, *This is Hollywood: An Unusual Guide* (Redlands, CA: Schlessler, 1993), p. 31.

11. Leslie A. Fiedler, *Love and Death in the American Novel* (New York: Dell, 1966). Further quotations will be cited parenthetically in the text.

12. See Mike Davis, *City of Quartz: Excavating the Future in Los Angeles* (New York: Verso, 1990) on the rhetoric of Southern Californian "seduction" and "prostitution" (p. 18). For a discussion of the influx of writers to Hollywood in the 1930s and 1940s, see Richard Fine, *Hollywood and the Profession of Authorship, 1928–1940* (Ann Arbor: UMI Press, 1985).

13. William A. Cohen, "Manual Conduct in *Great Expectations*," in Charles Dickens, *Great Expectations*, Case Studies in Contemporary Criticism, ed. Janice Carlisle (New York: St. Martin's Press, 1996), p. 576.

14. Quigley's annual survey of motion picture exhibitors places Mae West and Shirley Temple in the "Top Ten Moneymakers" in 1934. Temple topped the chart from 1935 to 1938. Reprinted at www.reelclassics.com/articles/general/quigleytop10-article.html.

15. Krin Gabbard, *Jammin' At the Margins: Jazz and the American Cinema* (Chicago: University of Chicago Press, 1996).

16. For discussion of Armstrong's complex role in the popular performance of racial identity, see Donald Bogle, *Toms, Coons, Mulattos, Mammies and Bucks: An Interpretive History of Blacks in American Films* (New York: Continuum Publishing, 2003); Ralph Ellison, *Shadow and Act* (New York: Vintage, 1972); and Gabbard, *Jammin'*.

17. See Kevin Starr, *Inventing the Dream: California Through the Progressive Era* (New York: Oxford University Press, 1985), pp. 89–92, and Davis, *City of Quartz*, who discusses the "great influx of Middle Western babbitry between 1900–1925" as one of the "great internal migrations of American history" (p. 114).

18. Schlesinger transposes this assessment of Homer's wardrobe to Faye and the final party scene, but Homer wears outrageous and inappropriate outfits in both scenes in the film.

19. See Jay Martin's discussion of the title of the novel in *Nathanael West: The Art of His Life* (New York: Hayden, 1970), pp. 318–319.

20. A contemporary bestselling detective novel, Michael Connelly's *Angels Flight* (1999), ends with a Los Angeles race riot in which the sounds of a siren and a character screaming are indistinguishable, a clear allusion to *The Day of the Locust*.
21. Joan Didion, "Los Angeles Notebook," in Didion, *Slouching Toward Bethlehem* (New York: Modern Library, 2000), p. 201.
22. Mike Davis, *Ecology of Fear: Los Angeles and the Imagination of Disaster* (New York: Holt, 1998), p. 98.
23. Ibid., p. 281.

4   *Ship of Fools*: from novel to film

Robert H. Brinkmeyer, Jr.

Both the author of *Ship of Fools*, Katherine Anne Porter (1890–1980), and the director and producer of the novel's film adaptation, Stanley Kramer, had grand expectations for their works. Porter envisioned her novel (the only one she published) as her crowning achievement, the work that would finally put to rest the carping critics who had dismissed her as "merely" a writer of short stories. *Ship of Fools*, moreover, would be the fullest expression of the major themes and issues that she had been exploring all along in her short stories, her culminating statement on life in the twentieth century, and, more generally, on the human condition. As the centerpiece of her career, the novel would look both backward to her previous work and forward to posterity.

Kramer, likewise, had high hopes for his film. As he recalled in his autobiography, he read *Ship of Fools* not long after its publication in 1962 and was immediately struck by its potential as a motion picture, observing that while reading the novel "ideas for filming kept flooding into my head. The characters, the subcharacters, the mature but tragic love story, all appealed to me. And the technique of telling the stories with a narrator who would function like a Greek chorus occurred to me in what I thought was a brilliant flash."[1] In contrast to how he felt about the two films he produced during the time when he was making plans and preparations for filming *Ship of Fools*, *A Child Is Waiting* (1963) and *Invitation to a Gunfighter* (1964), Kramer believed that Porter's novel "had everything necessary to be a smashing success" and that "it had the promise of being one of the greatest pictures ever made" (Kramer, *Mad World*, 203, 202). Perhaps appropriately, and certainly ironically, given the novel's withering portrayal of the foolishness of human aspiration and the tainted nature of even the purest-seeming motives, the hopes and dreams of both Porter and Kramer went unrealized. In the end, *Ship of Fools* brought Porter lots of money, but not the praise she desired; and Kramer's film, released in 1965, brought him neither big money nor lasting praise, even though the picture did initially receive a good deal of attention, landing nine Oscar nominations.

Figure 5. Lee Marvin and Vivien Leigh are two of the mismatched misfits voyaging to no good end in Stanley Kramer's *Ship of Fools*, a 1965 Columbia Pictures release.

Porter's problems with the novel started almost as soon as she began writing. Its origins lie in a long, diary-like letter that Porter wrote to her friend Caroline Gordon during a 1931 ocean crossing she took from Veracruz to Bremerhaven. Initially, Porter planned to rework her observations to Gordon into a long story (or a very short novel), entitled "Promised Land," for inclusion in a collection which was eventually published as *Pale Horse, Pale Rider: Three Short Novels* (1939). But while "Promised Land" did not spin entirely out of her control, Porter, who was known for piercingly taut artistry, found its ever-enlarging narrative and cast of characters too unwieldy for a long story, a form (of which she was a master) characteristically demanding tight control and lean expression. "I was baffled and frustrated because I wasn't able to work my material into the shape it wanted to become," she commented much later,[2] and it was only with great reluctance that she finally accepted the fact that "Promised Land" demanded the scope and size of a novel. No doubt her reluctance stemmed in part from what she knew about herself as a writer: that she typically wrote in quick bursts, sometimes finishing a story in a single sitting, and that she then might go for weeks, months, even years before writing something else. Porter's work habits (if they can be called that, so easily distracted was she from writing) were better suited for stories rather than novels; and she knew well her limitations with long projects, having recently failed to complete a biography of Cotton Mather and at least one other novel.

Nonetheless, rather than abandoning "Promised Land" for shorter works (she typically revised portions of her uncompleted longer works for publication as stories), Porter decided in 1940 to push ahead with the novel, which she was now calling "No Safe Harbor." Within two years, she had written more than two hundred pages and was hoping to be done within another two. But at this point her work on the novel essentially stopped, and it would be another twenty years before she finally completed it. During these twenty years, Porter was only rarely working on the novel; as she did with her stories, she wrote in fits, though, faced with a long and complicated novel, she tried to extend those fits to complete what she was now seeing as both her crowning achievement and her albatross. "I'd work on it and push it away," she later said of her efforts. "I separated myself from it for two or three years at a time; I'd quit in the middle of a paragraph and start again months or years later, and I thought it was going to look like a piece of restored pottery dug out of a prehistoric midden."[3] Of the psychological toll exacted over the many years of writing, Porter concluded after finishing *Ship of Fools*: "I think I sprained my soul."[4]

Despite her troubles writing *Ship of Fools*, once it was completed Porter claimed that the novel had grown sinuously, even organically, saying that the entire process had "been like making a tapestry, really. Weaving on a shuttle. You use threads of different colors, but the work itself is all of a piece." Whenever she had returned to the unfinished manuscript, she said, she had immediately picked up the thread "with no break in the novel's continuity or style."[5] She asserted, furthermore, that over the many years of the novel's composition her fundamental beliefs had remained constant. "It's astonishing how little I've changed," she said in a 1963 interview: "nothing in my point of view or my way of feeling . . . We change, of course, every day; we are not the same people who sat down at this table, yet there is a basic and innate being that is unchanged."[6]

Setting aside the issue of sincerity, Porter's comments are woefully inept if not flat-out mistaken. Her finished novel is less organic than mechanical; or, put another way, it is less woven than stitched together, less a tapestry than a patchwork quilt. One of Porter's most observant critics, Janis Stout, aptly observes that if *Ship of Fools* succeeds at all, "it does so as a collection of separate episodes, not as a whole." Stout characterizes the novel "as a sequence of short episodes stitched onto an overly predictable linear form, the allegorical journey," a sequence that reiterates ad nauseam humanity's collusion with evil. "With virtually no growth by the characters and little surprise, after the first few episodes, either of incident or of emotion," Stout concludes, "the whole becomes less than the sum of its parts."[7]

Even more troubling is Porter's claim that her fundamental attitudes and beliefs remained unchanged over the many years during which she worked on *Ship of Fools*. In fact, a number of her basic beliefs, particularly with regard to politics, changed dramatically during this time, and these changes weighed heavily on the vision underpinning the novel, pushing it toward unrelenting bitterness and cynicism. By the mid-1930s, Porter's early leftist sympathies had given way to disenchantment with socialist politics and the communism of the Soviet Union. Her antifascism of the early 1930s had evolved by the end of the decade into a thoroughgoing antitotalitarianism. To Porter's eyes (and indeed to many Americans' eyes at the time), all authoritarian governments, no matter what their professed ideologies, were fundamentally the same, an idea that she expressed succinctly, somewhat later, to one of her correspondents: "I feel indeed that Communism and Fascism are two names for the same thing . . . [both are] factions of totalitarianism."[8]

So obsessive had Porter's antitotalitarianism become by the start of World War II that she had convinced herself that fascists were in control of much of American government and business, and that these infiltrators were hell-bent on destroying individual liberties in the name of patriotism. "When that Dope Goering remarked en passant that America would be an inside job, well, I could only hope it wasn't so," Porter wrote to a friend in 1942. "But now I lie awake at nights fearing it may be true . . . God knows the air is full of signs and portents" (Porter, *Letters*, 228). "The very thing we are fighting in Europe is seeping up here among us like a kind of miasma out of the very earth under out feet," she wrote to her nephew in 1943, concluding later in the letter: "There never was such a concerted assault on human liberty as we see now, since the first idea of human liberty was ever fought for. And our worst enemies are here at home, most dangerous because you can't walk over them with an army" (Porter, *Letters*, 271). Porter was convinced that, in particular, the State Department and the FBI (which she sometimes identified as the Gestapo) were under fascist control. Before long, she was finding fascists just about everywhere she looked, most notably in the Republican Party and the Catholic Church. One can only wonder what the novelist J. F. Powers, a Roman Catholic who had gone to prison during World War II as a conscientious objector, thought when Porter wrote to him in 1947 that she feared fascism more than communism because "it has the Pope at its head, and is Protean in its forms, and I hear people talking Fascism and acting it without knowing what name to call it by" (Porter, *Letters*, 350). Even if fascism was the graver danger, Porter deeply feared the communist threat, and believed that communists, like the fascists, were quietly infiltrating all areas of American society. In another letter from 1947, Porter wrote that communists had strategically located themselves "not only in departments of government here and abroad, but in our schools and universities, the press, the publishing business, industry, the motion pictures. You find them everywhere; they mean business and they are dangerous."[9]

Underlying Porter's political paranoia, and no doubt in large part fueling it, was a forbidding vision of humanity's fundamentally evil nature, a vision that characterized people, whatever their apparent goodness, as vicious, bestial, and hateful. Apart from her political comments, Porter's misanthropy surfaced most virulently in her private comments on blacks, Jews, and Germans. They do not bear repeating. More significantly, her misanthropy also surfaced in, and indeed permeated, *Ship of Fools*. In full flower during most of the time she was writing the novel, Porter's loathing of the general run of humanity (at times, drawing on what she falsely claimed was her aristocratic heritage, she could find honor and dignity in an elite few) is the work's defining element, shaping and coloring just about every aspect of the narrative. She was not shy in talking about her and her novel's central vision. In a letter written a few years before she finished the book, she described *Ship of Fools* as:

A long exposition of the disastrous things people do to each other out of ignorance, prejudice, presumptuousness, self-love and self-hate, with religion, or politics, or race, or social distinctions, or even just nationality or a difference in customs . . . and this is the other side of the question, out of inertia, moral apathy, timidity, indifference, and even a subconscious criminal collusion, people allow others to do every kind of wrong, and even, if the wrongdoers are successful, finally rather approve of them, perhaps envy them a little. (Porter, *Letters*, 546–547)

Porter's right-on-the-money description points to the scope of *Ship of Fools*'s subject: evil in all its manifestations, from the psychological to physical violence, and to a misanthropic disgust with humanity, particularly disgust with the human propensity for self-deception, for voicing goodness while acting otherwise. No one in the novel finally acts with genuine compassion and dignity (with the possible exception of the unnamed bride and groom, whom we never really get to know; and the thrust of the novel suggests that they, too, along with everyone else, are on the same voyage to death and despair); every interaction, from chance meetings to lifelong relationships, suffers from the insidious evil that makes up the human heart, the evil of which Ric and Rac, the twin six-year-old terrors from the Spanish dance group, are the walking, talking embodiments. Ric and Rac suggest that Porter's world is the flipside of Rousseau's: her children begin not in innocence but in malice; and as they mature and enter into society, they do not learn evil but instead learn how to mask it, tucking it away behind custom and social grace. The long-suffering Frau Schmitt knows something of this process, observing that even the simplest relationship masks insidious desire and conflict: "She had always believed so deeply that human beings only wished to be quiet and happy, each in his own way: but there was a spirit of evil in them that could not let each other be in peace. One man's desire must always crowd out another's, one must always take his own good at another's expense."[10]

Individual evil paves the way for the social evil of authoritarian societies. Although set before Hitler's ascension to power, the novel has as its backdrop Germany's coming fate; sometimes that future is very visible, as when Herr Rieber, the vile German publisher, mouths off, but more often it merely haunts the text flittingly, suggesting a larger context for the novel's action. For Porter, the authority of authoritarianism rested primarily in the collusion of the oppressed; people willingly gave themselves to authoritarian dictates through indifference, self-interest, or fear. The dynamics of authoritarianism thus in a sense appear everywhere in the text, as one after another character bends and twists their conscience in order to maintain their peace and stability. Those dynamics get their fullest expression near the end of the novel when the Spanish dance company organizes a gala and then, through public ridicule and shame, coerces people to come. Arne Hansen's words not only speak of the ugly occasion that night but also look forward to the ugly world under which most of Europe would soon be suffering: "All is crooked, everything, look at these Spaniards! You know they are whores and pimps, nobody wants their party – but here we are, we all pay and we all go, like sheep! They blackmail, they cheat, they lie, they steal from everybody all over Santa Cruz, everybody sees, knows – what do we do? Nothing" (Porter, *Ship of Fools*, 412).

"Don't forget I am a passenger on that ship," Porter said in one of her interviews, a statement truer than she was ever willingly to admit publicly in any detailed fashion. During the time she was writing *Ship of Fools*, Porter was guilty of, and was no doubt later haunted by, her own collusion with what she had identified as an authoritarian enemy, and this fact probably goes far in explaining the self-disgust that lies behind the novel's misanthropic vision. In May 1942, with *Ship of Fools* well underway, Porter was interviewed by an FBI agent seeking information on Josephine Herbst, a longtime friend of Porter who had recently begun work in the federal government. Despite her concern for individual liberties and her fear of the FBI's infiltration by fascists, Porter not only provided damning information on Herbst's radical past, but also made up stories about her. She never publicly acknowledged her betrayal of Herbst, continuing to correspond with her friend as if nothing had happened, even writing to her to express what she said was her horror upon hearing that Herbst had been dismissed from her job. Two years after the interview, in a letter to her nephew, Porter advised him on a matter about which she knew all too well, writing that "very few people are capable of faithfulness to a love or an idea, and everybody in the long run loves himself the best of all. And there is a natural Judas sleeps in the heart of too many" (Porter, *Letters*, 283–284). Eighteen tortured years later, she finally completed the novel that externalized the natural Judas in her own heart.

It is somewhat ironic, then, that Stanley Kramer, a pioneering director who frequently gave himself and his art to liberal causes, would be so excited about adapting a novel that owes much of its origins to the author's betrayal of a leftist friend and more generally to her deep-seated prejudice against what she saw as the filthy, disposable masses, particularly the Jews. Kramer, of course, could not have known about Porter's betrayal of Herbst, but it is hard to believe that he missed the ugly anti-Semitism that percolates through the novel, primarily in the depiction of Herr Löwenthal, a Jewish merchant who at one time or another displays just about every demeaning Jewish stereotype. Löwenthal is not merely mean and bitter, he is foolish. At one point in the novel, angry over Herr Rieber's scorn for him, he spits disdainfully when he sees a group of Catholics celebrating mass, but right into the wind, so that he sprays his own face.

What, then, attracted Kramer to the novel? Other than his comments cited at the beginning of this essay, focusing on the richness of the characters and the tragic love affair between Dr. Schumann and La Condesa, Kramer remained vague about the great potential that he saw in *Ship of Fools*. Certainly, the tremendous fanfare that greeted the novel upon its publication must have had some impact (the screen rights were bought almost immediately, within a month of the book's appearance). Porter's novel made such a huge initial splash in part because its appearance had been so long anticipated; for decades the literary world had known that Porter was working on a novel and tantalizing excerpts had been surfacing in magazines. *Ship of Fools*'s publication on All Fools Day, 1962, then, was something of a literary sensation, and most early reviews were overwhelmingly positive. Mark Schorer's opening sentences, from his front-page review in the *New York Times Book Review*, captures this initial hoopla:

This novel has been famous for years. It has been awaited through an entire literary generation. Publishers and foundations, like many once hopeful readers, long ago gave it up. Now it is suddenly, superbly here . . . It is our good fortune that it comes at last still in our time. It will endure, one hardly risks anything in saying, far beyond it, for many literary generations.[11]

Almost certainly, Kramer envisioned adapting what was being proclaimed as the great American novel into the great American film. Signaling his ambitions was the star-studded cast he began assembling, which in the end included Vivien Leigh (Mary Treadwell), Simone Signoret (La Condesa), Jose Ferrer (Herr Rieber), Oskar Werner (Dr. Schumann), Lee Marvin (Tenny), George Segal (David), Elizabeth Ashley (Jenny), José Greco (Pepe), and Heinz Ruehmann (Herr Löwenthal).

To adapt the novel into film, Kramer faced the daunting but necessary task of trimming its overwhelming length (497 pages) and its immense cast of characters (there are so many characters that Porter prefaced the novel with a list to help the reader). Even more basic and crucial to the film's final shape, however, was the question of what to do with the novel's heavy-handed allegorical elements. Porter intended *Ship of Fools*, with its title echoing that of Alexander Barclay's 1509 translation of Alexander Brant's allegorical poem *Das Narrenschiff* (1491), to portray the human condition on a level transcending specific history; it was, she said in an interview, "a parable, if you like, of the ship of this world on its voyage to eternity."[12] And indeed, as Josephine Herbst pointed out in comments to friends, *Ship of Fools* sacrificed historical accuracy for allegorical schematization. "It's all overschematized," Herbst wrote in a 1962 letter:

This is 1931, she centers it on the Germans and there is only one question – the Jewish question. Her Germans have never heard of the Weimar republic, its glories or its disgraces. The issues that even Hitler had to hurdle before he could get around to the Jewish question are not present, none of the actors that Isherwood documents in the Berlin Stories. But then, of course, she puffs it all up as allegory.[13]

Porter also completely missed, Herbst pointed out, the possibilities for radical change that marked the times; despite the many crises facing the world, many reformers believed that those crises signaled the collapse of oppressive political and economic systems and the possibility of revolutionary reform. Hope as much as despair distinguished the period.

The allegorical and ahistorical aspects of Porter's novel clearly had little appeal to Kramer, a director known for his commitment to liberal causes and social justice. By the time he began work on *Ship of Fools*, he was already known as a maker of "message films" – films that explored specific social issues frankly and directly, if perhaps too simplistically for some people's tastes. He despised the designation, for he knew that critics used it to brand his films as heavy-handed and didactic; at the same time, he affirmed his commitment as a filmmaker to confronting significant social problems ("Perhaps I should have been a social worker," he once jokingly said),[14] commenting that "if to make a film contemporary and provocative, if to make drama out of what is already drama, if to translate that into film is to communicate a 'message,' then I am guilty. I think everything has a message; I don't care what it is."[15]

Kramer ultimately jettisoned almost entirely Porter's allegorical framework to ground his film's vision more thoroughly in a frightening portrayal of the crippling weakness of people to live by their ideals and of the terrifying ends to which that weakness can be manipulated by authoritarian forces. Kramer shows almost everyone in *Ship of Fools* blindly following society's demands rather than conscience in order not to stand out, that is, not to appear foolish. It is Dr. Schumann, having failed in his commitment to La Condesa, who delivers the lines that haunt the picture and comment upon its action. "When I think of the things I have seen on this ship. The stupid cruelties, the vanities. We all talk about values. There's no values," he says, adding that unlike La Condesa, who ran great risks working to improve the lot of the impoverished, "respectable" people meekly toe the line. "We are the intelligent, civilized people who carry out orders we are given, no matter what they may be. Our biggest mission in life is to avoid being fools. And we wind up being the biggest fools of all." And such foolishness, Kramer suggested much more forthrightly than Porter ever did, has led to a nation of fools – Nazi Germany – a once-civilized people, now colluding with evil rather than opposing it, followers of Hitler's barbarism.

In choosing Abby Cohen to write the screenplay, Kramer signaled the direction in which he wanted to take *Ship of Fools* long before he began filming. He had recently worked with Cohen on *Judgment at Nuremberg* (1961), hiring him to revise his 1959 teleplay of the Nuremberg trials into the film's screenplay. Although Kramer later wrote that he chose Cohen for *Ship of Fools* because he "considered him an excellent writer who knew a lot about Germans and Germany" (Kramer, *Mad World*, 205), it is clear from how the film turned out that he wanted to reinvestigate the very subject – what in the human character made the evils of Nazism possible – that he had explored in *Judgment at Nuremberg*. *Ship of Fools*, in other words, was meant to be the prequel to *Judgment at Nuremberg*, and would explore the terrors of Nazism, as the earlier film had, by focusing not on major political figures but on everyday people who become involved in the corrupt system. Moreover, Dr. Schumann's central role in *Ship of Fools* mirrored that of Ernst Janning in *Judgment at Nuremberg*: both collude with evil by accepting things as they develop, eventually coming to understand their complicity and guilt; and achieving this understanding, both deliver passionate speeches that vigorously voice their films' – and Kramer's – primary concern or "message."

In adapting a novel primarily about the universal ugliness of humanity into a film primarily about the rise of Nazism, as made possible through human weakness, Kramer may have been influenced by Hannah Arendt's *Eichmann in Jerusalem: A Report on the Banality of Evil*, which first appeared in 1963. Kramer and Cohen (they worked very closely together on the screenplay) made numerous changes, large and small, to Porter's novel. For one, they moved the time of the novel from August 1931 (when Porter actually took her voyage) to March 1933, a time when Hitler was appointed Chancellor and the Nazi transformation of Germany had begun. While neither Hitler nor the Nazis are ever mentioned specifically in the film, Rieber's tirades against the Jews and his calls for their extermination, along with deformed children, the elderly, and people of mixed race, clearly look to Nazi racial policy. The coming changes in Germany, moreover, are hinted at in a conversation between the dwarf Glocken and the Jew Löwenthal when they refer to the national elections that Hitler had called for to cement his power in March 1933 (the action of the film takes place, we discover, the week following the vote). Again, while the Nazis are not mentioned specifically, it is clear what Glocken means when he speaks of "Herr Rieber's Party." But the most telling signal of the Nazi future – the destination toward which this ship is sailing – comes during the film's final scene when the passengers are disembarking at Bremerhaven; there a man in Nazi uniform, a prominent swastika on his armband, greets one of the travelers. And the band plays happily on.

Kramer chose to film in black and white because, he said later, he "thought it would convey the mood better than color" and because "the theme was just too foreboding for full color" (Kramer, *Mad World*, 205). That may be, but Kramer at the same time goes to remarkable lengths to clean up the disgusting extremes of Porter's novel, particularity the filth and deformity everywhere present on board the ship. Any number of cleansings could be cited – Herr and Frau Hutten's dog Bébé sitting happily at the dining table instead of wallowing in vomit, Herr Glocken's friendly manner and straight, rather than grotesquely humped, back, to name only two – but one literal cleansing, the turning of the hoses on the people of the steerage, stands nicely for the whole process. In Porter's novel sailors hose down steerage to clean up the filth from the writhing, seasick passengers. "Hundreds of people, men and women, were wallowing on the floor, being sick, and sailors were washing them down with streaming hoses. They lay in the film of water, just lifting their heads now and then, or trying to roll nearer the rail," Porter described the scene, adding a little later:

Some of the men were getting on their feet by then; they stood jammed together along the walls of the ship and at the rail while the sailors went on hosing down the filth of their sickness into the sea. They then piled back upon each other, on the wet canvas chairs in their wet clothes, and in the abominable heat a strange mingled smell of vegetable and animal rot rose from them. (Porter, *Ship of Fools*, 72, 73)

The film portrays the hosing scene, in contrast, as an expression of Dr. Schumann's compassion for the suffering. After seeing that the steerage does not have adequate facilities for washing, he orders a resistant officer to turn the hoses on. He wants to give everyone a shower. Once the water is turned on, all in the steerage dance about happily, offering themselves to the hoses' spray. The good doctor smiles at this happy, fiesta-like scene.

Almost everyone in the film is similarly cleaned up, even Rieber, who in a moment of weakness begrudgingly admits that, after all, Löwenthal, the hated Jew with whom he shares a cabin, is not such a bad person. Of all the characters' transformations, Löwenthal's most dramatically impacts on the thrust of the film. As already noted, Porter's Löwenthal is the stuff of anti-Semitic hate-mongering, a bitterly nasty man from a bitterly nasty race. In the film, however, Löwenthal is forever gracious, forgiving, happy, and optimistic; he stands throughout as an honorable rebuke to German prejudice. Nothing seems to faze him; he is nice to one and all. Shunned by the Germans, he nonetheless sees himself as a good German, and he has the evidence to prove it: he is a decorated war hero, holder of the Iron Cross (which he takes out when he wants to make himself feel better, during those rare moments when he is feeling rather down). To Glocken, he counsels patience in the face of prejudice, sure that the world is getting better all the time, sure that Germans will outgrow whatever prejudices they presently hold against the Jews and others. Joan Givner has remarked that Löwenthal's remaking plunges the film into simplistic melodrama (saintly Jew *vs.* blackguard Germans),[16] and certainly at times that seems true, though Kramer tries to work against that simplicity by having Glocken deliver several stinging comeuppances regarding

Löwenthal's blind optimism (particularly with regard to his views on the German situation), telling him at one point, "You may be the biggest fool on this boat."

Kramer wants us to like Löwenthal but makes clear, by Herr Glocken's rebukes together with a few of his own sometimes excruciating lines (including his comeback to the more knowing Glocken, "There are nearly a million Jews in Germany. What are they going to do? Kill all of us?"), that we are not to admire him: he is too naive for anybody's good, other than the few unhappy individuals, such as Elsa Lutz, whom he makes feel better about themselves. It is La Condesa, instead, whom Kramer wants us to admire, and to a lesser extent Dr. Schumann (who comes close to the heroic but finally succumbs to the demands of conformity by not joining her), which is why their relationship dominates the movie in a way that it does not in the novel. La Condesa represents the possibility of change through commitment, the possibility of not acting foolish – that is, she is the courageous reformer who takes a stand and does not compromise, and her entrance into and exit from the film, the former with a sea of cheering peasants parting to let her through, the latter with her walking in quiet dignity off the ship and into a waiting automobile taking her to imprisonment, are two of the film's most stirring moments.

It is precisely La Condesa's heroism, with its galvanizing potential to right social injustice, that Porter does not give us and that Kramer cannot do without. Kramer's film reconfigures Porter's condemnation of human folly (including the idea of the heroic), with its attempt to reach the universal through an allegorical structure, into a study of difficult choices involved in taking a stand for human values in a world that attempts to destroy those values. For Kramer, to conform when you know better is to die, spiritually if not literally; Dr. Schumann, utterly broken after deciding not to go with La Condesa, soon dies of a heart attack; Herr Freytag, torn by guilt for having rejected the Jewish wife he loves, wallows in self-pity and guilt. (The novel presents things quite differently – Dr. Schumann is alive if not well at the end; and Freytag, though troubled by the social difficulties caused by his wife's Jewishness, has not rejected her).

In the end, there is very little of Katherine Anne Porter's novel in the film other than the most general outlines of character and plot. There are two brief scenes, however, in which Kramer deliberately invokes Porter's novel: Glocken's addresses to the viewer at the beginning and the end of the film, both of which implicate the audience in the universality of foolishness. "This is the ship of fools," Glocken announces minutes into the film, and, after giving a brief rundown of the many fools on board, he adds, "And, who knows, if you look closely enough, you may find yourself on board." At the end, in the film's final words, he again addresses the viewer: "So, I can just hear you saying, What has all this to do with us?" He pauses, and then with a knowing look says, "Nothing," lapsing into laughter that of course signals he knows otherwise. Kramer may be tipping his hat to Porter in Glocken's addresses, but he should have found another way of doing that, or just accepted the fact that the credits would give Porter her due. Not only is Glocken's simplistic moralizing unnecessary and distracting, but his words threaten to undo all that Kramer worked so hard to put across in the rest of the film, redirecting its grounded social realism outward into the faraway country of allegorical abstraction.

NOTES

1. Stanley Kramer and Thomas M. Coffey, *A Mad, Mad, Mad, Mad World: A Life in Hollywood* (New York: Harcourt Brace, 1997), p. 204. Further quotations will be cited parenthetically in the text.
2. Quoted in James Ruoff, "Katherine Anne Porter Comes to Kansas," in Joan Givner, ed., *Katherine Anne Porter: Conversations* (Jackson: University Press of Mississippi, 1987), p. 67.
3. Quoted in Roy Newquist, "An Interview with Katherine Anne Porter," in Givner, ed., *Katherine Anne Porter: Conversations*, p. 116.
4. Quoted in ibid., p. 117.
5. Quoted in Maurice Dolbier, "I've Had a Good Run for My Money," in Givner, ed., *Katherine Anne Porter: Conversations*, pp. 76, 75.
6. Quoted in Barbara Thompson, "Katherine Anne Porter: An Interview," in Givner, ed., *Katherine Anne Porter: Conversations*, p. 96.
7. Janis Stout, *Katherine Anne Porter: A Sense of the Times* (Charlottesville: University Press of Virginia, 1995), p. 213.
8. Katherine Anne Porter, *Letters of Katherine Anne Porter*, ed. Isabel Bayley (New York: Atlantic Monthly Press, 1990), p. 394. Further quotations will be cited parenthetically in the text.
9. Katherine Anne Porter, "A Letter to the Editor of *The Nation*," in *The Collected Essays and Occasional Prose of Katherine Anne Porter*, p. 203.
10. Katherine Anne Porter, *Ship of Fools* (Boston: Little, Brown, 1962), p. 152. Further quotations will be cited parenthetically in the text.
11. Mark Schorer, review of *Ship of Fools*, *New York Times Book Review*, April 1, 1962, p. 1.
12. Quoted in Thompson, "Katherine Anne Porter: An Interview," p. 97.
13. Quoted in Joan Givner, *Katherine Anne Porter: A Life* (New York: Simon and Schuster, 1982), p. 454.
14. Quoted in Donald Spoto, *Stanley Kramer: Film Maker* (1978; rpt. Hollywood: Samuel French, 1990), p. 20.
15. Quoted in Donald McDonald, "An Interview with Stanley Kramer," in McDonald, ed., *Stage and Screen: Interviews with Walter Kerr and Stanley Kramer* (Santa Barbara: Center for the Study of Democratic Institutions, 1962), p. 45.
16. Givner, *Katherine Anne Porter*, p. 469.

5 *Intruder in the Dust* and the southern community

Mark Royden Winchell

When *Intruder in the Dust* was published in 1948, it was William Faulkner's first book to appear since *Go Down, Moses* in 1942. During that six-year period, Faulkner's literary reputation experienced a remarkable reversal of fortune. Although he had been held in high critical esteem throughout the1930s and had even graced the cover of *Time* magazine on January 23, 1939, his books began going out of print in the early to mid-1940s. In some cases the very plates on which those books were printed had been melted down for war material. Then, in 1946, the general reading public rediscovered the Mississippi novelist with the publication of Malcolm Cowley's *The Portable Faulkner* – a selection of fiction set in the author's mythical Yoknapatawpha County. In editing this volume, Cowley paid scant attention to the formal distinction between stories and excerpts from novels. Believing that Faulkner (1897–1962) was less the careful craftsman than the grand mythmaker, Cowley arranged the contents of his book according to narrative chronology, giving us a history of Yoknapatawpha County over a period of two centuries.

Faulkner's newly acquired fame (which included his receiving the Nobel Prize for Literature in 1950) coincided with the birth of the post-war civil rights movement in America. Two months before *Intruder in the Dust* was published, the Democratic National Convention in Philadelphia had split over the party's stand on race. At the urging of the fiery young Mayor of Minneapolis, Hubert Humphrey, the convention committed the party to support strong federal action on behalf of civil rights. As a result, delegates from several southern states walked out. When the smoke had cleared, the dissident southerners had formed the State's Rights (or Dixiecrat) Party and had nominated Strom Thurmond of South Carolina for president and Fielding Wright of Faulkner's home state of Mississippi for vice-president. Because Faulkner was a southern novelist who had written with sensitivity about race, the intellectual community was curious to see what, if anything, his new novel had to say about the controversy over civil rights. Not surprisingly, there was enough in *Intruder in the Dust* to intrigue and infuriate just about everybody.

78

Figure 6. *Intruder in the Dust* emphasizes the unusual relationship between a young white boy, Chick Mallison (Claude Jarman, Jr.) and an older, independent black man, Lucas Beauchamp (Juano Hernandez). A 1949 M-G-M release.

The general action of Faulkner's new novel was congenial to northern liberal sensibilities. A proud black man is accused of a murder he did not commit. While he is in danger of being lynched for his uppity ways, the black is defended by a white lawyer, a boy still too young to have been completely tainted by racial bigotry, and an independent old spinster woman, who has always behaved decently toward African Americans. By defying community sentiment, this trio proves the black man's innocence and forces the mob to back down. Make the lawyer a bit more idealistic, and (just over a decade later) you have Atticus Finch in Harper Lee's *To Kill a Mockingbird* (1960). Faulkner is clearly on the side of the liberal angels. Or is he? The closer we look at the lawyer, Gavin Stevens, the more flaws he seems to have as both an attorney and a man. Without even speaking to his client, he assumes the man's guilt and plans only to seek a change of venue in the hope of copping a plea and sparing his life. What is even worse, Stevens is constantly lecturing his nephew on the evils of federal intervention and the need to allow the South to solve the race problem in its own way and its own time. Critics began to suspect that Faulkner was posing as a liberal in order to make the same old conservative argument for local autonomy.

The critics who were troubled by what they considered to be Faulkner's political stance included several of his more discerning admirers. Malcolm Cowley thought that *Intruder in the Dust* should have been either less political or more politically correct. Writing in the *New Republic,* he concluded that "the tragedy of intelligent Southerners like Faulkner is that their two fundamental beliefs, in human equality and in Southern independence, are now in violent conflict."[1] In an even stronger statement in *Partisan Review,* Elizabeth Hardwick argued that Faulkner's "states rights pamphlet . . . falsifies and degrades his fine comprehension of the moral dilemma of the decent guilt-ridden Southerner."[2] But the most extended discussion of the author's political transgressions came in Edmund Wilson's review in the October 23, 1948, issue of the *New Yorker.* While finding much to admire in the novel, Wilson believed that it ultimately descended to the level of a tract whenever Gavin Stevens opened his mouth. In an ingenious twist of logic, Wilson contends that, all arguments to the contrary notwithstanding, southerners do respond to outside pressures regarding race. Otherwise, Faulkner (the southerner) would never have written such an overtly political book as *Intruder in the Dust.*[3]

The problem with this analysis is not that it is inaccurate, but that it is insufficient. Even if Faulkner has written a social protest novel or novel of ideas, it is still a novel, and the statements made within that context ought not to be read as if they appeared in an essay or an interview. (This is a less obvious version of the error made by people who rip a speech made by Polonius or Falstaff out of context and preface it with the words "Shakespeare believes.") In *The Well Wrought Urn* (which was published the year before *Intruder in the Dust*), Cleanth Brooks maintained that "a poem does not *state* ideas but rather *tests* ideas."[4] If we extend this generalization to prose fiction, then any given statement that Faulkner's novel makes about race must be seen not in isolation but as part of the larger dramatic action of the story. Not surprisingly, Brooks himself interprets Gavin Stevens's political observations in precisely that light in his own analysis of *Intruder in the Dust.* According to Brooks, *Intruder* is essentially a tale of initiation, in which young Chick Mallison finds his place in the community to which he has been born. "Gavin is the person who would naturally talk to the boy about the problems that are disturbing him," Brooks writes, "and the adult's notions about the community, the Negro, and the nature of the law and justice represent for the boy at once

a resource and an impediment. It is against these that his own developing notions must contend and it is these views which he must accept,
repudiate, or transcend."[5]

What then does *Intruder in the Dust*, as a novel, say about race in the
American South? The fact that young Chick Mallison is Faulkner's primary center of consciousness is an important part of the answer to that
question. Although Chick is not a first-person narrator, his relationship
to the black man Lucas Beauchamp is not unlike the situation of the
peripheral observer in any number of modern novels. Such an eyewitness
(Joseph Conrad's Marlow, F. Scott Fitzgerald's Nick Carraway, and even
Herman Melville's Ishmael) observes another person's story and seeks to
understand that person through what Robert Scholes and Robert Kellogg call "an imaginative sharing of his experience." Contending that "this
has been a very fruitful device in modern fiction," Scholes and Kellogg
note that "the story of the protagonist becomes the outward sign or symbol of the inward story of the narrator, who learns from his imaginative
participation in the other's experience." Consequently, "the factual or
empirical aspect of the protagonist's life becomes subordinated to the
narrator's understanding of it." Thus "not what really happened but
the meaning of what the narrator believes to have happened becomes
the central preoccupation."[6] If you substitute the word "observer" for
"narrator," you have a fairly accurate description of Faulkner's technique
in *Intruder in the Dust*.

Chick's first encounter with Beauchamp comes when the young white
boy, who is out hunting, falls into an icy pond on the old Negro's property.
When Beauchamp takes him in and provides him with both warm clothes
and supper, Chick does not know how to respond. Beauchamp's proud
rejection of payment for these services suggests a kind of social equality
that Chick finds unsettling. Every time he tries to reestablish a position
of superiority by sending Beauchamp a gift, Chick receives a gift of equal
or greater value in return. (This game ends only when Beauchamp is
plunged into grief by the death of his wife.) As Chick indignantly observes,
"We got to make him be a nigger first. He's got to admit he's a nigger.
Then maybe we will accept him as he seems to intend to be accepted."[7]
Clearly, "being a nigger" is more a matter of social construction than
of biology. If Beauchamp is too obstinate or proud to play his assigned
racial role, it is up to the white folks of the community to put him in his
place. Even in the most earnest propaganda novel, Chick would start out
believing such things, if only so that he could unlearn them as he matures
morally.

If Beauchamp has no intention of being a "nigger," he is no conventional crusader for black civil rights either. This became evident in an

encounter he had had with some white working men at a crossroads grocery store three years before the present action of the novel had even begun. Taking exception to his swagger and his indifference to their presence as he purchases and starts to eat a package of ginger snaps, one of the white men jumps up and accosts Beauchamp, saying, "You goddamn biggity stiffnecked stinking burrheaded Edmonds sonofabitch." Showing what he most objects to in this diatribe, Beauchamp replies, "I aint a Edmonds. I dont belong to these new folks. I belongs to the old lot. I'm a McCaslin"(19). Readers of *Go Down, Moses* will know what Beauchamp is talking about. He is the grandson of a wealthy local planter, who is patriarch to a line of black and white descendants. Beauchamp's racial pride derives not from any notion that black is beautiful but from his heritage as a *male* McCaslin. (The bulk of the McCaslin inheritance is now owned by the Edmonds family, a white clan descended from a McCaslin *daughter*.) Unlike Malcolm X, Beauchamp has not "learned to hate every drop of that white rapist's blood that is in me."[8] To compound the irony, Carothers McCaslin had represented everything that was most loathsome about race relations in the antebellum South.

The black McCaslin progeny are yet another reminder of how difficult it is to find a biologically "pure" African in the South or, indeed, in all of America. At one time, the racial caste system stigmatized anyone with the slightest taint of African ancestry. As a consequence, the tragic mulatto became a stock figure in our literature, while the phenomenon of "passing" through both racial worlds became the subject of novels as diverse as Mark Twain's *Puddn'head Wilson* (1894) and James Weldon Johnson's *The Autobiography of an Ex-Coloured Man* (1912). In the figure of Lucas Beauchamp, Faulkner demonstrates even further ambiguities of race and class. In antebellum times, slaves who were owned by an aristocratic family often felt socially superior to free white trash. (Consider Mammy and Uncle Peter in Margaret Mitchell's *Gone With the Wind* [1936].) If Beauchamp is capable of condescending to the Edmondses because they represent a distaff line of the McCaslin family, one can only imagine the contempt that he feels for the decidedly nonaristocratic whites he encounters in the crossroads grocery. Not only does Beauchamp refuse to act like a nigger, he puts on the airs of an aristocratic white man.

Even if he is neither heroic enough nor victimized enough to be the sacrificial Negro of northern liberal mythology, Beauchamp's plight does *test* some indigenous southern approaches to the race problem. One is the lynch mentality represented by Crawford Gowrie and many of the townspeople. Another is the ostrich-like indifference of Chick's parents. A third is the much-maligned gradualism of Gavin Stevens. A fourth is exemplified by the rustic professionalism of Sheriff Hampton. A fifth and final paradigm is provided by Miss Eunice Habersham. It is from these various white role models that Chick must learn how to deal with the enigmatic Beauchamp and, in the process, find his own place in the community of Yoknapatawpha County.

No serious observer believes that Faulkner is advocating lynch law. His entire canon disparages the knee-jerk white supremacy that has all too often dehumanized American blacks. Nor can he be accused of ignoring the situation. Although some of the most accomplished southern literature is monochromatic in content, Faulkner's work does not fall into that category. What is perhaps more to the point is that Chick is never tempted to join the mob and refuses to let sloth or cowardice dissuade him from helping Beauchamp. If his Uncle Gavin and Sheriff Hampton seem more plausible role models, each leaves much to be desired. Unlike Stevens, Chick is genuinely interested in the question of Beauchamp's guilt or innocence. The sheriff may be an exemplar of courage and decency in protecting Beauchamp from the mob, but he does not think to examine the bullet in Vinson Gowrie's body until sometime after Chick, his black friend Aleck Sander, and Miss Habersham have dug up the grave in which Vinson was presumed to be lying.

Miss Habersham is the one character in the novel who believes unwaveringly in Beauchamp's innocence. She also leads the exhumation party to the empty grave and holds Crawford Gowrie and the mob at bay with only the moral force of her presence. It may be naive, even sentimental, to build a political platform on Miss Habersham's example, but she is clearly the moral center of Faulkner's novel. If Stevens can be said to speak for the public Faulkner, Miss Habersham is closer to the author's most deeply held intuition when she says to Chick, "Lucas knew it would take a child – or an old woman like me: someone not concerned with probability, with evidence. Men like your uncle and Mr. Hampton have had to be men too long, busy too long" (89).

For all the male bonding in Faulkner's fiction (and Beauchamp and Chick are surely an example of that phenomenon), it is invariably the women who show the way in Yoknapatawpha County. Consider, for example, the title narrative of *Go Down, Moses*, a story that immediately preceded *Intruder in the Dust* in the Faulkner canon and included some of the same characters. In this tale Stevens represents both the possibilities and limits of what a later public figure would call "compassionate conservatism." He raises money among the white people of Jefferson so that the body of Lucas Beauchamp and Mollie Beauchamp's grandson can be returned home. (Butch Beauchamp was a career criminal who had been executed for murder in Chicago.) Nevertheless, for all his good intentions, Stevens indulges the elitist notion that he knows what is best for the Beauchamp family and is decidedly uncomfortable in the presence of Mollie's overt emotionalism.

If Stevens's sincere concern is accompanied by incomplete understanding, a more elemental bond unites Mollie with her longtime white friend Miss Belle Worsham. (As Arthur Mizener points out, "Miss Worsham speak[s] quite unconsciously of the grief, which is primarily her Negro sister Mollie's, as 'our grief.'"[9]) Although elderly black women (such as Dilsey in *The Sound and the Fury* [1829] and Mollie in *Go Down, Moses*) may be Faulkner's primary moral exemplars, it is encouraging that a white woman such as Miss Worsham can occasionally achieve an empathy that crosses racial lines. It is perhaps because both Miss Worsham and Miss Habersham are said to have grown up with Mollie Beauchamp that the critic Edmund L. Volpe is convinced that the two white women were meant to be one and the same and that Faulkner had simply forgotten the character's name in the six years between his two books.[10]

Although it is possible to consider *Intruder in the Dust* as a self-contained literary artifact, it is neither necessary nor particularly desirable to do so. As I have tried to suggest, placing it within the larger context of Faulkner's Yoknapatawpha fiction sheds useful light on recurring characters and recurring themes. But there is another sense in which the novel version of *Intruder in the Dust* lacks a fully independent existence. Two months before the novel was published, Bennett Cerf of Random House negotiated a $50,000 deal for film rights to the story. In a sense, *Intruder* was a potential movie even before it was an actual book.

Intruder in the Dust lent itself to film adaptation in a way that some of Faulkner's more obviously literary novels did not. The author's initial intention was to write "a blood-and-thunder mystery novel which would sell."[11] Although he eventually did more than that, *Intruder* became his bestselling novel since *Sanctuary* in 1931. We are so accustomed to think of Faulkner as a difficult high modernist that we sometimes forget that the journal in which he published most frequently was the *Saturday Evening Post*, the magazine that Leslie Fiedler supposes was "most likely to be picked up by the common man when he had seen all the movies in town." Although Faulkner was capable of doing hackwork for much-needed money, some of his best fiction was in fact written for a popular audience. While textual scholars have created a cottage industry by publishing "restored editions" that track every stray comma in his original manuscripts, Faulkner himself frequently agreed to publish truncated versions of his work. As early as 1948, he tried to secure a magazine serialization of *Intruder in the Dust* that would have completely excluded Chapter 9.[12]

By the time the movie was released in 1949, Faulkner's tale of a young white boy's initiation into manhood had been transformed into a character study of an eccentric old black man's near-fatal refusal to be a "nigger." Not your usual cinematic adaptation, the film version of *Intruder* was made with Faulkner's approval and assistance. Ninety percent of the movie was shot in Oxford, Mississippi, with townspeople used as extras and cast in small speaking roles. Perhaps even more important was the fact that the film was produced and directed by Clarence Brown. By 1949 Brown had been directing films for nearly three decades. In addition to being a highly respected craftsman, he was also a specialist in literary adaptation.

Brown's second film (released on November 16, 1920) was a silent version of *The Last of the Mohicans* (1826). While there have been at least three subsequent adaptations of James Fenimore Cooper's classic novel, Brown's film is the one most faithful to the original text. Over the next twenty-seven years, Brown brought more than forty literary works to the screen. Although most of his sources are eminently forgettable, they also include such undeniable classics as Eugene O'Neill's *Anna Christie* (1930) and *Ah, Wilderness!* (1935), Leo Tolstoy's *Anna Karenina* (1935), Robert E. Sherwood's *Idiot's Delight* (1939), William Saroyan's *The Human Comedy* (1943), and Marjorie Kinnan Rawlings's *The Yearling* (1946). Like Faulkner, Brown was a native southerner with his own distinctive artistic and moral vision. When a reporter asked the author if he believed the movie was true to his book, Faulkner replied, "I do. Of course you can't say the same thing with a picture as you can with a book any more than you can express with paint what you can with plaster. The mediums are different. Mr. Brown knows his medium and he's made a fine picture. I wish I had made it."[13]

Faulkner had reason to be pleased with the film version of his novel. While staying remarkably faithful to the original text, Brown and screenwriter Ben Maddow made several changes that rendered the action more coherent. When Chick, Aleck Sander, and Miss Habersham dig up the purported grave of Vinson Gowrie in the novel, they discover the body of an extraneous character who had witnessed the murder and was blackmailing Crawford Gowrie. By the time Sheriff Hampton has the grave officially reopened, Crawford has dug up and disposed of the body of his second victim and filled in an empty grave. (Cleanth Brooks finds this bit of tomfoolery to be one of the most egregious flaws in the novel.[14]) Brown and Maddow wisely dispose of the blackmailer and leave the grave empty to begin with. In another gesture toward narrative economy, the film has Vinson Gowrie (rather than an unidentified white man) attack Beauchamp in the crossroads grocery store. This makes it more plausible for the townspeople to believe that Beauchamp killed Vinson Gowrie out of revenge.

Technically speaking, both the novel and the film begin *in medias res* with the captured Beauchamp being brought into town on Sunday morning. After ten lines, however, Faulkner moves into a flashback that depicts Chick's first encounter with Beauchamp. In contrast, Brown introduces the community of Jefferson with shots of men in the barbershop and of families singing a hymn in church. (Because there is no artificial soundtrack, all the background noises are an integral and literal part of the plot.) If our view of the church service is meant to emphasize the sanctimoniousness of the townspeople, the one in the barbershop serves an expository function. As the center of male gossip, it is the place where Beauchamp's plight would naturally be discussed. Moreover, the absence of the shine boy is an indication of how the frightened blacks of the community are lying low. Then, when the sheriff's car crosses a temporarily empty town square, we notice that he is driving with a flat tire. Whether this is meant to symbolize a malfunctioning system of justice, the flat raises suspicions of sabotage and thus increases the general sense of foreboding in the scene.

After the opening sequences in the town, which find their climax in Beauchamp's request that Chick summon his uncle, the lad returns home for Sunday dinner. Disturbed by Beauchamp's situation and irritated by his parents' treating him as a child, Chick abruptly leaves the dinner table and heads for his room. His uncle (called *John* Stevens in the film) immediately follows him in an effort to console and gently reprove the highstrung adolescent. Visually, this action suggests a bond between uncle and nephew. That fact is further emphasized when Stevens enters the room and finds Chick desultorily tossing a baseball in the air and catching it. Wordlessly, the two throw the ball back and forth, as Stevens's calm demeanor clashes markedly with Chick's growing agitation. It is only then that Chick reveals to his uncle (and to us) the circumstances of his first meeting with Beauchamp and of the altercation he had witnessed in the grocery store. Not only does this delayed exposition increase the narrative tension, it also gives us a cinematic equivalent of an interior monologue. Because Stevens is a perfectly logical audience for these recollections, Brown avoids the clunky artifice of having Chick address the audience directly or speak to no one in particular.

One could go through this film scene by scene demonstrating the formal aptness of the choices that Brown made. The very decision to shoot the picture in black and white, ultimately bleeding into shades of gray, accentuates the atmosphere of stark realism. So, too, does the setting of Oxford and the participation of so many of its citizens. Although the movie is not literally a documentary, there is an aura of danger in some of the crowd scenes that could not have been obtained in a Hollywood studio with a cast of professional extras. When Beauchamp is brought from the sheriff's car to the steps of the jail and, again, when Crawford Gowrie runs that same gauntlet, the camera moves with them rather than cutting back and forth to close-ups of the crowd. If Faulkner was never able to capture the grammar and poetry of film in his own screenwriting career, he could recognize it when he saw it in the work of Clarence Brown.

The fact that Brown has created a film that is remarkably faithful to its source should not delude us into thinking that his vision is identical to Faulkner's. To begin with, there is a difference in point of view. The kind of peripheral narration that Scholes and Kellogg describe has never been successfully translated onto the screen. When a good movie is made from a novel that employs this technique, the moral education of the observing character is inevitably reduced in significance as the enigmatic protagonist takes center stage. Remove the narrator Jack Burden from Robert Penn Warren's *All the King's Men* (1949), and you are left with a political melodrama. In adapting Warren's novel for the screen, Robert Rossen did essentially that. Although Burden (as played by John Ireland) remains a vestigial figure in the film, he is completely overshadowed by Broderick Crawford's performance as Willie Stark. By the same token, Chick Mallison is not so much the protagonist of Clarence Brown's film as he is a transparency through which the audience sees Lucas Beauchamp. This is accomplished at least in part by reducing the cautionary rhetoric of Chick's Uncle Stevens. Thus there is no compelling *middle way* between Chick's bonding with Lucas and his joining the mob. Although Chick comes of age in the film, he does so with less dramatic complexity than in the novel.

In the film, as in the novel, Lucas is an example of what Pauline Kael calls "the maddening Negro . . . He refuses to accept condescension or patronage, he insists on his right to be no better than a white man, and what is truly intolerable – he acts as if he *were* white."[15] But, of course, the novel makes the point that Lucas not only *is* part white but is of aristocratic descent as well. Faulkner emphasizes that fact in the confrontation at the crossroads grocery. In Brown's rendering of that same scene, Beauchamp's white ancestry is never mentioned. If there is any racial ambiguity, it lies in the fact that the part of Lucas is being played by a Puerto Rican actor, Juano Hernandez. The poor whites in the grocery and the lynch mob (dominated by Gowries in both cases) are attacking a man of color, not a McCaslin who haughtily refuses to act like a "nigger".

Whereas Faulkner merely assumes that lynching is a bad thing and proceeds from there, Brown was more intent on filming an anti-lynching polemic. Ben Maddow explained the director's intentions as follows: "He had witnessed when he was a young man of perhaps sixteen or seventeen, a so-called 'race riot' in which blacks were shot down on the streets and piled onto a flatcar at the railway station, and then dumped in the woods miles away from the scene of the slaughter. To him the film was a kind of payment of his conscience."[16]

Without lawyer Stevens's pleas to allow the South to solve the racial problem in its own way, the viewer of the film might be more apt to conclude that outside action is necessary – although that particular argument is never explicitly made. Brown, however, is no self-loathing southerner. Beauchamp is freed not by some fast-talking civil rights attorney from Chicago, but by the combined efforts of Chick, Aleck Sander, and Miss Habersham, with the assistance of lawyer Stevens and Sheriff Hampton. These people are all as much southerners as the Gowries, who are themselves not even uniformly despicable. Nub Gowrie genuinely mourns the death of his son and refuses to make Beauchamp a scapegoat after his innocence is demonstrated. Moreover, Brown's southerners are finally apolitical, in that they speak neither for nor against federal civil rights legislation.

In the penultimate scene of the film (which corresponds to the final scene of the novel), Beauchamp shows up at Stevens's office to insist on paying what he owes. Stevens deflects this gesture by saying that Beauchamp's debt is really to Chick and Miss Habersham. He advises his "client" to thank the old lady by buying her some flowers, but not to pay Chick anything for fear that the boy will be charged with practicing law without a license. Finally, the exasperated and bemused Stevens agrees to accept two dollars to repair the pipe he had dropped in Beauchamp's jail cell. Beauchamp counts out the money, the last fifty cents of which is in pennies, and then asks for a receipt. This legalistic charade is surely recognized as a joke by the people involved. Faulkner's point would seem to be that no balance scale will ever determine what black and white southerners owe to each other. Beauchamp himself had emphatically made that point when he refused Chick's payment for his hospitality at the beginning of the story.

Although the novel ends with this farcical accounting, the film continues with some additional dialogue. Chick and Stevens watch Beauchamp as he leaves the law office and crosses the town square. "Proud, stubborn, – insufferable: but there he goes," Stevens says: "the keeper of my conscience." To which Chick quickly adds, "Our conscience, Uncle John." These lines were supplied by Dore Schary, the liberal M-G-M executive who persuaded Louis B. Mayer to make the film. Critics who dismiss this exchange as an overly sententious way of driving home the film's message assume that Schary is tacking on a homily about the race problem being a universal *American* obligation.[17] If, however, Chick's reference is to the South (or perhaps only to Yoknapatawpha County), he is making a point that rises naturally from the action of the story, which is insistently local in scope. In that case, Chick has become part of a truly promising *southern* community. If Lucas is indeed the keeper of its conscience, that community may well be capable of finding its own way. At least in the late 1940s, that seemed a distinct possibility to William Faulkner and Clarence Brown.

NOTES

1. Malcolm Cowley, "William Faulkner's Nation," *New Republic* (October 18, 1948), pp. 21–22.
2. Elizabeth Hardwick, "Faulkner and the South Today," *Partisan Review* 15 (1948), pp. 1130–1135.
3. Edmund Wilson, "William Faulkner's Reply to the Civil-Rights Program," *New Yorker* (October 23, 1948), pp. 120–121, 125–128.
4. Cleanth Brooks, *The Well Wrought Urn: Studies in the Structure of Poetry* (New York: Reynall and Hitchcock, 1947), p. 229.
5. Cleanth Brooks, *William Faulkner: The Yoknapatawpha Country* (New Haven, CT: Yale University Press, 1963), p. 288.
6. Robert Scholes and Robert Kellogg, with the assistance of Alex Haley, *The Nature of Narrative* (New York: Oxford University Press, 1966), pp. 261, 261–262.
7. William Faulkner, *Intruder in the Dust* (New York: Random House, 1948), p. 18. Further references will be cited parenthetically in the text.
8. Faulkner, *Intruder*, p. 19. Malcolm X, *The Autobiography of Malcolm X*, with the assistance of Alex Haley (New York: Grove Press, 1965), p. 2.
9. Arthur Mizener, "The Thin, Intelligent Face of American Fiction," *Kenyon Review* 17 (1955), p. 517.
10. Edmund L. Volpe, *A Reader's Guide to William Faulkner* (New York: Farrar, Straus, 1964), p. 259.
11. Mizener, "The Thin, Intelligent Face," p. 517.
12. Volpe, *A Reader's Guide*, p. 259.
13. See Regina K. Fadiman, *Faulkner's Intruder in the Dust: Novel into Film* (Knoxville: University of Tennessee Press, 1978), p. 9.
14. See Brooks, *William Faulkner*, p. 280.
15. Pauline Kael, *Kiss Kiss Bang Bang* (Boston: Little, Brown, 1968), p. 284.
16. E. Pauline Degenfelder, "The Film Adaptation of Faulkner's *Intruder in the Dust*," *Literature/Film Quarterly* 1 (Spring 1973), p. 138.
17. For Maddow's screenplay, see Fadiman, *Faulkner's Intruder*, pp. 95–303. For a discussion of Schary's role in shaping the ending of the film, see Gene D. Phillips, *Fiction, Film, and Faulkner: The Art of Adaptation* (Knoxville: University of Tennessee Press, 1988), pp. 94–95.

6   Dramatizing *The Member of the Wedding*

McKay Jenkins

On March 19, 1946, after seven drafts, nearly six years of artistic distress, and a series of terrible physical and emotional impairments, Carson McCullers (1917–1967) finally published her third novel, *The Member of the Wedding*. The new novel received wide and largely positive praise, cementing a literary reputation built on the success of her remarkable 1940 debut, *The Heart is a Lonely Hunter*. But eleven days after *The Member of the Wedding* appeared, Edmund Wilson published a review in the *New Yorker* that cut McCullers to the quick. Under the headline "Two Books That Leave You Blank: Carson McCullers, Siegfried Sassoon," Wilson wrote that McCullers was "a writer of undoubted sensibility and talent" but seemed to have "difficulty in adjusting her abilities to a dramatically effective subject." The new novel was "a formless chronicle" that had no internal structure and did not "build up to anything." The book "has no element of drama at all," Wilson wrote. "I hope that I am not being stupid about this book, which has left me feeling rather cheated."[1]

McCullers, dangerously frail her whole life, learned of the review while she was in residence at the Yaddo writer's colony. She became so unnerved that she descended into a period of acute physical and psychological agony, suffering chronic attacks of dizziness and a terror of fainting in public. But Wilson's review also apparently knocked McCullers's artistic sensibilities askew. His critique led directly to her decision to adapt her novel into a play, a surprising decision for someone with virtually no experience in the genre. But far more surprising was the way his critique moved McCullers to abandon temporarily the central component of her voice as a writer – a philosophically complex understanding of the fluidity of human identity – and replace it with a series of gross and even pandering caricatures. Searching for a way to satisfy Wilson's appetite for an "element of drama," McCullers discovered the narrative usefulness of gaudy racial and gender stereotypes.[2]

Throughout her fiction, McCullers had an uncanny ability to create characters who immediately unsettle norms of physical appearance, ethnic heritage, and gender. Men gradually become feminine, women

Figure 7. Fred Zinnemann's *The Member of the Wedding* is a sentimental coming-of-age story, featuring a charismatic girl-child played by Julie Harris. A 1952 Stanley Kramer Productions/Columbia Pictures release.

become masculine; whites accrue black characteristics, blacks morph into whites. Even household pets are androgynous: there is a cat in *Wedding* who goes by both "Charles" and "Charlina." It is not just that her characters are empathetic toward people who are their racial or sexual "opposites"; they *are* their racial or sexual opposites. There are no binaries in McCullers's fiction. Each character has within himself or herself the seeds of his or her complementary half; they are human yin-yang, with traits and instincts and impulses in continuous flux. If her characters are chronically alienated, it is only because they live in a world where such fluidity, such mixing, is considered suspect, rejected, even persecuted. In *The Heart is a Lonely Hunter*, the roughneck white outcast Jake Blount drunkenly pronounces that he is "part nigger and wop and bohunk and chink. All of those . . . And I'm Dutch and Turkish and Japanese and American . . . I'm one who knows. I'm a stranger in a strange land." The café owner Biff Brannon, who secretly enjoys putting on his wife's perfume, wonders "why was it that the smartest people mostly missed that point? By nature all people are of both sexes . . . old men's voices grow high and reedy and they take on a mincing walk. And old women sometimes grow fat and their voices get rough and deep and they grow dark little mustaches."[3]

In *The Member of the Wedding*, the novel's three primary characters spend much of their time sitting around a kitchen table musing on the nature of human identity. Berenice is a black nanny who wears a blue glass eye. Frankie is a twelve-year-old white girl who cannot decide whether to run away to California to become a starlet or to New York to become a marine. John Henry, a seven-year-old white boy named for the legendary black railroad worker, spends a good deal of time dressed in a tutu. As they prepare to celebrate the wedding of Frankie's older brother, each member of the odd trio muses about a "perfect world." Berenice dreams that "there would be no separate colored people in the world, but all human beings would be light brown color with blue eyes and black hair." Frankie "planned it so that people could instantly change back and forth from boys to girls, which every way they felt like and wanted." John Henry thought "that people ought to be half boy and half girl, and when the old Frankie threatened to take him to the Fair and sell him to the Freak Pavilion, he would only close his eyes and smile."[4]

Although it has moments that mark its geographical and historical place as a novel of the World War II American South, *The Member of the Wedding*, like all McCullers's fiction, is less concerned with contemporary racial politics than it is with the irreducible complexity, or ambiguity, or indeterminacy, of human identity itself. McCullers writes of a world in which people are both brown-skinned *and* blue-eyed, black *and* white, male *and* female. And while there are some heated spoken exchanges on race or gender, much of McCullers's power comes from a decidedly novelistic technique: the ruminations that carry on inside her characters' heads. Recounting a visit to the Freak pavilion at the Chattahoochee Exposition, Frankie finds herself captivated – and recognized – by The Half-Man Half-Woman:

This Freak was divided completely in half – the left side was a man and the right side a woman. The costume on the left was a leopard skin and on the right side a brassiere and a spangled skirt. Half the face was dark bearded and the other half bright glazed with paint. Both eyes were strange. Frankie had wandered around the tent and looked at every booth. She was afraid of all the Freaks, for it seemed to her that they had looked at her in a secret way and tried to connect their eyes with hers, as though to say: we know you. (18)

Words like "freak" and "queer" occur repeatedly in McCullers's fiction, and the words do not simply describe the rejection that eccentrics feel when boxed in by a conservative cultural landscape: they also mark characters who recognize the multiplicity of their own personalities, and who recognize each other.

Particularly given the cultural conservatism of mid-century America, the popularity that McCullers's strange novels enjoyed seems somewhat bewildering. Edmund Wilson was only the most powerful critic to gripe that *Wedding* lacked dramatic tension. Mid-century reviewers had a hard time even finding words to describe what she was up to. Most positive reviews considered her novel an attempt "to recapture that elusive moment when childhood melts into adolescence" (*Time*, April 1, 1946), but George Dangerfield, writing in the *Saturday Review*, said this was "like writing about a tent pole and forgetting to describe the tent." McCullers's characters "invariably remind one of faces one may have seen, in a dream perhaps, in a tabloid newspaper possibly, or out of a train window."[5] It was nearly two decades before the critic Robert Phillips argued that something more was going on. "Instead of romantic couples or brave heroes and heroines we find homosexuals and lesbians, flowers of evil dotting a grotesque landscape," he wrote in 1964. "The perverted and pusillanimous characters of McCullers's experience no love of permanent value." Even excusing his florid rhetoric, Phillips missed a larger point, that these grotesque characters were precisely representative of McCullers's art, where heaven – unlike the 1940s South, where the work was produced – is a place where identity, particularly racial and gender identity, is multivalenced, changeable, amorphous.[6]

Over the several years following the novel's publication, McCullers, still hurt and angered by Wilson's review, turned her novel into a play. For months she struggled with a genre of writing she had never attempted (except as a teenager, when she performed in her family's living room a sketch called "Fire of Life," featuring Jesus and Nietzsche, with herself in the role of the German philosopher). Now, consciously writing against Wilson's critique, McCullers sought anxiously for a source of dramatic tension to enliven a story that even her admirers recognized was languorous and overly cerebral. She decided she needed to fit her complex and often ethereal ideas of identity into more recognizable forms.

"It seemed to me after my first experiences that the theatre was the most pragmatic of all art media," she wrote in "The Shared Vision," a piece for *Theatre Arts* in April, 1950. "The first question of ordinary producers is: 'Will it get across on Broadway?' The merit of a play is a secondary consideration and they shy from any play whose formula has not been proved a number of times."[7] In an interview with Harvey Breit in the *New York Times*, McCullers confessed to feeling bewildered by the playwriting process. "Paradoxically, I had to forget the novel," she said:

It all has to spring from another medium. It was fascinating. The play has to be more direct. The inner monologue has to become the spoken word. It has to be more naked emotionally, too. I'd say that the play is transposed on a sharper, more immediate point. I wouldn't say the play gains, but in a strange way the play becomes more emotional because those lines in the novel needed to be spoken.[8]

Apparently, McCullers's instincts hit the mark. The play, directed by Harold Clurman and starring Ethel Waters as Berenice, Julie Harris as Frankie, and Brandon de Wilde as John Henry, premiered at Philadelphia's Walnut Theater on December 22, 1949. It went on to a fourteen-month, 501-performance run at Broadway's Empire Theater, and then a national tour. "I have never before heard what happened last night at the curtain calls, when hundreds cried out as if with one voice for Ethel Waters and Julie Harris," wrote William Hawkins, in the *New York World Telegram.* The play "has incomparable insight, grace, and beauty," Brooks Atkinson wrote in the *New York Times.* "Anyone who loves acting ought to be grateful for such acting and direction." The play won the New York Drama Critics Circle Award, though not the Pulitzer Prize, which went to *South Pacific.* In February 1951 McCullers sold the film rights to the play for $75,000 to the producer Stanley Kramer. All three primary actors from the play signed on, Fred Zinnemann, the director of *High Noon,* agreed to direct, and the script adaptation was assigned to Edward and Edna Anhalt, who had won an Oscar for writing Elia Kazan's 1950 thriller *Panic in the Streets.*[9]

Reviews of the 1952 film were mixed. The "vibrant and sensitive sketches of an adolescent girl, a warm-hearted Negro mammy and an amiable little boy that were drawn with such skill and perception" on stage were "considerably less arresting or pervasive in the picture medium," Bosley Crowther wrote in the *New York Times.* "All that Fred Zinnemann has been able to contrive in the way of camera angles, lighting and cutting has not been sufficient to disguise the paucity of dramatic action and the weight of repetition in the film." Moved by such complaints, Columbia cut about twenty minutes of footage, restoring it only some twenty years later. The film nonetheless became a minor hit, secured an Oscar nomination for Harris, and continued a revival of Waters's career that had begun with the play.[10]

If McCullers's novel was embraced by the mainstream despite its eerie, even subversive notions of identity, the stage and film versions of the work succeeded precisely because these notions were watered down, stripped out, or reversed altogether. Thadious Davis has written that the novel is a work of "defamiliarization," while the play (and, I will argue, the film) are works of "familiarization," and this gets it just right.[11] The novel effectively dissolves traditional markers of racial and sexual identity;

characters are vessels that leak all over the place. But as she anxiously sought to create the "element of drama" that Wilson found lacking in her novel, McCullers rejected her own artistic instincts about race and gender. She created characters that were variously firm or fragile, but they never leaked. Part of this may have been due to McCullers's own inexperience as a playwright. Part of it may have been due to the narrative requirements of stage- and filmcraft. But part of it was certainly due to the political riskiness of adapting a novel that had at its very core two subjects about which mid-century America still had great ambivalence: race and sex.

Heating up the race

In the novel Frankie spends a lot of time walking down her village streets, looking into people's eyes and experiencing what she can only describe as an "unnamable connection": a flow of recognition, understanding, and compassion that washes between her and the people she meets. This happens when she walks by the Freak Pavilion ("we know you," their eyes say) and it happens again when she sees "an old colored man, stiff and proud on his rattling wagon seat, (who) drove a sad, blindered mule down toward the Saturday market." McCullers continues:

F. Jasmine looked at him, he looked at her, and to the outward appearance that was all. But in that glance F. Jasmine felt between his eyes and her own eyes a new unnamable connection, as though they were known to each other – and there even came an instant vision of his home field and country roads and quiet dark pine trees as the wagon rattled past her on the paved town street. And she wanted him to know her, too. (50)

The "connection" that the young white girl feels with the old black man is not empathy *per se*; it is a recognition of unity, an understanding that she and the black man, to use a Buddhist expression, "are not two." It is precisely this sense of unity that is eviscerated from the theatrical and film versions of the novel. In both adaptations lines of identity are thickened to the point of caricature, and any chances of a character finding an "unnamable connection" are irrevocably lost. Characters are no longer yin-yang, they are sealed off, impermeable and isolated.

This change is most apparent in the ways McCullers altered her own black characters for the play. Where readers of the novel discovered characters of dignity and complex sensitivity, audiences were given caricatures from central casting. In the novel T. T., an older black man and Berenice's sometime consort, is "a well-off colored man who owned a colored restaurant." Honey is a melancholic horn player, "a sick-loose person" whose isolation and deep physical suffering are offered up right away: "The army would not include him, and he had shoveled in a gravel pit until he broke one of his insides and could not do heavy work any more." To young Frankie, Honey is also elegant, self-educated, and highly romantic. He "had been first in his studies at the colored high school," had "ordered a French book from Atlanta and learned himself some French," and could "talk as well as any human she had ever heard," with lavender lips that "could move as light as butterflies." If anything, the novel's black characters represent the only family and community ever experienced by Frankie, whose mother died in childbirth and whose father is passive and neglectful. When she visits Berenice's house, Frankie always saw "that there would be many people in the room – the family, various cousins, friends. In the wintertime they would sit by the hearth around the draughty, shivering fire and talk with woven voices" (35–36; 122, 125).

In the play, and later in the film, all this changes. T. T. is no longer a small businessman; he is a shuffling waiter at the wedding reception, seen mostly polishing wine glasses. Honey, "very high-strung and volatile," is described as having served time on a road gang, and is now a reefer-smoking (in the play) or a gin-drinking (in the film) addict with a razor in his pocket. His love of music is emblematic not of romance or melancholy, but of rebellion, and even violence. Early on in the play (and the film), T. T. and Honey enter the kitchen, Honey carrying his trumpet and fingering a large welt on his head. He has just been in a "ruckus" with a drunken soldier, and got himself cracked on the head by a white military policeman Honey is furious: "Times like this I feel I got to bust loose or die," he says. T. T., ever obsequious, tries to paper over the racial energy of the moment. "It was one of those accidents can happen to any colored person."[12]

Oblivious to Honey's rage, little John Henry picks up Honey's horn and blows a few inept notes. Honey flies into a fury. "You got it full of slobber inside and out. It's ruined!" he screams, shaking John Henry violently. Berenice slaps Honey. "You ain't mad because John Henry is a little boy. It's because he's a white boy."

Leaving aside the absurdity of a trumpet being "ruined" by spit, this scene is only in place to establish Honey as a "race man," a political hot-head, whose anger is so indiscriminate that he is a danger even to a child. But the scene, created for the stage version and repeated in the film, is only a warm-up. A later scene is even more grossly overdone. Frankie's father, who had been a vaguely inattentive (and decidedly minor) character in the novel, enters the kitchen through a hall door as Frankie is trying on her dress for the wedding. He barely notices her outfit, and Frankie takes offense: "Papa, why is it you don't ever notice what I have on or pay any serious mind to me? You just walk around like a mule with blinders on, not seeing or caring."

But Mr. Addams, continuing to ignore his daughter, instead turns his attention to T. T. and Honey, who he hopes will help him down at the store. T. T. offers graciously, but then demurs when he remembers he has a previous commitment: "I promised to work for Mr. Finney, sir. I can't promise anything, Mr. Addams. But if Mr. Finney change his mind about needing me, I'll work for you, sir." T. T.'s subservience again infuriates Honey, whose own response is curt. "I ain't got the time," he says.

Honey's insolence enrages Mr. Addams. "I'll be so glad when the war is over and you biggety worthless niggers get back to work. And furthermore, you *sir* me! Hear me?" Moments later, after Mr. Addams has stormed off, John Henry turns to Berenice. "Uncle Royal called Honey a nigger. Is Honey a nigger?"

"Be quiet now, John Henry," Berenice responds. "Honey, I got a good mind to shake you till you spit. Not saying *sir* to Mr. Addams, and acting so impudent."

Honey turns his anger on Berenice. "T. T. said sir enough for a whole crowd of niggers," he says, removing a blade from his pocket. "But for folks that calls me nigger, I got a real good nigger razor. Don't touch it, Butch, it's sharp. Liable to hurt yourself." Begging some money from Berenice, he says, "Gimme, Berenice. I'm so tensed up and miserable. The nigger hole. I'm sick of smothering in the nigger hole. I can't stand it no more" (66–69).

In the film the scene is modified. Honey's addiction is now gin instead of marijuana, and Mr. Addams is no longer a virulent racist. With Berenice and John Henry outside hanging laundry, Honey pulls out his trumpet and plays a snappy jazz riff. Berenice is unimpressed.

"You on that stuff again?" she asks.
"Course not."
"Stop lyin' Satan. That much wind ain't natural. That's gin blowing."

At this point, Frankie's father emerges, and respectfully asks Honey to help him down at the store. Honey begs off, saying he has a job playing music at Sam's Club. The father meekly turns away. As soon as he is gone, Berenice turns on Honey, calling him a liar: he's at Sam's, all right, but he's not getting paid, and when he's not playing he's "drumming up liquor parties."

"But I feel good when I play," Honey whines, then asks Berenice for a dollar. "One of these days I'ma get me a good job. Save my money. Get out of this town." "At least it'll stop you from stealin'," she says.

The two scenes are remarkable for several reasons. Most obviously, the word "nigger" does not appear in the film. Davis wrote that the word does not appear in the novel, but it does, once, and in its way it fits the book's tone. Crushed when her brother and his bride leave their wedding without her, Frankie wishes "the whole world to die." Then, turning to her beloved Berenice, she "used the word she had never used before, nigger – for now she hated everyone and wanted only to spite and shame." The word in the novel is an audible mark for a poisonous emotion, a manifestation of rage and humiliation that reflects Frankie's paralyzing anxiety and self-loathing. "Herself she hated the worst of all, and she wanted the whole world to die" (135).

In the play the word seems a clumsy effort to sharpen the identities of both white and black characters and, perhaps, at best, to capture the racial tension that had begun to arise with the end of World War II. Mr. Addams's invocation of the war, and his rage at "worthless niggers," seems especially crude given that black soldiers, having helped to fight a war against ethnic cleansing in Europe, were returning to a country still in the throes of legal segregation. Honey's youthful anger over T. T.'s instinctive humility may also have served to reflect a demographic and political transition, a hint of the civil rights battles now just a few years away. Even Honey's horn became a potent political symbol, which it was not in the novel. In the late 1940s and early 1950s, the trumpet (and the saxophone) became more than instruments of artistic expression, they became instruments of reinvention. In the hands of Dizzy Gillespie and Miles Davis (and Charlie Parker), the be-bop of the postwar era rejected both the melodic traditions of jazz and the social niceties of the supper club. Honey in the play and the film is far angrier, far more alienated, far more "racialized" than he is in the novel, and all three traits are amplified by the horn.

But mostly, the word "nigger" in the play and the "racializing" of the characters in both the play and the film serve only as narrative tricks to keep the viewer's pulse beating. Honey's isolated "blackness" is further exaggerated toward the end of the play, when he is shown hiding from the police. In the novel, just two pages from the end, Honey's fate is revealed indirectly, almost in passing, and seems to absolve Honey of criminal responsibility. "First it was Honey. Made crazy one night by a marihuana cigarette, by something called smoke or snow, he broke into the drugstore of the white man who had been selling them to him, desperate for more" (151). Honey's crime is breaking and entering, not violence, and if there is a hint of race in the moment it is a white man, not Honey, who seems sinister. It is not the cigarette that made Honey crazy; it was the additives put into the cigarette by his white dealer. By the time the novel ends, Berenice has gotten a lawyer and visited Honey in jail.

In the play the police are after Honey because he has pulled a razor on a bartender after being refused a drink. Frankie, using Honey's nickname, offers this advice: "Lightfoot, if you drew a razor on a white man, you'd better not let them catch you." Berenice, raising the specter of a lynching, agrees, "Already I feel that rope." But Honey, whose predatory violence seems to have satisfied his racial fury, appears almost relieved. He has fulfilled his destiny as a violent black man. "Don't you dare cry," he tells Berenice. "I know now all my days have been leading up to this minute. No more 'boy this – boy that' – no bowing, no scraping. For the first time, I'm free and it makes me happy." By the play's end, Honey has been arrested and has hanged himself in jail (109, 114).

In the film, once again, the racial drama remains in place, but its sharpest edges have been dulled. Honey is a drinker, not a drug addict. He has not slashed a white man with a razor but inadvertently run over a white man with his car. He is afraid of being put in a road gang by the police, not of being lynched by a mob. "Berenice, you gotta help me!" he cries, bursting into the kitchen. "They'll put me on the road again for this for sure. If I'm lucky they'll put me on the road." By the end of the film, Honey has been sentenced to ten years in jail, his racial identity as firmly boxed in – and immovable – as he is.

Cooling down the sex

Ironically, for a novel that is far more "about" gender and sexuality than it is about race, the play and film versions of *Wedding* are utterly oblique and even frightened of a subject that surely offered as many dramatic possibilities as racial conflict. If McCullers and her producers thought that race would bring audiences to theaters and cinemas and keep them there, they apparently felt that overt images of interracial longing, homosexuality, preadolescent intercourse, and incest would scare them away. If the heating up of the story's racial tension reflected the country's mid-century comfort with racial stereotypes, the cooling down of the story's sexuality reflected the opposite.

Early on in the novel, Frankie convinces her little cousin John Henry to come to bed with her, and proceeds to rub "Sweet Serenade" down the inside of her shirt and on John Henry's body.

They went to bed . . . She heard him breathe in the darkness, and now she had what she wanted so many nights that summer; there was somebody sleeping in the bed with her. She lay in the dark and listened to him breathe, then after a while she raised herself on her elbow. He lay freckled and small in the moonlight, his chest white and naked, and one foot hanging from the edge of the bed. Carefully she put her hand on his stomach and moved closer; it felt as though a clock was ticking inside him and he smelled of sweat and Sweet Serenade. He smelled like a sour little rose. Frankie leaned down and licked him behind the ear. The she breathed deeply, settled herself with her chin on his sharp damp shoulder, and closed her eyes: for now, with somebody sleeping in the dark with her, she was not so much afraid. (13)

Heightening the sexuality of the moment is "the sad horn of some colored boy" that Frankie hears drifting through an open window. Suddenly, the music stops:

Then, without warning, the thing happened that at first Frankie could not believe. Just at the time when the tune should be laid, the music finished, the horn broke off. All of a sudden the horn stopped playing. For a moment Frankie could not take it in, she felt so lost. She whispered finally to John Henry West: "He has stopped to bang the spit out of his horn. In a second he will finish." But the music did not come again. The tune was left broken, unfinished. And the drawn tightness she could no longer stand. She felt she must do something wild and sudden that never had been done before. She hit herself on the head, but that did not help at all. (14)

If young Frankie is "wild," in other words, she is wild with sexual frustration. Just as the tune should be "laid," the horn "broke off" so that the man could "bang the spit out of his horn" (14). The music would not "come again" (14). Frankie, who "could not take it in" (14), goes wild with sexual frustration years before she would even have a name for the feeling.

In the play Frankie and John Henry never even make it to the bedroom. Standing in the yard between their two houses, Frankie calls up to John Henry, still in his room, and suggests that they put up her "Indian teepee and sleep out here in the yard" (47). But the teepee is never built, the children never lie down, and there is not even the suggestion of physical contact. The trumpet plays, but it is background music, and ignored.

For the film, Zinnemann apparently decided to play the scene for a laugh. To a ludicrous, slapstick score, John Henry scampers across the lawn to Frankie's house. This time, he actually makes it inside her house and into her bedroom, but the scene is completely stripped of sexuality – unless you consider the sight of Julie Harris's 26-year-old body in a negligée. Harris was more than twice the age of the girl she had been cast to play, and the muscles in her shoulders and calves are nothing like those of a twelve-year-old. Nonetheless, her Frankie and de Wilde's John Henry never get into bed together here, either. John Henry kneels to recite the Lord's Prayer while Frankie stands by the window with her back to him.

She hears the trumpet, but instead of eroticism, the moment raises the possibility of – yes – racial conflict that did not even appear in the play. Why did Honey stop playing the horn? John Henry has an idea: "I bet a policeman stopped him."

Such incidental gestures not only fabricate racial tension that did not exist in the novel, they toss out the novel's interest in sexual ambiguity and ambivalence in favor of gender stereotypes. If there is anything even vaguely risqué in the filmed bedroom scene, it is entirely domesticated: Frankie and John Henry speak to each other like an old (and sexless) married couple; they are a comical simulacrum of the hypertraditional couple formed by Frankie's brother and his fiancée. In the novel even the seven-year-old John Henry is sexually curious: having already (unwittingly) received Frankie's nocturnal massage, John Henry pulls up a doll's dress "and fingered the real panties and body waist"(15). In the play his interest in the doll is merely parental: "Lilly Belle is taking a nap," he says, "so don't talk so loud" (28). In the film he is both desexed and masculinized: he grabs the doll, declares, "I will call her Belle," and then punches it in the face.

Later, in the novel, Berenice counsels her young charges on the complexities of love. "I have heard of many a queer thing," she says:

"I have knew mens to fall in love with girls so ugly that you wonder if their eyes is straight. I have seen some of the most peculiar weddings anybody could conjecture. Once I knew a boy with his whole face burned off so that – "

"Who?" asked John Henry.

Berenice swallowed a piece of cornbread and wiped her mouth with the back of her hand. "I have knew womens to love veritable Satans and thank Jesus when they put their split hooves over the threshold. I have knew boys to take it into their heads to fall in love with other boys. You know Lily Mae Jenkins?"

F. Jasmine thought a minute, and then answered: "I'm not sure."

"Well, you either know him or you don't know him. He prisses around with a pink satin blouse and one arm akimbo. Now this Lily Mae turned into a girl. He changed his nature and his sex and turned into a girl." (76)

In perhaps its only moment of adherence to the spirit of the novel, the play keeps much of this language intact. But the film completely pulls the punch, once again playing the scene for a laugh and adding an odd jab at Honey. "I've known men to fall in love with girls so ugly you'd wonder if their eyes are straight," Berenice says. "Even known boys to fall in love with women older than their mothers. Take Honey – he's in love with that horn." Wondering about men who fall for older women or a musician attached to his music hardly compares to considering characters who are openly homosexual and even transgendered. As elsewhere, the film makes a gesture toward the risky complexity of the novel, but the gesture is empty, gratuitous.

Especially given Wilson's original complaint that the novel lacked dramatic tension, the strangest change of all in both the play and the film is the utter neglect of the novel's one narrative component that actually *does* drive the story forward, at times with real terror: the relationship between Frankie and the drunken soldier who tries to seduce her. Both the play and the film reinforce not only Frankie's heterosexuality but her innocence, so fetishizing the rituals of her brother's wedding that Frankie seems desperate only to be a blushing bride. In fact, in the novel Frankie is terrified of sex, and not because she is a virgin.

In the novel Frankie meets the soldier at the Blue Moon café in the morning of the day before the wedding, and converses with him over the course of five or six pages. She is naive and trusting, he is drunk and flirtatious: "Which way are we going?" he asks her, thick-tongued. "Are you going my way or am I going yours?" (63). His request for a "date" later that night virtually guarantees trouble, and trouble Frankie gets. Sixty pages later, roaming the town's streets late at night, Frankie wanders back to the Blue Moon and goes inside with the soldier. He invites her into a back room, pulls her down on a bed, and puts his arms around her. "He was not rough, but it was crazier than if he had been rough – and in a second she was paralyzed by horror. She could not push away, but she bit down with all her might upon what must have been the crazy soldier's tongue." After metaphorically castrating the soldier, Frankie crashes a water pitcher on his head, crumpling him, and leaves not knowing "whether he was dead or not" (130).

In the novel the scene is given extra power not by Frankie's sexual innocence but by her sexual experience. Earlier, she alludes to having "committed a queer sin" in a garage with a neighbor named Barney MacKean. "The sin made a shriveling sickness in her stomach, and she dreaded the eyes of everyone. She hated Barney and wanted to kill him. Sometimes alone in the bed at night she planned to shoot him with the pistol or throw a knife between his eyes" (23). In the novel Frankie is not only philosophically obsessed with questions of gender and sexuality, she has already had, at the age of twelve, at least two experiences that have left her terrified of heterosexual sex.

In the play and the film, the two long scenes with the soldier are cut to a single short one, the tongue-biting is omitted, and the whole thing seems to be played simply to show how dangerous the world of grown-ups can be. And Barney MacKean, who in the novel was the very source of Frankie's sexual ambivalence and dread, returns as a masculine, heterosexual ideal. At the end of the play and the film, Frankie describes

Barney as a "Greek god," a football star whom she invites to ride with her on a moving truck to her new house. In effect, even as the play and the film do their best to turn Honey Brown into a source of danger, the actions of the two people who actually threaten Frankie – both white – are either diluted or entirely refigured. And the ambivalence about traditional gender roles displayed by Frankie and everyone else in the novel is replaced by lockstep conformity to the married heterosexual ideal. "Does marrying really stop your growth?" Frankie asks Berenice in the novel. "It certainly do," Berenice replies (25). In the film Berenice's answer is reversed, and revealing. "Marriage," she says, "don't stop nuthin."[13]

NOTES

1. Edmund Wilson, "Two Books That Leave You Blank: Carson McCullers, Siegfried Sassoon," *New Yorker*, March 30, 1946, p. 80. Virginia Spencer Carr discusses McCullers's reaction is detail in her *The Lonely Hunter: A Biography of Carson McCullers* (Garden City: Doubleday, 1975), p. 259. McCullers was plagued by illness for most of her life. At fifteen she was diagnosed with rheumatic fever that required several weeks of convalescence in a sanitarium. By the mid-1930s she had begun smoking three packs of cigarettes a day and losing weight and was plagued by pneumonia, a bone infection in her jaw, a kidney infection, and, before she reached thirty, three strokes, one of which temporarily affected her vision, another permanently paralyzing her left side. Carson spent most of December 1946 in the Neurological Institute of Columbia Presbyterian Hospital in New York City, then spent three weeks in Manhattan's Payne Whitney Psychiatric Clinic in Manhattan for attempted suicide. Several years later, she was treated for a broken hip, diagnosed with breast cancer, and had her right breast removed. For most of her adult life she fought chronic depression, alcoholism, and severe pain in her useless left arm.
2. Josyane Savigneau, *Carson McCullers: A Life*, trans. Joan E. Howard (New York: Houghton Mifflin, 2001), pp. 156–158. Wilson's review came out in a year in which his own reputation had reached a high point with the publication of *Memoirs of Hecate County*. F. Scott Fitzgerald considered Wilson "the most heeded and lucid" American literary critic at work.
3. Carson McCullers, *The Heart is a Lonely Hunter* (New York: Houghton Mifflin, 1940), pp. 16, 18–19, 112–113.
4. Carson McCullers, *The Member of the Wedding* (New York: Houghton Mifflin, 1946), p. 92. Further references will be cited parenthetically in the text.
5. George Dangerfield, "An Adolescent's Four Days," *Saturday Review*, March 30, 1946, rpt. in Beverly Lyon Clark and Melvin J. Friedman, eds., *Critical Essays on Carson McCullers* (New York: G. K. Hall & Co.), 1996, p. 31.
6. Robert S. Phillips, "The Gothic Architecture of *The Member of the Wedding*," *Renascence: Essays on Values in Literature*, 16.2 (Winter 1964), pp. 59–72.
7. Carson McCullers, *The Mortgaged Heart* (Boston: Houghton Mifflin, 1971), p. 264.

8. Harvey Breit, "Behind the Wedding: Carson McCullers Discusses the Novel She Converted Into a Stage Play," *New York Times*, January 1, 1950. McCullers's frustration over Wilson's review was partially alleviated by a surprising source. Tennessee Williams claimed that he stayed up all night reading her novel, stopping only to wipe tears from his eyes. Unable to sleep, he composed for McCullers what he claimed was his first fan letter, and later invited her to visit him at his house on Nantucket, where he was struggling to complete his play *Summer and Smoke*. McCullers accepted nervously, though she had seen perhaps six plays in her life, a list that did not include *The Glass Menagerie*. The two hit it off immediately. McCullers so charmed Williams that he pushed through his block and completed the play. He did more: he bought McCullers a typewriter and convinced her to try her hand at writing drama. Sitting across from one another, often passing a bottle of bourbon back and forth, the two worked in independent harmony. "She was the only person I have ever been able to work in the same room with, and we got along beautifully," Williams said. "In no sense of the word was I Carson's mentor. If she wanted to ask me something or read some lines aloud for my reaction, she would. But that was rare. Carson accepted almost no advice about how to adapt *The Member of the Wedding*. I did not suggest lines to her more than once or twice, and then she would usually have her own ideas and say, 'Tenn, honey, thank you, but I know all I need to know'" (Carr, *The Lonely Hunter*, pp. 271, 275).

9. For details, see Carr, *The Lonely Hunter*, pp. 33, 345, 367. The play, and then the film, provided a major comeback for Ethel Waters, who at fifty was unknown to a generation that had not heard her as an international jazz singer. Julie Harris had made her Broadway debut five years earlier, with Burgess Meredith in Synge's *The Playboy of the Western World*, but her roles had been minor. McCullers had seen her in *The Glass Menagerie* in Nyack, and perhaps because of her admiration for Tennessee Williams, decided that Harris would be perfect. Brandon de Wilde would go on to a successful career on Broadway, in Hollywood, and as a folk singer, until he was killed in a car crash in 1972. Edward Anhalt would win an Oscar for Best Screenplay for *Becket* in 1964, and Edward and Edna received an Oscar nomination for *The Sniper* in 1952. Edward also wrote the 1962 Elvis Presley vehicle, *Girls! Girls! Girls!*, and *The Boston Strangler* (1968), and co-wrote *Jeremiah Johnson*, starring Robert Redford, in 1972. The Austrian-born Zinnemann would go on to make *From Here to Eternity* (1953), *Oklahoma!* (1955), the Oscar-winning *A Man For All Seasons* (1966), and *Day of the Jackal* (1973).

10. *New York Times*, December 31, 1952.

11. Thadious Davis, "Erasing the 'We of Me' and Rewriting the Racial Script: Carson McCullers's Two Member(s) of the Wedding," in Clark and Friedman, eds., *Critical Essays on Carson McCullers*, p. 217

12. Carson McCullers, *The Member of the Wedding: A Play* (New York: New Directions, 1949), pp. 42–43. Further references will be cited parenthetically in the text. In the film even Berenice seems to lose economic autonomy. When John Henry digs her blue glass eye out of her bag, she admonishes him, saying, "I still owe $64.23 on this eye." Frankie, laughing, mocks her: "Maybe the finance company will come and take it back!"

13. For Broadway, the director Harold Clurman decided to cut the entire bar-room scene between Frankie and the drunken soldier, despite the fact that an entire set had already been built for it. McCullers found this change difficult to accept, in part because it was one of the scenes that Tennessee Williams had helped her to write (Carr, *The Lonely Hunter*, p. 340).

7   Film and narration: two versions of *Lolita*

Robert Stam

As Wayne Booth points out in *The Rhetoric of Fiction* (1983), we react to narrators as we do to persons, finding them likeable or repulsive, wise or foolish, fair or unfair. Narrators vary widely on a broad spectrum, not only in terms of likeability but also in terms of reliability. Some are honest brokers, while others are pathological liars. On a scale of trustworthiness, narrators range from those who are almost completely suspect (such as Jason Compson in *The Sound and the Fury* [1929]) to those who are more or less reliable (Nick Carraway in *The Great Gatsby* [1925], Bras Cubas in *Posthumous Memoirs of Bras Cubas* [1880]) to those who serve as dramatized spokespersons for the implied author and whose values conform to the norms of the text (Joseph Conrad's Marlow in *Heart of Darkness* [1902]).[1]

What interests me here is a particular kind of narration, to wit *unreliable* narration. The modern period has been especially fond of 1) changing narrators and 2) unreliable narrators. Changing narrators alter their discourse and ideas as they narrate; they mutate before our eyes. This trait is especially true of the *Bildungsroman* or novel of development (for example, *Great Expectations* [1851]); part of the plot, in such novels, is not just *what* happens but how the narrator changes *as a result of* what happens, for example when Pip learns about the true source of his fortune. Although the technique of unreliable narration can be traced back to the prose fictions of antiquity, it is modern novelists since Dostoevsky who have especially exploited the device. The challenge of reading, with unreliable narration, consists in divining the narrator's inconsistencies and neuroses, penetrating the veil set up by the narrators to hide their vices (or even their virtues). Sometimes the reliability of a narrator becomes a "crux" in interpretation, as is the case with Ellen Dean in Emily Brontë's *Wuthering Heights* (1848) or of the Governess in Henry James's *The Turn of the Screw* (1898). In the cinema Akira Kurosawa's *Rashomon* (1951), in which the story of a crime is told in four radically different, yet equally plausible ways, constitutes a tour de force of problematic narration.

Figure 8. Humbert Humbert (James Mason) is in sexual bondage to a largely unconcerned postpubescent Lolita (Sue Lyon) in *Lolita*, a 1962 Anya/Harris-Kubrick/Seven Arts release.

Here we will examine this process as it operates in two versions of Vladimir Nabokov's (1899–1977) novel *Lolita* (1955). The story told in this masterwork about a middle-aged European intellectual absorbed in the pursuit of murder and nymphets is well known, so I will not rehearse its details here, since the very name "Lolita" has become synonymous in the popular mind with exactly the kind of story that the novel tells. Despite Nabokov's expressed hostility toward the work of Dostoevsky, his narrator in *Lolita* clearly carries the genetic traces, the literary DNA, as it were, not only of Cervantes's Don Quixote (since the memoirs are the ravings of a hyperliterate obsessive), but also of Dostoevsky's Underground Man. Like the narrator of *Notes from Underground* (1864), the narrator of *Lolita* is unreliable in the extreme. Indeed, he is self-declaredly mad, sometimes "losing contact with reality" and given to what he himself calls "bouts of insanity."[2] As with *Notes from Underground*, here again the perverse pleasure of the text partially consists in reading between the lines, in detecting the inelegant, not to say grotesque, behavior hidden "beneath" the murderer's fancy prose style. Yet one of the dangers of unreliable narration is that hermeneutically challenged readers will take liars at their word. Thus some readers were seduced by the murderer's fancy style, as when the critic Robertson Davies summed up the story as "the exploitation of a weak adult by a corrupt child."[3] It is ultimately up to us to discern, in the interstices of all *Lolita*'s circumlocutions and literary allusions, exactly what is going on. Indeed, at times we have to figure out precisely what sexual acts are being performed, to realize that when Humbert's tumescent prose speaks of being "proud like a Turk in his tower" as Lolita sits in his lap, for example, he is referring to his erection, and that going "over the abyss" means he is having an orgasm.

Lolita is written in the first-person, confessional point of view, a latter-day descendant, in a long literary-historical perspective, of the celebrated "confessions" of St. Augustine and Jean-Jacques Rousseau. Like some of his forebears, Nabokov, too, was skeptical about the possibilities of autobiographical revelation, even within the intimacy of a diary. (Hermann, the narrator of Nabokov's *Despair* [1966], calls the diary "the lowest form of literature."[4]) Nabokov picks up his narrational technique, more particularly, from the neurotic, unreliable, self-deconstructing narrators of Dostoevsky novellas such as *Notes from Underground*. Divinely egocentric and solipsistic, the Humbert of the novel controls his own self-presentation, with the result that we get only glimpses of what Nabokov called "the vain and cruel wretch" who "manages to appear touching." So the challenge is to distinguish between the authorial voice, which Nabokov calls "an anthropomorphic deity impersonated by me," and the narrational voice of the character Humbert.[5]

Nabokov's imaginary had always been shaped by the cinema. Already in the 1920s, he was writing scenarios. In the early 1930s the former Moscow Art Theater director Sergei Bertenson invited Nabokov to Hollywood to devise storylines. Both *Camera Obscura* in 1932 and the rewrite *Laughter in the Dark* in 1938 revolve around a man who falls in love with an usherette who dreams of becoming a film star. An early avatar of the Humbert Humbert character in the novel *The Enchanter* (1977) watches young girls at play but perceives only the "senselessly smooth movement of slow-motion film."[6] Nabokov's *Bend Sinister* (1947) includes camera notations such as "photographed from above" and notes to the "actors."

By crowding *Lolita* with references to movies and stars and spectatorship, Nabokov brings René Girard's notion of "triangular" and "mimetic" desire into the age of the mass media.[7] The societal imaginary is no longer inflected by romantic literature, as in *Madame Bovary*, but rather by Hollywood films. Everyday life is shown as shaped by cinematic art. The film industry functions as pedagogue. Behavior, too, is learned from movies;

in *Lolita* kissers close their eyes "as Hollywood teaches." Humbert, after a lover's spat with Valechka, regrets having merely slammed the door, when he could have delivered the "backhand slap" more in conformity with "the rules of the movies." As Alfred Appel, Jr. lovingly delineates in *Nabokov's Dark Cinema* (1974), the novel is littered with movie references.[8] Humbert describes himself, for example, as "a great big handsome hunk of movieland manhood." Here the narrator's abuse of a poetic device – alliteration – becomes the aesthetic correlative of the clichés of fan magazines. Allusions to movie stars, at this point in literary history, become a kind of descriptive shorthand premised on readerly cine-competence, as in Humbert's account of Charlotte as "a weak solution of Marlene Dietrich."

Interestingly, Humbert Humbert himself thematizes the issue of the narrative capacities of film vis-à-vis novel. Humbert at one point calls himself an idiot for not having *filmed* Lolita: "Idiot. Triple idiot. I could have filmed her. I would have had her now with me, before my eyes, in the projection room of my pain and despair." Witnessing such a scene, Humbert imagines himself "a humble hunchback abusing [himself] in the dark." In the "seduction" scene Humbert notes that he "seemed to have shed [his] clothes and slipped into [his] pajamas with the kind of fantastic instantaneousness which is implied when in a cinematographic scene the process of changing is cut." In another suggestive passage Nabokov's narrator expresses a kind of envy of the cinema. Gleefully reporting his wife Charlotte's providential death by car crash, Humbert deplores the fact that he:

has to put the impact of an instantaneous vision into a sequence of words; their physical accumulation on the page impairs the actual flash, the sharp unity of impression . . . At this point, I should explain that the prompt appearance of the patrolman, hardly more than a minute after the accident, was due to their having been ticketing the illegally parked cars in a cross lane two blocks down the grade; that the fellow with the glasses was Frederick Beale Jr., driver of the Packard . . . and finally that the laprobe on the sidewalk (where she had so often pointed out to me with disapproval the crooked green cracks) concealed the mangled remains of Charlotte, who had been knocked down and dragged several feet by the Beale car as she was hurrying across the street.

Humbert laments the incorrigible, frustrating linearity of the linguistic signifier, the plodding deliberateness of prose fiction, with its subordination to linear consecution, its congenital incapacity to seize the moment in its multifaceted simultaneity. At the same time, style itself becomes symptomatic of a severely disturbed sense of human values. The meaning of the "mangled remains" of a person well known to the narrator (and who had shown him only kindness) is obscured by an obsessive attention to the trivial details of green cracks and laprobes. Charlotte's death is subordinated to a writer's maniacal obsession with getting the details right. The very syntax is perverse, as Charlotte is "killed off" in a dependent, subordinate clause ("Charlotte, who had been knocked down . . .") The same moment as staged by Stanley Kubrick's *Lolita* (1962), in contrast, *does* offer simultaneity: we see the crash as we hear it, along with the commentative music, which conveys a tragically suspenseful atmosphere that matches and underlines the events presented. Yet I would in no way argue the superiority of the Kubrick rendition. Nabokov, paradoxically, conveys more sense of discontinuity between theme and style, that is, between the tragic motif of untimely death on the one hand and the flip, cynical style of Humbert's presentation of that death on the other, than does Kubrick, who decides not to take advantage of the potentially discontinuous multiplicity of tracks available to the filmmaker.

In another passage of the novel, Humbert tries his hand at genre criticism. Delineating Lolita's tastes in movies, the narrator explains:

Her favorite kinds were, in this order: musicals, underworlders, Westerners. In the first, real singers and dancers had unreal stage careers in an essentially grief-proof sphere of existence wherefrom death and truth were banned, and where, at the end, white-haired, dewy-eyed, technically deathless, the initially reluctant father of a show-crazy girl always finished by applauding her apotheosis on fabulous Broadway. The underworld was a world apart: there, heroic newspapermen were tortured, telephone bills ran to millions, and, in a robust atmosphere of incompetent marksmanship, villains were chased through sewers and storehouses by pathologically fearless cops . . . Finally, there was the mahogany landscape, the florid-faced, blue-eyed roughriders, the prim pretty schoolteacher arriving in Roaring Gulch, the rearing horse, the spectacular stampede, the pistol thrust through the shivered windowpane, the stupendous fistfight, the crashing mountain of dusty old furniture, the table used as a weapon, the timely somersault, the pinned hand still groping for the dropped bowie knife, the grunt, the sweet crash of fist against chin, the kick in the belly, the flying tackle; and immediately after a plethora of pain that would have hospitalized a Hercules . . . nothing to show but the rather becoming bruise on the bronzed cheek of the warmed-up hero embracing his gorgeous frontier bride.

The passage vividly evokes readerly memories of hundreds of cinematic scenes. Nabokov's mimetic prose conveys not only the images but also the feel of the editing of the films, as in the quick-cut succession of "close shots" in the account of the western, where the gutturals and the fricatives and the dentals and the sibilants and the plosives – the *thr*ust *pistol*, the *stu*pendous *fistfigh*t, the *crash*ing *furniture*, the *grunt* and the *crash* and the *kick* and the *tack*le – convey the visceral violence of the genre. Although couched in parodic terms, the passage in some ways provides a sterling example of genre criticism, in that it zeroes in on a

number of genre criticism's principal concerns: 1) degree of verisimil-
itude ("unreal stage careers"); 2) recurrent plot formulae (the show-
girl's apotheosis); 3) typical characters (roughrider and schoolteacher); 4)
spectatorial response (the "grief-proof" musical); 5) characteristic decors
(sewers and warehouses); 6) typical props (bowie knife); 7) shots and
gestures; 8) the spectatorial pleasures mobilized. All that is missing are
more technical notations about camera movements (crane shots in westerns), sound techniques (cabaret sound in musicals) and editing (montage versus *mise-en-scène*).

As the previous passage suggests, Nabokov is also an extraordinarily
sound-sensitive writer. In the screenplay to *Lolita*, Nabokov requests that
the director reproduce the "the hot, moist sound . . . the tickle and the
buzz, the vibration, the thunder of [Lolita's] whisper" (110). The same
acoustic sensitivity is evident in the account of the seduction night in the
Enchanted Hunters Hotel:

There is nothing louder than an American hotel . . . the corridor would brim
with cheerful, resonant and inept exclamations ending in a volley of goodnights.
When that stopped, a toilet immediately north of my cerebellum took over. It
was a manly, energetic, deep-throated toilet, and it was used many times. Its
gurgle and gush and long afterflow shook the wall behind me. Then someone in
a southern direction was extravagantly sick, almost coughing out his life with his
liquor, and his toilet descended like a veritable Niagara, immediately beyond our
bathroom. And when finally all the waterfalls had stopped, and the enchanted
hunters were sound asleep, the avenue under the window of my insomnia, to the
west of my wake . . . degenerated into the despicable haunt of gigantic trucks
roaring through the wet and windy night.

If we could "see" the films described in the earlier passage about genre,
here we can virtually "hear" the sounds evoked, thanks to the use of
onomatopoeia ("gurgle" and "gush") and to the evocative, anthropomorphic language (the "manly" and "energetic" toilet). In an uncanny way,
Nabokov anticipates innovations in multitrack and Dolby sound, which
came to the cinema only decades later. (Dolby sound, for theorist Michel
Chion, added "three octaves to what had been a five-octave piano."[9])
Nabokov's almost comic precision about directionality – "north of my
cerebellum . . . in a southern direction . . . to the west of my wake" – provides the literary equivalent of stereophonic and later Dolby sound, where
one becomes conscious of the location and thrust and directionality of
sound. (One possible way of adapting such a passage would be to have the
screen go blank, while the various noises emerge from the speakers spread
around the screen and the cinema). We are reminded of the multilayered
sound practiced by sound editors such as Walter Murch, who parcels out
sound, for example in the opening sequence of *Apocalypse Now* (1979),

into scores of tracks, mingling "objective" and "subjective noises," so that the sound of the hotel fan gives way to remembered helicopter blades, while car horns transmute into birds, and flies into mosquitoes.

Before becoming a film, *Lolita* the novel took an intermediate narrative form, that of Nabokov's 400-page screenplay, conceived by its author as a "vivacious variant" of the novel, of which Kubrick used but a small portion. The screenplay is rather more audacious than the film, though Nabokov himself recognizes in the preface that the "author's goal of infinite fidelity" may be a "producer's ruin" (xiii). In the published screenplay Nabokov comments wittily on the process of filmmaking, contrasting what he sees as the beatific solitude of literary writing with the chaotic collectivity of filmmaking, which Nabokov compares to a "communal bath where the hairy and the slippery mix in a multiplication of mediocrity."[10] Speculating on how he might have directed the film himself, Humbert imagines himself as a kind of *auteur*-tyrant of the kind imagined by certain versions of *auteur* theory: "I would have advocated and applied a system of total tyranny, directing the play or the picture myself, choosing settings and costumes, terrorizing the actors, mingling with them in the bit part of guest, or ghost, . . . prompting them, and in a word, pervading the entire show with the will and art of one individual."[11]

The screenplay makes frequent allusion to Edgar Allan Poe, which is appropriate given both the gothic tone of the story and the nympholeptic tendencies of the American writer. The screenplay also includes a cameo role for Nabokov himself, a Hitchcockian touch that recalls his guest appearance in his own *Despair*, and which would have constituted the filmic equivalent of his anagrammatic presence in *Lolita* in the form of "Vivian Darkbloom."

The Nabokov screenplay also develops the embedded narration featured in the book. It expands the role of the pedantic Dr. John Ray, Jr., developing a constant interplay between Ray's presentation of Humbert's notes and Humbert's self-presentation. The screenplay in this sense creates a dual alter-ego narration, another doubling similar to the one that compares Humbert to Clare Quilty, his nemesis. The screenplay also promotes a dialectical interplay between direct and indirect narration. His wife Valeria screaming, "I hate you!" at Humbert segues to Ray's voice commenting that "she had never been more voluble." The screenplay is more prone than the Kubrick film to comic interruption and dedramatization. For Charlotte's fateful car crash, the screenplay has the film cut to traffic policemen examining diagrams of the accident, a narrative dislocation that visually translates the nonchalantly perverse syntax of Humbert's account of his wife's death. The stress in the Nabokov screenplay is on mediations of all types: photographs that come alive, a tape-recording of

a Humbert lecture. The narrator of the screenplay is more intervention-
ist than his counterpart in the Kubrick film; he requests specific shots,
a technique "faithful" to certain passages in *Lolita* where the narrator
actually addresses any future adaptor of the book: "If you want to make
a movie of my book, have one of those faces gently melt into my own,
while I look." The suggestion anticipates precisely the technique adopted
two years later by Alfred Hitchcock in *The Wrong Man* (1957), where the
face of the wrongly accused Henry Fonda is lap-dissolved into that of the
actual thief.

The screenplay also features completely fantastic images: a "ripply"
shot shows a knight in full armor riding a black horse, Humbert's mother
floating to heaven gripping a parasol, a vignette anticipatory of Woody
Allen's mother floating in the sky over Manhattan in *New York Stories*
(1989). Had these vignettes been filmed, they would have formed part of
a completely different film, featuring an anti-illusionistic aesthetic, more
reminiscent of Federico Fellini or Woody Allen than of the early Kubrick.
Nabokov's screenplay constantly anthropomorphizes the camera as well,
having it "glide," "slide," and "slither" – in a way that suggests a very
active, constantly moving camera functioning as a kind of narrator. One
Rear Window-like sequence, entitled "Various Rooms," has the camera
"glide from room to room at dawn [so as to] construct a series of situations
contrasting with the atmosphere in Room 342."[12]

The Nabokov screenplay also brings up interesting questions relevant
to the theory of adaptation. It reveals the instabilities of textual production, the fact that so-called definitive works are actually only one version arbitrarily frozen into definitive status. The screenplay, for example,
includes scenes rejected from the final draft of the novel yet reinstated
in the screenplay, as well as dialogue unlike anything in the novel, all of
which elicits a fascinating question: if a novelist has written a novel, but
also provided a screenplay which is already "unfaithful" to the novel, to
which text is the filmmaker to be "faithful"?

Nabokov's reaction to the Kubrick film was contradictory:

I discovered that Kubrick was a great director, that his *Lolita* was a first-rate film
with magnificent actors, and that only ragged odds and ends of my script had been
used. The modifications, the garbling of my little finds, the omission of entire
scenes and all sorts of other changes may not have been sufficient to erase my
name from the credit titles but they certainly made the picture as unfaithful to the
original script as an American poet's translation from Rimbaud or Pasternak.[13]

Nabokov also offered his own analysis of the Kubrick film in the form of
a poem, entitled "Pale Film" in an allusion to his own *Pale Fire* (1962).
In the poem, anatomized by Richard Corliss in his 1995 BFI study of

Lolita, Nabokov speaks of himself as the "novelist who watched/as each of his books-into-films was botched," where "similes were debased into a smile," where he "intersected with the movies' gaze/as Humbert saw the young Dolores Haze." Nabokov continues:

> I saw my words made whispers, twelve made teen
> Back roads made backlots, US made UK
> And green made gold, and me an émigré
> From Lo, whom I conceived but could not save

Speaking of his work as an extra in German cinema, Nabokov compares himself to "the larval author lurking in costume/as Hitchcock did, or Vivian Darkbloom." Applying his "writer's sleight-of-hand" to these "film-besotted wretches," Nabokov finally consoles himself with an assertion of the ultimate superiority of the verbal medium of literature: "nitrate reels will decompose, but each good reader will preserve my prose."[14]

Kubrick cleans up Nabokov's "messy" protagonist and "mainstreams" the relationship with Lolita. Partially as a sop to the censors, the Kubrick version makes an important structural change, also made in Nabokov's screenplay, by creating a circular structure whereby the murder of Quilty begins and ends the film. The change generates a shift in genre from erotic confession to murder mystery: the hermeneutic tease is no longer *who* killed Quilty or who Quilty is but rather *why* a specific person – Humbert – killed Quilty. Through this framing device, Kubrick downplays the novel's eroticism, thus giving Kubrick a strategic advantage in his inevitable struggles with potential censors. In the novel we know that Humbert is a murderer, but we do not know whom he has murdered. In the film we know whom he has murdered, but not why he has murdered him.

The generic shift has the corollary benefit of placing Quilty center stage, thus authorizing more space for the mercurial Peter Sellers. (Kubrick's long-take style, furthermore, allows room for Sellers to spread his wings as a performer). Along with Quilty, Sellers also plays the unnamed guest in the Enchanted Hunters Hotel, the psychologist Dr. Zemph, and the salacious unseen phonecaller from the morality squad. The Quilty character becomes a shape-shifter, incarnating some of the protean, Menippean spirit that animates the novel. Sellers, who emerged as a performer out of the world of stand-up comedy, from radio parody sketches and *The Goon Show*, thus shares an affinity with the genre that surreptitiously permeates Kubrick's later *Dr. Strangelove* (1963), where many of the routines could easily have been drawn from the repertoires of stand-up comics such as Mel Brooks or Sid Caesar, Mike Nichols, or Elaine May. Through a kind of displacement from narrative to character, Quilty becomes something of an ambulatory intertext, a performative embodiment of the Nabokovian style, no longer as literary citation but rather as allusive improvisation. Many of the specific features of the Kubrick adaptation can be partially explained by the pressures of censorship. The film combats the censors, or better censors itself, for example, by normalizing the relationship between Humbert and Lolita. Unlike both the novel and the Nabokov screenplay, the film offers no explanation as to the origins of Humbert's nympholepsy. Everything conspires to create the impression, when Humbert first meets Lolita (Sue Lyon), of love at first sight, the only taboo being an age difference slightly greater than was conventionally seen as acceptable between two lovers. In sum, the film offers what seems more a case of an adult's normal lust for an attractive teenager than a case of incest or nympholepsy. (Could it be this reluctant "normalization" that triggers Sellers/Quilty's obsessive repetition of the word "normal" in the dialogue between Quilty and Humbert in the Enchanted Hunters Hotel?)

The theme music by Nelson Riddle subliminally reinforces this normalization effect, by supplying a static, premodernist, rather syrupy muzak-style love theme. The very lack of dissonance and discontinuity in the music, and the fact that it does not change or progress either rhythmically or melodically, implies a lack of dissonance in the relationship; it empties the relationship of the tantalizingly taboo atmosphere that renders the affair deliciously illicit and scrumptiously dangerous. In a sense, the standardized "love-theme" music "blesses" the relationship, wrapping the incest in an innocuously romantic glow. The choice of James Mason, as opposed to the other players contemplated as possibilities (Laurence Olivier, David Niven, Marlon Brando), also contributes to this normalization. Understated, stern, paternal, Mason through most of the film seems more the harried father than the dirty old man, though he does at least fit Nabokov's description of Humbert as "attractively Simian, and boyishly manly" sporting "thick black eyebrows and a queer accent," even if one might not want to attribute to Mason "a cesspoolful of rotting monsters between his slow boyish style." But here, too, the film transforms the process of readerly/spectatorial inference. In the film we witness Humbert's clumsiness, including his *verbal* clumsiness, resulting in a reversal: while in the novel we have immediate access to Humbert's verbal brilliance, and have to *infer* his clumsiness, in the film we witness his clumsiness, and have to infer his brilliance.

The film also makes a significant adjustment in narrational technique. The novel features twenty-nine passages of direct address by Humbert to the reader, variously referred to as "readers" as well as "jury," "doctor," and even "printer." Humbert is aware of his dependency on the reader –

"I shall not exist if you do not imagine me." He reminds him that his "gloomy good looks" should be "kept in the mind's eye if [the] story is to be understood." Humbert also asks for the collaboration of "learned readers" in "the scene I am about to replay." Thus Nabokov's technique mingles the direct address of a Henry Fielding narrator with the ongoing swirl of internal self-consciousness of a Dostoevskyean character.

In the film, in contrast, Humbert's voiceover narration is only intermittent, and it exercises much less control over the point of view. The unreliable narrator of the novel, whose neurotic voice echoes with the overtones of *Notes from Underground* tradition, becomes the reliable narrator of the film, in that the film never casts any serious doubt on Humbert's account of events. The voiceover is generally only informative, providing basic exposition rather than glimpses into Humbert's feelings or imagination. The voiceover narration becomes an anchor of truth, unlike the novel, where the narration forms a shifting, unanchored space of mendacity and ambiguity. Kubrick achieves this normalization of narrational voice, in part, by eliding the more outrageous things that the Humbert of the book has to say. What is lost, unfortunately, is the novel's shrewdly constructed gap between the elegant, courtly style of the narrator and the sordid behavior of the child-abuser, the dirty old man lurking "behind" the style, hiding, as it were, in the interstices of the prose.

While the novel's narrator is what Gérard Genette would call "autodiegetic" – that is, the author generates and narrates a story within which he is the main protagonist – the film is closer to what Genette calls "homodiegetic," that is, the narrator is involved with the story but is no longer the only protagonist. What becomes clear in the film versions both of *Notes from Underground* and *Lolita* is that filmic narrators based on novels featuring unreliable narrators must struggle against a basic feature of the film medium. The discursive power of unreliable autodiegetic narrators is almost automatically relativized by film. In a novel the narrator controls the *only* track – the verbal track. In a film the narrator can partially control the verbal track – through voiceover – but that control is subject to innumerable constraints: the pressure to include voiced dialogue, to dramatize, to tell stories visually, and so forth. In a film the other characters instantly gain a physical presence denied them in the novel. Even minor figures such as Lolita's husband, completely marginalized in the novel, achieve, however briefly, a certain embodiment. They cannot be safely "solipsized," as Humbert solipsizes Lolita, since they are now present as speaking, moving, gesticulating characters. The narrator/character from the novel is also relativized through contextualization; he now has to compete for attention not only with the other characters but also with the decor, the music, the color, the light. I am not suggesting that it is impossible to relay unreliable first-person narration in the cinema; I am only saying that it would require relentless subjectification on various cinematic registers: uninterrupted voiceover, nonstop point-of-view editing, constantly motivated camera movements, always marked subjective framing, in a way that approximates to Pier Paolo Pasolini's "cinema of poetry." The Adrian Lyne version of *Lolita* (1997), as we shall soon see, takes a few, small steps in that direction.

Questions of narration are inseparable from questions of style. *Lolita* was made at a certain point in Kubrick's career, and at a certain point in film history. Kubrick in the early 1960s was primarily the "realistic" director of *The Killing* (1957), *Paths of Glory* (1957), and even *Spartacus* (1960). He was not yet the satiric reflexive director of *Dr. Strangelove* and *Clockwork Orange* (1971). At the time of *Lolita*, Kubrick had an instrumental view of novelistic style, as something a writer "uses" to convey his feelings and thoughts. Yet style in Nabokov's novel is not instrumental or decorative; it is arguably "of the essence," completely inseparable from content, and the means by which we find clues to Nabokov's attitude toward his character.

The Kubrick film, though made three years after Jean-Luc Godard's jazzy and polyrhythmic *A Bout de Souffle* 1959 and Alain Resnais's modernist *Hiroshima Mon Amour* (1959), deploys a relatively conventional pre-New Wavish style. While Godard renders car-driving sequences as a nervous, jump-cut orchestration of shrewd and discontinuous editing mismatches, Kubrick exploits the rather old-fashioned device of matte-shot (back-projection) effects. The mainstream fiction film's relative impermeability to reflexivity partially explains the film's aesthetic failure of nerve and its consequent incapacity to create a filmic equivalent to the novel's self-flaunting artificiality. While the novel constantly flaunts its own status as linguistic artifact, the film is largely cast in the illusionistic mold, presenting rounded characters in plausible settings, filmed by a self-effacing camera. While the book forms a veritable palimpsest of virtuoso parodic turns – Dostoyevsky, Sade, Poe, Proust are all spoofed – the Kubrick film is at best intermittently parodic, as we see in the clumsy homage to Charlie Chaplin's tussle with a bed in *One A.M.* (1916), in Quilty's allusion to Kubrick's own *Spartacus*, in the disorientingly direct cut to *The Curse of Frankenstein* (1957) – but never as consistently or as effectively so as the novel. In terms of cinematic allusion, paradoxically, the film is less "filmic" than the novel. Yet in another sense, however, the film displaces the literary spirit of Nabokovian wit onto the register of spoken performance, and especially that of Sellers as Quilty. Sellers's shape-shifting capacity to mimic diverse personages makes him a comic constellation of impromptu "quotations" whose very modus operandi is parodic in the best Nabokovian sense.

Occasionally, Kubrick does achieve a sense of the stylistic discontinuity of the novel, for example in the scene of Quilty's murder. In the book the scene takes roughly ten pages (discourse time) and portrays an hour in the fiction (story time). The film creates a certain gap between the decor and the lighting. Quilty's Pavor mansion is the gothic castle *par excellence*, yet the lighting is not expressionist, as would be the norm in horror films, but rather high key. The scene is beautifully choreographed, and more importantly reproduces the sense of a gap between style and content, since a very serious event – a murder – is treated in the tone of a black-humored prank.

Many sequences are brilliantly filmed and performed: Humbert drunk in his bath, sipping wine to commemorate Charlotte's death, while his friends and neighbors worry that he might be contemplating suicide (rather than nympholepsy) and where they encourage him to do exactly what he is doing anyway: "Try to think of Lolita." In a number of scenes, Kubrick "traps" Humbert in the act of voyeurism. Often we see Humbert, satyr-like, peeping at Lolita from behind books, newspapers, and flower arrangements. At one point, he is lasciviously ogling Lolita wiggling with her hula-hoop, when Charlotte takes his photo, so that he is caught *in flagrante*. A number of shots feature a triangular composition, ideal for a situation of "mediated desire." The shot where Humbert, making love to Charlotte, draws erotic inspiration from Lolita's photo strategically placed next to Charlotte's bed. This triangular structure informs the book as a whole, where Humbert marries one woman (Valeria) because he admires her father, marries another (Charlotte) because he lusts for her daughter, and desires Lolita because she reminds him of his lost love Annabel.

While Nabokov constantly highlights the verbal factitiousness of his text, Kubrick finds no filmic equivalent for this self-referential device. While the novel frequently plays with or violates the reader's expectations, the film rarely surprises (the sudden cut to the drive-in Frankenstein film constitutes a rare exception). The novel consistently disorients its reader, especially as to the degree of "sincerity" of the text, while the film gently guides the spectator by the hand. While the novel develops a systematic tension between the *what* being told and the *how* of tone and style of the telling, the film is, in the main, stylistically homogeneous. In short, Kubrick substitutes three-dimensional illusionism and stylistic continuity for the recklessly flamboyant anti-illusionism of the book. That is why the Kubrick film is more pleasurable on a second viewing. Lovers of the Nabokov novel have to forget its specifically literary qualities to better appreciate the film's pleasures: its fine-tuned performances and subtle *mise-en-scène*.

More than three decades after the Kubrick version, the Adrian Lyne adaptation of *Lolita* was made in a rather ambiguous social atmosphere that harmed the film's possibilities for distribution. On the one hand, the 1990s were less censorious than the early 1960s, for by now porn had entered the mainstream, with the result that the film looked relatively tame compared to what was available on cable television or even in Enchanted Hunters-style motels and hotels. On the other hand, the United States, at least, was obsessed with pedophilia and the sexual abuse of children by teachers and caretakers. It was the period of the Jon Benet Ramsay case, and of the Orin Hatch "Child Porn Prevention" bill. As a result, the film was denounced by conservatives in the United States and the United Kingdom and had trouble finding a distributor, finally premiering on cable television, so that Showtime became the contemporary media equivalent of Paris's Olympia Press.

Lyne's *Lolita* also went through various scriptwriters – James Dearden, Harold Pinter, David Mamet, and finally and definitively, Stephen Schiff. Each version entailed dramatically different choices. The Dearden version did not include Annabel, and had Humbert distributing books by Stephen King and Norman Mailer. David Mamet wanted to have the same actress play both Annabel and Lolita to stress the sense of ritual repetition and *déjà vu*. The Pinter version, interestingly, seemed to read *Lolita* through *Notes from Underground*, as suggested by the opening lines of the script: "My name is Humbert. You won't like me. I suffer from moral leprosy."

While the Kubrick *Lolita* treats a contemporaneous story, the thirty-five years that separate the original novel from the Lyne adaptation turn the film into a period piece, now set in the late 1940s. While the foreign-born Nabokov had shown himself to be a master observer of Americana, paradoxically, the American-born Kubrick had filmed the novel as if he were a foreigner, partially because Kubrick at that time was living in England, where his version was actually filmed (apart from some second-unit work). The Englishman Lyne, again paradoxically, shows a better grasp of Americana than did Kubrick, both in terms of an anthological soundtrack filled with pop hits by Louis Prima and Ella Fitzgerald, and in terms of locations which privilege the tackier aspects of an industrialized American landscape. What in the novel was *literary* allusion here becomes pop culture musical allusion. Pop songs are used to ironic effect; we hear "That's Amore" as Lolita is jiggled by a coin-operated massage-bed. And we hear Louis Prima's "barbaric yawp" against civilization – "Bongo, bongo, bongo/I don't want to leave the Congo"/Oh no, no, no!" – during the couple's picaresque journey across America, suggesting that Humbert prefers the uncivilized (that is, taboo) relationship with Lolita to a return to "civilization" and respectability.

Whereas one thinks of Kubrick as an antierotic and misogynistic director, who prefers the world of men alone and at war – *The Killing, Paths of Glory, Dr. Strangelove, Full Metal Jacket* – Lyne is associated with films laced with frank eroticism: *Foxes* (1980), *Flashdance* (1983), $9\frac{1}{2}$ *Weeks* (1986), *Indecent Proposal* (1993), and, most recently, *Unfaithful* (2002). Unlike the Kubrick version, but like the Nabokov screenplay, the Lyne version reserves a privileged place for the Annabel episode in the form of a sensuous, soft-focus French Riviera flashback. A voiceover reveals the traumatic effect of Annabel's untimely death: "Whatever happens to a boy the summer he's fourteen will mark him for life. The shock of her death froze something in me. The child I loved was gone, but I kept looking for her, long after I left my own childhood behind. The poison was in the wound, you see, and the wound wouldn't heal."

The sequence, seen as if through the soft-focus haze of memory, traces the genesis of Humbert's nympholepsy to a cruelly interrupted relationship: "If it wasn't for Annabel," Humbert's voiceover informs us, "there might never have been a Lolita." Thus Lyne, like Kubrick, normalizes, or more accurately "humanizes" Humbert, but differently. By positing Humbert as victim in the first instance, and repentant in the last, Lyne foregrounds both the trajectory of Humbert's moral growth and also his melancholy realization that he had abused Lolita. He thus closes the novel's gap between the narrator's self-presentation and the author's.

Drawing on a resource available only to film, the Lyne version also uses music to make a point about character. Lolita's character is very much identified with the late 1940s and early 1950s diegetic pop music *in* the film, which she sings, mouths, dances or otherwise performs. Humbert, meanwhile, is associated with the more complex and upscale romantic/modernist music scored *for* the film. The scored music is impressionist, harmonically complex, evocative of the ethos and psyche of the European intellectual and the aesthetics of the art film. As a hybridization of the romantic and impressionist modes, the Ennio Morricone music "carries" the melancholy and even tragic overtones of a dissonant romance. And the tragic sensibility belongs to Humbert, while the pop sensibility belongs to Lolita. The close shots in which complex and contradictory emotions play over Jeremy Irons's face, together with the music's evocation of interiority, all help to shape Humbert as a complex and ultimately moral figure. Yet this normalization of Humbert as a multifaceted and sensitive human being enters into conflict with another aspect of the film, its soft-core erotic aesthetic, the sensuous pastels, the filtered smoky lighting, reminiscent of champagne commercials, which make the spectator, and especially the voyeuristic male spectator, complicitous with Humbert's nympholeptic desire.

Music and close-ups are just a few of the many cinematic registers used to align us with Humbert's feelings. Both Kubrick and Lyne emphasize Humbert's voyeurism. But in Kubrick we do not peek with Humbert; rather, he has us watch Humbert watching, often catching him *in flagrante*, as when Charlotte photographs him as he is admiring Lolita's undulating hula-hoop. Many of the shots in the Kubrick version are pointedly *not* point-of-view shots, as when a shot of Lolita getting in a car on the way to camp, framed through Humbert's window, is subsequently revealed *not* to be from Humbert's point of view, since he is shown sleeping. Kubrick thus simultaneously identifies us with Humbert's voyeurism and distances us from it through the refusal of the reaction shot that might have sutured us into the character's gaze. Lyne, in contrast, rigorously identifies us with Humbert's perspective by having us look *with* Humbert through carefully constructed point-of-view shots. Countless shots show Humbert straining to get a glimpse of Lolita. Humbert peers from behind obstacles, looks through half-open bathroom doors to glimpse her bare legs and the unrolling toilet paper. Repeatedly, Humbert positions himself strategically in order to afford himself (and the spectator) the best possible view. Lyne in this sense reproduces Nabokov's quasi-Flaubertian precision about point of view, for the novel, too, posits precise vantage points: "I happened to glimpse from the bathroom, through a chance combination of a mirror aslant and a door ajar, a look on her face . . . an expression of helplessness." At times, Humbert's strategic scopophilia does, admittedly, take on a comic dimension, as when Humbert, seated on the porch swing with Charlotte, has to strain his neck to catch Lolita's whimsical Charleston, while the swinging has him pop up and down, in and out of the frame.

But even when not deploying literal point-of-view editing, the Lyne film aligns us with Humbert's feelings and sensibility. Humbert's first epiphanic vision of Lolita, for example, is rendered in aquatic, dripping, sprinkly slow motion. On other occasions, the film's canted frames render Humbert's "slanted" point of view. Even the leitmotif of impeded vision, or blocked scopophilia, lubricates the mechanisms of spectatorial desire, through a striptease of fragmented body parts. Here an aestheticized deviancy comes close to Pasolini's "cinema of poetry"; the implied author's style becomes virtually indistinguishable from the sensibility of the character. The net result is to give a much greater sense of what Genette calls "internal focalization" or of what Murray Smith calls "alignment," which weds us to Humbert's, rather than Lolita's, feelings and perspective.

Kubrick emphasizes the comic dimension of his source by casting stand-up comedian Peter Sellers in three distinct roles. The rather cold lighting in Kubrick tends toward the noirish, as in the seduction passage: "The door of the lighted bathroom stood ajar . . . a skeleton glow came through the Venetian blind from the outside arclights; these intercrossed rays penetrated the darkness of the bedroom." The Lyne film, in contrast, quarantines expressionist techniques to those sequences featuring Frank Langella as Quilty. (If Kubrick misses the style of the novel, Lyne misses its humor). And if the lighting of the Kubrick *Lolita* tends toward gothic chiaroscuro, the Lyne version prefers the pastels of a commercialized version of painterly impressionism. The Kubrick aesthetic, speaking more generally, favors depth of field, with a fairly static camera, and shots of relatively long duration, while Lyne prefers an aesthetic of glimpses and close ups, with a constantly moving camera crawling along surfaces. In generic terms, the Lyne film adheres to a relatively timid version of the conventions of the European art film (the genre with which Irons had become associated), while the lighting favors backlit sunbeams and overly pretty landscapes. At times, the light becomes impressionist, almost pointillist, as when the hazy filtered gaseous and smoky look favored by Lyne literalizes the haziness of the memory of the adolescent tryst with Annabel. In the Lyne film a love affair with filtered light and textured style in some ways substitutes for Nabokov's love affair with language. Just as the sophisticated elegance of Humbert's style is a form of seduction that masks his perversity, so the filtered light, smoky effects, and sunlit nymphetry of Lyne's film obscure the sordid nature of the events depicted.

While Nabokov in *Lolita* was self-declaredly "not concerned with so-called sex at all" – a fact which led the true porn-lovers to be disappointed with his novel – Lyne is very much concerned with sex. This concern is reflected in the soft-core porn aesthetic, in the gratuitous states of undress for Dominique Swain playing Lolita, and in the generally "tasteful" titillation characteristic of the film. The result is a kind of aestheticization of child molesting. But the contemporary prevalence of real porn has had the perhaps salutary effect of revealing soft-core porn's basic falsity, as if real porn's "money shots" had torn away the fig leaf of the fake artsiness of so-called "erotica." In an erotic version of Marshall MacLuhan's "rear view mirror" theory, real porn has had the retroactive effect of revealing the basic dishonesty of soft-focus "erotica."

In terms of character, Lyne's Lolita is more spontaneous, lively, and intelligent than Kubrick's somewhat bland heroine, more in keeping with Nabokov's own notion of "courageous, undefeated Lolita." Swain shows a talent for improvisation, as when she exhibits her skill in chin wobbling. When Humbert stumbles in his attempt to find the right word to characterize their relationship, Swain's Lolita supplies the precise substantive – "incest." In her singing and dancing and acting, she is more creative than Kubrick's Lolita. Her unrelenting attack on Humbert's body, along with her constant verbal mockery, constitutes a form of agency, since it puts Humbert on the defensive even while charming him. Interestingly, Lolita often impedes Humbert's ability to see, whether by knocking off his glasses, or by wrapping her legs around his face, or by placing a bag over his head while he drives. But what Lolita gains in agency she loses in dignity and autonomy. Whereas the novel repeatedly stresses that Lolita "never vibrated to my touch," Lyne portrays Lolita as seductive and taking sexual pleasure from the relationship with Humbert. In the Lyne version, then, Lolita seems more accomplice than victim. She even seems, on rare occasions, a victimizer.

The derisive portrayal of Charlotte, in both the Kubrick and the Lyne adaptations, not only conveys the narrator's attitude but also points to our own perversity as spectators. Like the novel, neither of the two adaptations prods us to sympathize with Charlotte (Shelley Winters, Melanie Griffith). While conventional morality would have had us side with the exploited mother and sincere wife Charlotte, the structure of the film and the dynamics of the performances lead us to empathize with Humbert. We as spectators, not unlike the novel's murdering protagonist, begin to see Charlotte as an annoying obstacle to a liaison that we desire as well. (It is partially that desire, after all, that has brought us into the cinemas). Lyne also downplays the role of Quilty. While Quilty is a major player in the Kubrick *Lolita*, in the Lyne version he seems like a generic extraterrestrial, someone who seems to have wandered in from another studio's backlot.

While the voiceover narration in Kubrick is pedestrian, giving us little more than basic information, the voiceover in Lyne is poetic in style and emotional and soul-baring in content, still another way in which the film aligns us with Humbert. At the same time, the adaptation "translates" Nabokov's poetic prose through audio-visual correlatives for poetic devices. And here an approach to the film through the devices and tropes of classical rhetoric becomes fruitful. At times, Lolita's off-screen voice, or her shadow, synecdochically "stands in" for her real presence. When she escapes from Humbert, she remains present through cherished vestiges – chewed gum, bottle caps, photographs. But other characters and emotions, too, are evoked through partial objects; suds in a car wash, for example, evoke Humbert's tears. Even the electric bug-zapper can be seen as a metaphor, whereby Humbert is the moth attracted to the "light" of Lolita.

Both the beginning and the end of the film show Humbert's drunkenly weaving car, which clearly metaphorizes a man out of control; the violation of traffic rules evokes the violation of more serious taboos such as incest and murder. In fact, the sequence picks up on Humbert's own analogy: "Since I had disregarded all laws of humanity, I might as well disregard the rules of traffic." Lyne literally conveys Humbert's description of driving on the wrong side of the road: "Gently, dreamily, not exceeding twenty miles an hour, I drove on that queer mirror side . . . Cars coming towards me wobbled, swerved and cried out in fear . . . With a graceful movement I turned off the road, and after two or three big bounces, rode up a glassy slope, among surprised cows, and there I came to a gentle, rocking stop." The Lyne version renders this sleepy, strangely peaceful finale – including the surprised cows – with great aplomb. One almost has the feeling that Humbert, as his pursued car shudders to a halt, is relieved to be caught. The finale has Humbert contemplate the landscape as he remembers Lolita, just as the police catch up with him. What in the novel is presented as a transtemporal memory here becomes present time. Everything about the sequence – the point-of-view shot, the hilltop vantage point, the music, the voiceover, screams: epiphany! In words that vary slightly from Nabokov's, the voiceover tells us: "What I heard then was the melody of children at play, nothing but that. And I knew that the hopelessly poignant thing was not Lolita's absence from my side, but the absence of her voice from that chorus." This moment, more than any other, seals Humbert's redemption as a character. It is the "moral apotheosis" promised by Dr. John Ray, Jr. in the preface, the "socially redeeming" message that rescues the film from its kiddie-porn indulgences. The scene fulfills the drift of the entire film, the trajectory that leads from Humbert's initial victimization – in the Annabel episode – through his exploitative relationship (but with which we are made complicitous) – through his final repentance and redemption.

In defense of the film, however, it might be said that the film's style also makes its point by matching theme to aesthetic. Throughout the film, an aesthetic of close-ups – the synecdochic film technique *par excellence* – provides a formal corollary to the protagonist's fetishistic pathology, rooted in a "cut off" synecdochic experience of adolescent love interrupted by Annabelle's sudden death. Here we see the metonymic displacements typical of fetishism. Humbert is portrayed as literally a fetishist, seen for example in his dive into Lolita's closeted clothing after her departure for camp, a dive that provokes the maid's sarcastic "What's he doing in there?" But beyond that, the film itself constantly deploys "fetishistic" close-ups of objects. Throughout, the Lyne film develops an aesthetic of synecdoche, of part for whole, whereby objects come to stand for persons or feelings. Lolita especially is evoked through objects that render her as an object of desire and nostalgia – ink pot, insect zapper, typewriter, telephone, hotel fan, braces. Many shots take on metaphorical resonances, standing in for characters or ideas: the bobby pin as a souvenir of Lolita, her dripping underwear, and (by now an advertising cliché) the ejaculatory milk on the lip. We are constantly given body parts – Lolita's knees, elbows, etc. – and partial views.

The film also proliferates in metonymical slidings in various forms: sexual innuendo, where words suggest something taboo ("Has Lolita been keeping you up?"); names that slide into other names (Lola into Dolly, Dolores, Lolita; Quilty into Vivian Darkbloom); the sliding appearance of Swain as Lolita, as she shifts in appearance from girl to woman to adolescent to child to mother; Quilty's ever-changing signature and his sliding homophones ("you lie, she's not" becomes "July was hot"). Moreover, the camera slides metonymically over Lolita's body, much as her body slides up and down Humbert's when she says goodbye on her way to camp. Lyne transposes the poetry of the novel, its rhetoric of stylistic devices, into a homologous rhetoric shaped for another medium; Nabokov's poetic prose style is now rendered as cinema. The only difference is that while Nabokov's poetic prose is distanced and ironic, Lyne's is painfully sincere and sometimes overwrought.

NOTES

1. See Wayne Booth, *The Rhetoric of Fiction* (Chicago: University of Chicago Press, 1983), and Gérard Genette, *Narrative Discourse: An Essay in Method*, trans. Jane E. Lewin (Ithaca: Cornell University Press, 1972).
2. Vladimir Nabokov, *Lolita* (New York: Berkeley, 1971).
3. Robertson Davies, "Mania for Green Fruit," *Victoria Daily Times*, January 17, 1959.
4. Vladimir Nabokov, *Despair* (New York: Capricorn Press, 1966).
5. See Vladimir Nabokov, Preface to Nabokov, *Lolita: A Screenplay* (New York: McGraw-Hill, 1974).
6. Vladimir Nabokov, *The Enchanter*, trans. Dimitri Nabokov (New York: G. P. Putnam's Sons, 1986).
7. Many of these references are detailed by Alfred Appel, Jr. in *Nabokov's Dark Cinema* (New York: Oxford University Press, 1974).
8. See ibid.
9. See Michel Chion, *Audio-Vision: Sound on Screen*, trans. and ed. Claudia Gorbman (New York: Columbia University Press, 1994), p. 153.

10. Nabokov, *Lolita: A Screenplay*, p. x.
11. Quoted in Appel, *Nabokov's Dark Cinema*, p. 237.
12. Nabokov, *Lolita: A Screenplay*, pp. 111–112.
13. Ibid. pp. xii–xiii.
14. The poem is included, and commented on in Richard Corliss, *Lolita* (London: BFI, 1995), pp. 9–11.

8   World War II through the lens of Vietnam: adapting *Slaughterhouse-Five* to film

William Rodney Allen

By 1972, the year the film adaptation of his 1969 novel *Slaughterhouse-Five* premiered, Kurt Vonnegut (b. 1922) was well on his way to becoming one of the most famous writers in the world. After more than two decades of hard work as a short story writer and novelist, he had expanded his notoriety far beyond his limited core audience of science fiction fans and college hipsters and was connecting with millions of readers, especially with those disillusioned over the ongoing war in Vietnam. Although *Slaughterhouse-Five* was a fictionalized account of Vonnegut's experiences in World War II, the book's audience also read it as a critique of America's long and painful conflict in Southeast Asia – one that had taken the lives of tens of thousands of its young men and seemed on the verge of tearing the country apart. Vonnegut had encouraged this "contemporary" reading by including references to Vietnam in his novel ("Every day my Government gives me a count of corpses created by military science in Vietnam," as well as to the assassinations of Dr. Martin Luther King, Jr. and Bobby Kennedy.[1] This contemporary relevance, combined with the wide distribution of the movie version of his novel, led even more people to read not only *Slaughterhouse-Five*, but often Vonnegut's entire literary output, which by that time included dozens of short stories and half a dozen novels. Noting his seeming cultural omnipresence, *Time* magazine referred to the rumpled writer with the sad eyes and curly hair as "ultra-Vonnegut." In the early 1970s there was no doubt that Vonnegut had become – in the then-new parlance of the times – a superstar.

A "perfect storm" of sorts, if there is a positive sense of that phrase, came together to make the movie *Slaughterhouse-Five* a watershed point in Vonnegut's career as well as an artistic success. In addition to coming out at the height of opposition to the war in Vietnam, and besides being an adaptation of the masterpiece of an extremely popular writer, the film was created by a talented cinematic team determined to be as faithful as possible to Vonnegut's artistic vision. The movie's director was George Roy Hill, fresh from the extraordinary success of *Butch Cassidy and the*

Figure 9. *Slaughterhouse-Five* is in part an outrageously humorous sci-ence fiction tale, with Michael Sacks and Valerie Perrine playing two kidnapped earthlings inhabiting an off-world human zoo in this 1972 Universal Pictures/Vanadas Productions release.

Sundance Kid (1969), starring Paul Newman and Robert Redford. Hill had been nominated for an Oscar for Best Director for that film, though the award that year would ultimately go to John Schlesinger for *Midnight Cowboy*. The *Slaughterhouse-Five* screenplay adaptation was assigned to Stephen Geller, a young writer whose offbeat, black-comic first novel had been made into the film *Pretty Poison* (1968), starring Tony Perkins and Tuesday Weld. Geller got the job after producer Paul Monash saw and admired *Pretty Poison* and read another of Geller's screenplays circulating around Hollywood. Despite some later conflicts between the two men, Geller was given a great deal of artistic freedom by Universal studios, and he produced an adaptation that showed none of the flaws of screenplays written by committee. Geller clearly *got* Vonnegut. Even while producing an adaptation that is in some ways quite different from the novel, he was able to capture Vonnegut's signature black-comic tone to the extent that Vonnegut himself was pleased with the result. As Vonnegut remarked of *Slaughterhouse-Five*, "this picture and 'The Godfather' [which won the 1972 Academy Award for Best Picture] have to be considered by their authors as the best possible adaptations of their books."[2]

But before the movie reached cinemas, some problems arose. It seems that the course of Hollywood screenwriting ne'er did run smooth. In a telephone interview in 2003 Geller talked to me about some of his struggles with his producer Monash – arguments that threatened to derail the whole project. While initially supportive and "a wonderful editor" in Geller's words, Monash shocked Geller one day by demanding that he share screenwriter credit with him. As Geller describes Monash, "He was a writer: he went out to L.A. as a writer from New York and he had some short stories published and I guess he felt that that meant more to him than being a producer."[3] But according to Geller, Monash had not written any of the *Slaughterhouse-Five* screenplay. Geller contacted his agent, Dick Hyland, who advised Geller to demand that Monash submit any pages of the screenplay he had supposedly written to the Screen Writers Guild for arbitration. Meanwhile, in meetings over the course of the next few days, Monash was telling Hill that "30 percent of Geller's screenplay needed to be rewritten." Geller observed in our interview that "according to the Writers Guild, a shared credit would exist if one person had written at least 30 percent. I mean it [Monash's estimate of how much rewriting was necessary] was literally a right-on-the-button figure." At this point, the film's executive producer Jennings Lang intervened and urged Hill to put pressure on Monash to back down from his demand to share writing credit, which Hill did. After a final blow-up in which Monash wadded up part of Geller's script and threw it at him, Monash relented under the dual threats of facing the Screen Writers Guild arbitration board and possibly having Hill leave the project. Geller was then free to finish the screenplay on his own, and he ultimately retained full screenwriter credit (Geller).

Aside from turf battles at the studio, any adaptor of a novel into a screenplay obviously faces serious artistic problems, regardless of whether he or she was the author of the original source. Moreover,

Slaughterhouse-Five presented a special range of challenges. First of all, it was anything but a conventional novel. While it was in some senses representative of a familiar genre – the semiautobiographical war novel of an Ernest Hemingway or James Jones or Norman Mailer – in other ways it was very different. To start with, it was pointedly metafictional, repeatedly calling attention to its own fictionality. Vonnegut wrote himself into the novel, especially in his framework first and last chapters, describing some of what had happened to him since his survival of the bombing of Dresden on February 13, 1945; commenting on current events; and, most importantly, detailing his struggles with trying to find an effective way to structure the novel he was writing. To an important degree, *Slaughterhouse-Five* is a self-referential novel about the difficulties of writing a novel about something so absurd as the "greatest massacre in European history" (*S-F*, 101)

Early on, Geller made the decision that the whole metafictional apparatus of the novel had no place in his screenplay. To try to include it, he said, would have turned the project into an experimental film that simply "couldn't have happened, in the industry," especially given the "prosaic" nature of Universal pictures at the time. As he put it bluntly, "To push the film as meta film – I would have had no reading" (Geller). Good meta films would appear in the next decade, for example the cult classic *The Stunt Man* (1980), directed by Richard Rush and starring Peter O'Toole; and in the 1990s, with Tim Burton's arch tribute to real-life B-movie director *Ed Wood* (1994), starring Johnny Depp. Now, in the twenty-first century, the genre has reached maturity in films such as E. Elias Merhige's *Shadow of the Vampire* (2001), starring John Malkovich, an *hommage* to the classic silent film (1922); and the brilliantly *Nosferatu-* executed *Adaptation* (2003), directed by Spike Jonze, written by Charlie Kaufmann, and starring Nicolas Cage. But back in the early 1970s, the highly experimental metafiction of *Slaughterhouse-Five* never got a chance to make it to the screen.

Likewise, Vonnegut's somewhat autobiographical character Kilgore Trout does not appear in the film. Trout is Vonnegut's most famous recurring character, one who appeared early in his fiction and kept showing up all the way until his last novel, *Timequake* (1997). Trout is a kind of metafictional alter-ego of Vonnegut, a disparaging self-portrait of what Vonnegut feared he might have become had he been consigned as a writer to the disreputable paperback world of zany space novels with the obligatory number appearing in the titles. Trout, or at least his fiction, first shows up in *Slaughterhouse-Five* while Vonnegut's hapless protagonist Billy Pilgrim is recuperating after the war from a mental breakdown. The patient in the bed next to Pilgrim in the hospital is Eliot Rosewater, another recurring character who first appeared in Vonnegut's previous novel, *God Bless You, Mr. Rosewater* (1965). Rosewater introduces Pilgrim to Trout's novels. The down-and-out science fiction hack Trout has written dozens of books, all published by different fly-by-night publishers, about the "big ideas" entertained by writers in his genre. The problem is that "his prose was frightful. Only his ideas were good" (*S-F*, 101).

One of Trout's books that Pilgrim reads in the hospital is *The Gospel from Outer Space*, in which Trout has a space alien come to earth to study Christianity. The alien decides that the message of the Gospels is, "Before you kill somebody, make absolutely sure he isn't well connected" (*S-F*, 109). The space visitor then decides to write a new version of the New Testament, in which "Jesus really *was* a nobody, and a pain in the neck to a lot of people with better connections than he had. He still got to say all the lovely and puzzling things he said in the other Gospels" (*S-F*, 109). This message becomes important to Pilgrim, who clearly turns into an antiheroic, ironic Christ figure in the novel. Vonnegut introduces this important motif in his epigraph to *Slaughterhouse-Five*, which is from the familiar Christmas carol "Away in a Manger": "The cattle are lowing/The baby awakes/But the little Lord Jesus/No crying he makes." In the novel Vonnegut observes that Pilgrim "resembled the Christ of the carol" (*S-F*, 197), and that he lay "self-crucified" (*S-F*, 80) on a brace in his POW boxcar on the ride to Dresden. Later, Pilgrim will become a Christ-like prophet of sorts, explaining to crowds the meaning of life as he has come to understand it through his experiences in the war, Trout's novels, and his travels to the planet Tralfamadore. Like Christ, he unresistingly goes to his death when he is executed by those who do not understand his message. Yet none of the novel's frequent references to Pilgrim as an ironic Christ figure appears in the film. Geller also decided that Trout was part of "the more literary aspects of the novel [that] had to fall by the wayside, in favor of Billy's character" (Geller). Including Trout would have been a distraction in a screenplay already filled with characters and incidents ranging over the whole span of Pilgrim's lifetime. Further, Geller would cover Trout's ideas about space and their implications for ethics on earth in his treatment of the Tralfamadorians and their philosophy.

Geller decided that the Tralfamadorians themselves would be *heard* in the film rather than *seen*. In the novel Vonnegut describes them as "two feet high, and green, and shaped like plumber's friends. Their suction cups were on the ground, and their shafts, which were extremely flexible, usually pointed to the sky. At the top of each shaft was a little hand with a green eye in its palm" (*S-F*, 26). In making them appear so cartoonish, Vonnegut encourages the idea that the Tralfamadorians may have simply been cooked up in Pilgrim's brain, which has been addled by war trauma, depression, shock treatments, and even a severe concussion in a plane crash. In Geller's screenplay, since the action is dramatized rather than narrated, the effect is to make the Tralfamadorians seem more "real" than they do in the novel. To add to this sense of realism, Geller wisely decided not to depict them on screen: Pilgrim and his kidnapped partner, the actress Montana Wildhack, hear their cosmic kidnappers/instructors but do not see them. As Geller put it, "we couldn't actually show them because they looked like toilet plungers, kind of like in an acid [Walt] Disney country" (Geller).

Yet another casualty of adaptation was the most famous signature phrase in Vonnegut's fiction, "So it goes." One of Vonnegut's critics once claimed that the phrase appears exactly 100 times in *Slaughterhouse-Five*, but another counted 103.[4] Geller could logically have included it in the film during the Tralfamadorians' lectures to Pilgrim about the true nature of space and time, since Vonnegut attributes the expression to them in the novel. Since Tralfamadorians "live in the fourth dimension," they do not experience time the way earthlings do, existing only in the present: instead, they "see" the past, present, and future simultaneously. Stars are not points, but look like spaghetti; people look like millipedes, with a baby's form at one end and an old person's at the other. Pilgrim's modified version of the Tralfamadorians' simultaneous experience of past, present, and future is his "time tripping." The unexplained premise of the novel is that Pilgrim has "come unstuck in time" (*S-F*, 23) and finds himself living different parts of his life in random, nonchronological order. Although this strange experience certainly prepares Pilgrim for what the Tralfamadorians will tell him about simultaneity, Vonnegut does not have the aliens take credit for making Pilgrim jump around in time. He just *does*, even to the point of fast-forwarding to the exact date of his death, when he is shot by a fellow soldier from the war bearing an irrational grudge. But Pilgrim learns from the Tralfamadorians not to fear his death by murder, or try to avoid it. When anyone dies, the Tralfamadorians do not grieve but simply say "So it goes," since they can still see that the person is "alive" in the past. When anyone dies in the novel, Vonnegut uses the phrase as a sort of benediction/shrug. Yet, surprisingly, the words "So it goes" are never spoken in the film. Geller perhaps felt that the catchphrase gained its resonance in the novel from its frequent repetition, and that simply inserting it once in the screenplay was not a good idea.

Another difference between the novel and the film is that the latter has far fewer "time trips." Geller was faced with presenting a nonchronological narrative with hundreds of time shifts that could potentially have been extremely confusing for a movie audience, but he wisely chose to start the film with Pilgrim's typing a letter to the editor of his local newspaper in which he explains his travels to Tralfamadore and his time tripping. The audience sees his typing of the words "I have come unstuck in time," and then Geller inserts a sound "match cut": the clacking of Pilgrim's old manual typewriter blends into the sound of German armored vehicles as the scene changes to those vehicles moving through a forest. A young Private Pilgrim, unarmed and wrapped in a blanket like a baby, watches from behind the trees as the vehicles go by, then flounders around in the snow, trying to avoid capture. What follows is a movie filled with perhaps the most extensive use of sound and visual match cuts in the history of film. Visual match cuts, in which an object at the end of one scene is prominent at the opening of the next scene, may simply provide transitions, but they can also highlight important themes. The classic match cut in film history occurs in Stanley Kubrick's *2001: A Space Odyssey* (1968), when an ape-man from several million years ago hurls a bone into the air, which then, as the scene changes, seems to turn into a spaceship of approximately the same shape. The point is that once primitive tools appear, spaceships will eventually follow. In terms of his use of this device, Geller said in our conversation that "every one of those [match] cuts was written into the script" rather than having been created independently by the director or the editor (Geller). Recurring visual match cuts add to the nonchronological film's sense of continuity, with important matching images including boots, blankets, cameras, and masks. Match cuts in *Slaughterhouse-Five* act as metaphors for the associations in Pilgrim's mind that seem to trigger his time trips.

Geller simplified Pilgrim's time traveling into four distinct segments: his experiences before, during, and after World War II, and his trip to Tralfamadore. In our interview Geller said, "I arced all four timelines as if they were separate films" (Geller). "Arcing" is a Hollywood term for the narrative "shape" formed by the rising action, climax, and falling action present in typical plots. In order to reduce the confusion, Geller presented the crucial World War II segment in chronological order, and periodically interrupted it with nonchronologically ordered sections from the other three timelines. The links between these segments were the aforementioned sound and visual match cuts. While Vonnegut had gone to great lengths to suggest that he was not writing a conventionally "arced" novel – intentionally diffusing suspense, mixing "story" with metafiction, constantly jumping back and forth in time – *Slaughterhouse-Five* still operates as a traditional narrative in the sense that it builds up slowly to the bombing of Dresden, which occurs in Chapter 8 of a ten-chapter novel. Geller reasonably chose to do the same thing, with the three main nonchronological storylines buzzing like electrons around the steadily advancing nucleus of the Dresden plot.

Even though a good portion of *Slaughterhouse-Five* takes place in Germany during World War II and many of the films lines are spoken in German by Nazi soldiers, the film offers no subtitles. Some movies about the war had included subtitles (which inevitably detract from the audience's visual appreciation of the film), while others used the unrealistic convention of having the actors speak English in German accents. The makers of *Slaughterhouse-Five* avoided either of those distractions, simply letting the context of a scene convey the approximate meaning of what the Germans were saying. Since Pilgrim and his fellow soldiers speak little or no German, an English-speaking audience shares their experience of being strangers in a strange land, where linguistic misunderstandings may turn comic or deadly. About the only German that Pilgrim masters is *"Schlachthof-funf,"* the no. 5 address of the Dresden slaughterhouse where he and his fellow POWs are imprisoned. Ironically, this underground meat locker/prison, both in real life and in the film, offers one of the few effective bomb shelters in the city. During the bombing, Dresden became a figurative slaughterhouse, but Pilgrim and Vonnegut ironically escaped death by taking shelter in a literal one.

On the level of characters other than Pilgrim, Geller had rich material with which to work, and he had no trouble converting Vonnegut's lively "cast" to the screen. In addition to featuring such well-known actors as Rod Leibman, who played Paul Lazzaro, the angry soldier bent on revenge against Pilgrim, and Valerie Perrine, who played Montana Wildhack, the film was strengthened by effective casting across the board. Pilgrim's chubby wife Valencia; their troubled son Robert, who ends up as a soldier in Vietnam; Pilgrim's mentor in the war, Edgar Derby, who is shot for looting in the Dresden ruins; and Howard W. Campbell, Jr., the American Nazi/double agent who has a cameo role following on from his original appearance in Vonnegut's novel *Mother Night* (1961): all are efficiently adapted from the book to the screen and portrayed vividly by the respective actors. Geller recalled that "every character who was active, who had an intention, I never had to rewrite. Lazzaro is exactly the way he was in the first draft, and Edgar Derby, and Billy's father and mother, and all the characters. But Billy was an absolute dud" (Geller).

Geller's initial cinematic problem with Pilgrim was that he was so passive that it was difficult to get a handle on him. Passive characters' interior lives are more easy to reveal through fictional narration than on screen, so Geller needed some sort of positive motivation for Pilgrim in order to make him come alive. Monash suggested that Geller call Vonnegut, whom Geller had yet to meet, and ask for some advice. When Geller did so, he told Vonnegut about his problems with Pilgrim and asked, "'Isn't there anything Billy is passionate about? Isn't there anything that he loves?'" Vonnegut replied, "'Sure – he loves his dog'" (Geller). Although at first puzzled by this revelation, even wondering if Vonnegut had been joking, Geller finally decided to write into the film a love story of sorts between Pilgrim and the classically named Spot, who is Pilgrim's constant companion, even on Tralfamadore, and who seems to mean more to Pilgrim than his human family. While Valencia bakes pies and cakes by the dozen in an early montage, Pilgrim raises Spot from a pup. Late in the film, after Valencia dies from carbon monoxide poisoning after a car crash as she rushes to Pilgrim's side after *his* plane crash, Pilgrim goes home and is greeted by his aged but still faithful dog. The two of them mount the stairs, sit on the bed, and are then transported to Tralfamadore. Montana soon shows up, and Spot serves as their go-between while they get acquainted as a sort of cosmic Adam and Eve who eventually produce a child.

If the dog portraying Spot in the film did a good job in his role, Michael Sacks was even better as Pilgrim. Appearing in nearly every scene, he has to carry the film, and he does. Sacks perfectly captures Pilgrim's Chaplinesque quality of comic sorrow, and it is impossible not to root for him despite his fecklessness and naiveté. The comic antihero was a familiar character in the films of the period – Dustin Hoffman as *The Graduate* (1967) springs to mind – but Sacks as Pilgrim has a believability and pathos that is quite striking. The Oscar nominees for Best Actor for 1972 were Michael Caine and Sir Laurence Olivier for *Sleuth*, Peter O'Toole for *The Ruling Class*, Paul Winfield for *Sounder*, and Marlon Brando (who won but refused to accept the award) for *The Godfather*. The competition was certainly stiff, but Sacks would still have been a worthy nominee.

Slaughterhouse-Five would not be nominated for Best Picture either. *Cabaret*, *Deliverance*, *The Emigrants*, *Sounder*, and *The Godfather* were the nominees, with *The Godfather* taking the Oscar. The lack of a nomination was not surprising, given the fact that the reviews of *Slaughterhouse-Five* had been decidedly mixed. Some reviewers thought highly of the film, but others clearly did not. Although it had won the Jury Prize at Cannes, many American critics, according to Geller, used their reviews "as a stick to beat up Vonnegut" (Geller). They did so in part because a critical backlash against Vonnegut's enormous popularity was developing, and in part because some reviewers who did not like the antiwar "counterculture" found Vonnegut's stance unpatriotic in the light of the deteriorating situation in Vietnam. Geller maintains that rather than the film's being reviewed, "Vonnegut was being reviewed, and the antiwar movement was being reviewed" (Geller).

Some of the controversy was surely due to the uncomfortable truth presented in both the novel and the film: the bombing of Dresden on February 13, 1945, by British and American planes was an atrocity. Another uncomfortable truth in 1972 was that American foreign policy in Vietnam had led to the deaths of hundreds of thousands of people, but was on its way to ending in utter defeat. The reason Dresden was an atrocity was that so many civilians were killed, and they were in fact the intended targets of the bombing, as civilians were soon to be at Hiroshima and Nagasaki. But questions remain about just how large an atrocity Dresden actually was. In his novel Vonnegut had cited the casualty figures in David Irving's *The Destruction of Dresden*, which were that 135,000 died in the raid. Those numbers would have made the Dresden bombing more costly in terms of civilian deaths than either of America's atomic bomb attacks on Japan. A recent book by Frederick Taylor, *Dresden: Tuesday, February 13, 1945*, however, questions those figures. Taylor argues that the actual number of civilians killed was between 25,000 and 40,000; and that far from having no strategic significance, as Irving had argued, Dresden was a vital communications and transport hub supplying the Eastern Front.[5] Hindsight makes Dresden look more like an atrocity than it really was, Taylor argues, because we now know that the war was close to being over early in 1945 – knowledge that the Allies lacked at the time.[6]

But whatever the actual numbers of dead, Dresden was a horror, and *Slaughterhouse-Five* captures that horror vividly. Near the end of the film, Pilgrim and his fellow POWs and their captors retreat to their underground meat locker as the bombs begin to fall. The lights flicker, then go out. The scene then changes to the future, when Pilgrim's daughter is driving him home after Valencia's accidental death. When they reach the house, the aging Spot is there to greet his melancholy master. The scene then changes back to the meat locker where, in the silence, matches are struck that illuminate the faces of the dazed Americans and their worried German guards. As all of them slowly mount the stairs, the scene alternates with shots of Pilgrim's climbing the stairs to his bedroom, carrying Spot in his arms. When Pilgrim and the others emerge from their bomb shelter, they come upon a shattered moonscape of a city – a city that had been so beautiful just hours before, as the film had earlier depicted in an uplifting montage set to the music of Bach, who was from the Dresden region. To a contemporary viewer revisiting the film, the broken skeletons of the Dresden buildings eerily resemble the ruins of the World Trade Center Twin Towers destroyed in 2001 in the worst single atrocity (so far) of this young century. Geller dramatizes the Germans' reaction to the devastation by having one of the young guards yell "You American pigs!"

then run through hundreds of yards of the ruins before finally coming upon the burning remains of his parents' apartment building. He dashes inside but is dragged out by firefighters as he despairingly screams "Papa! Papa!"

Back in the future, Pilgrim and Spot sit calmly on the upstairs bed, looking out of the window. They see a mysterious light in the night sky that gets larger and larger, until it engulfs them and makes them vanish. They are on their way to Tralfamadore. Because of its juxtaposition with the scenes of Dresden destroyed, this scene makes it clear that the trip to Tralfamadore is psychologically an "escape" from the absurdities of a world that has produced so many Dresdens. Tralfamadore offers Pilgrim a radically new philosophical way of dealing with human tragedy, the tragedy and its aftermath that we see unfolding on the screen as he and his fellow soldiers gather up what is left of the bodies of the city's dead, pile them high, douse them with gasoline, and burn them. Behind masks – scarves wrapped around their faces to keep out the smell and smoke – Pilgrim and the others grimly watch the bodies burn. These masks echo the Mardi Gras masks (Dresden was bombed on Mardi Gras, February 13, in 1945) that the children of Dresden had worn the day before. The day after, ironically and appropriately, was Ash Wednesday, a day when Christians bear a cross marked with ashes on their foreheads to remind themselves of their mortality. After Dresden, Pilgrim will never need reminding again.

The novel's last chapter begins with Vonnegut musing on the murders of Dr. King and Bobby Kennedy. He then recalls how Pilgrim and his fellow soldiers had burned the remains of the Germans killed in the Dresden bombing. And he again tells us that "somewhere in there the poor old high school teacher, Edgar Derby, was caught with a teapot he had taken from the catacombs. He was arrested for plundering. He was tried and shot. So it goes" (*S-F*, 214). Finally, one morning in the spring, Pilgrim wakes up to discover that his German guards have fled, and that the war is over. Out in the street it is pretty quiet, but "the birds were talking. One bird said to Billy Pilgrim, "Poo-tee-weet?" (*S-F*, 215).

The film, on the other hand, ends with a big Hollywood finish, albeit one that Geller's screenplay treats ironically. Geller called his finale "a parody of a Hollywood ending."[7] In the film's last scene, Pilgrim and Montana are snuggled up together with their newborn baby on the couch in their geodesic dome on Tralfamadore. The Tralfamadorians, who have been wanting them to "mate" since they brought the two of them together, are pleased. Despite having only one hand, as Vonnegut describes them, they applaud the couple's fecundity. Pilgrim and Montana acknowledge the applause by calmly waving like the king and queen of England.

Outside the dome, in the cyanide-laden atmosphere of Tralfamadore (which incongruously includes the planet Jupiter), decidedly earth-like fireworks explode in a celebratory counterpoint to the earlier bombs of Dresden as the exuberant music of Bach takes us into and through the credits.

As Vonnegut has the Tralfamadorians tell Pilgrim, it is better "to concentrate on the happy moments of his life, and to ignore the unhappy ones" (*S-F*, 194–195).

NOTES

1. Kurt Vonnegut, *Slaughterhouse-Five* (New York: Delacourt/Lawrence, 1969), p. 210. Further quotations will be cited parenthetically in the text as *S-F*.
2. William T. Noble, "'Unstuck in Time' . . . A Real Kurt Vonnegut: The Reluctant Guru of Searching Youth", in William Rodney Allen, ed., *Conversations with Kurt Vonnegut* (Jackson: University Press of Mississippi, 1988), p. 60.
3. Stephen Geller, unpublished telephone interview with William Rodney Allen, August 30, 2003, transcribed by Nicholas Hite. Further quotations will be cited parenthetically in the text.
4. William Rodney Allen and Paul Smith, "An Interview with Kurt Vonnegut," in Allen, ed., *Conversations*, p. 299.
5. Frederick Taylor, *Dresden: Tuesday, February 13, 1945* (New York: Harper Collins, 2004).
6. Laura Miller, "*Dresden: Tuesday, Feb. 13, 1945* by Frederick Taylor," *Salon*, March 1, 2004; www.salon.com/books/review/2004/03/01/Dresden/print.html.
7. Stephen Geller, email to William Rodney Allen, March 28, 2004.

9   John Huston's *Wise Blood*

Matthew Bernstein

Peter S. Greenberg: "The movie *Wise Blood* didn't exactly make you rich either, did it?"

John Huston: "No, but it was one of the finest movies I think I've ever made."

–Peter S. Greenberg, "'Saints and Stinkers':
The *Rolling Stone* Interview" (1981)[1]

John Huston may have regarded *Wise Blood* highly, but film studies has had comparatively little interest in it, favoring other, "classic" Huston films.[2] In some ways, this is understandable. *Wise Blood* is an acquired taste: a low-budget, independently financed film with no stars that closely follows the Georgia author Flannery O'Connor's (1925–1964) bizarre, comic-horrific account of the southern orphan Hazel Motes's futile rebellion against his religious heritage. The characters are wholly unsympathetic, their interactions unpredictable and highly episodic, and the film, like O'Connor's novel, adopts a cool, ironic, and blackly humorous tone toward their truly outlandish antics.

Yet the more closely one examines the film, the more one is struck by how artfully it conveys O'Connor's highly symbolic, theologically imbued story. While adaptation studies has taken stock of and dismissed the notion of a film's "fidelity" to a source-text,[3] *Wise Blood* is one adaptation where fidelity was the keynote principle of the filmmakers and the film itself. Equally compelling is how well its concerns coincide with those of many of Huston's other films – even though Huston himself did not write the film's screenplay. For the film features an uncanny conjunction of O'Connor's distinctive view of southern male identity gone awry with Huston's much-appreciated debunking of American masculine ethos. By considering *Wise Blood*'s production context, its script, and Huston's visualization of O'Connor's setting and characters, we can better appreciate the film's achievement.

Figure 10. Hazel Motes (Brad Dourif) confronts "blind" preacher Asa Hawks (Harry Dean Stanton) in John Huston's *Wise Blood*, a 1979 Anthea/Ithaca release.

Production background

Wise Blood was financed, produced, and shot entirely outside of Hollywood. Its production began with Michael and Benedict Fitzgerald, the sons of O'Connor's friends and literary executors Robert and Sally Fitzgerald. Robert Fitzgerald was a highly regarded literary critic and translator of Homer's epic poems; his wife Sally was the editor of a celebrated volume of O'Connor's letters (*The Habit of Being* [1979]), and editor of the Library of America's edition of O'Connor's works. The Fitzgeralds' connection to *Wise Blood* goes even deeper: O'Connor had written a draft of *Wise Blood* while staying with the Fitzgeralds in the late 1940s.

O'Connor died in 1964 of lupus. Fourteen years later, Michael Fitzgerald sent Huston a copy of O'Connor's book and asked him if he would be interested in making a film of it. Huston, then seventy-two and struggling with emphysema and heart trouble, immediately agreed. Fitzgerald (and his wife/co-producer Kathy Fitzgerald) spent nearly two years raising the $2 million needed to shoot the film from European (and especially German) film distributors and television production companies, since no American studio was interested in the project.[4] Meanwhile, Michael's brother Benedict Fitzgerald worked on the screenplay, which was revised with substantial input from Michael and Huston. (Benedict subsequently wrote scripts for television adaptations of major novels, such as *Heart of Darkness* [1994], *Moby Dick* [1998], and, most recently, he collaborated on the original screenplay for Mel Gibson's *The Passion of the Christ* [2004]. Michael went on to produce Huston's *Under the Volcano* [1984], as well as *Mister Johnson* [1990], *The Penitent* [1998] and *The Pledge* [2001].) *Wise Blood* was shot in early 1979 in Macon, Georgia, which stood in for Taulkingham, the big city where Hazel Motes arrives after finding his home abandoned and his family dead. Other scenes were shot in Atlanta and Tommsboro.[5]

Wise Blood is the last film that Huston discusses in his 1980 autobiography *An Open Book*, and it is a film he was clearly proud of. He credited first assistant director Tommy Shaw with bringing the film in for $1.6 million, in part by assembling a twenty-five-person crew (the smallest Huston had ever worked with), having costumes made by Sally and Kathy Fitzgerald, and securing the cooperation of Macon residents. "It all worked out to perfection," Huston wrote, perhaps mindful of the trials of making *The African Queen* (1951) and *Moby Dick* (1956).[6] The casting of well-established film actors who were also not stars was another money-saving device that ultimately resulted in the powerful lead performances. Hazel Motes was played by Brad Dourif, best known now perhaps as Grima Wormtongue in *Lord of the Rings: The Two Towers* (2002), and in the late 1970s acclaimed for portraying Billy Bibbitt in *One Flew Over the Cuckoo's Nest* (1975). Ned Beatty, who was featured in *Deliverance* (1972), *Nashville* (1975), and *Superman* (1978), among other films, played the deceptive radio preacher Hoover Shoates. Harry Dean Stanton (who had just finished work on *Alien* [1979] and would have a major leading role in Wim Wenders's *Paris, Texas* in 1984) played the ominous "blind" preacher Asa Hawks, who infuriates Hazel. The remainder of the cast were virtual unknowns in Hollywood, such as prominent Atlanta stage actor (and mother of stage actor Dana Ivey) Mary Nell Santacroce as the landlady Mrs. Flood and Dan Shor as the ape-like Enoch Emery. Hazel Motes impersonator Solace Mayfield was portrayed by William Hickey, whom Huston would later cast to great effect as the corrupt family don in *Prizzi's Honor* (1985). In 1980 in *An Open Book*, Huston commented that "[t]here were seven outstanding performances in *Wise Blood*. Only three of those seven actors have any reputation to speak of . . . The other four are unknowns. They are all great stars, as far as I'm concerned. Nothing would make me happier than to see this picture gain popular acceptance and turn a profit" (369).

But Michael Fitzgerald later recalled that "I couldn't sell it to anybody . . . Everyone was terrified of the story and felt that it was the least commercial movie ever made."[7] New Line Cinema, then a relatively new company, ultimately distributed the film to critical acclaim. Among its fans were Vincent Canby, who wrote several times about the film, which he called "one of John Huston's most original, most stunning, movies"; Julian Fox of *Films and Filming* in England ("a monolith among recent American movies"); *Horizon* ("unquestionably one of the most powerful films of the year and one of the finest in Huston's long career"); Robert Hatch in *The Nation* ("a triumph of adaptation from print to screen"); and John Simon of the *National Review* ("Miss O'Connor would have approved – which is praise enough").[8] The film, as its filmmakers predicted, earned minimal box office returns.

O'Connor's novel

Huston described *Wise Blood* concisely as "the story of a young religious fanatic's brief rebellion against Christ" (Huston, *Open Book*, 368–369). The novel, set in the 1950s, begins as Hazel Motes is riding a train to the big city of Taulkingham; he responds to polite inquiries by sneering at fellow passengers, "I bet you think you've been redeemed" and informing them, "I'm gonna do some things I've never done before."[9] Motes is in revolt against Christian religion, specifically his grandfather's preaching in rural Georgia. But his rebellion is not successful. When he trades in his army uniform for a new suit and hat, he is mistaken for a preacher. He embraces "sin" (sleeping with a local prostitute) but takes no real pleasure in it. He buys a car that provides him with a home and a pulpit like his grandfather's (he can stand on its hood to speak), but it constantly breaks down.

On the streets of Taulkingham, Motes becomes fascinated with the "blind" preacher Asa Hawks and his daughter Sabbath Lily, whom he meets in front of a potato peeler demonstration. Both intrigued and disgusted, Motes follows them while attempting to shake off the attentions of eighteen-year-old Enoch Emery, who like Motes is a stranger in town without friends, and who works at the zoo. Incensed at Hawks's preaching, Motes spontaneously announces the formation of a new church, the Church of Jesus Christ Without Christ, "where the blind don't see, the lame don't walk, and what's dead stays that way" (59). He takes a room in the boarding house where the Hawkses reside.

After discovering that Hawks only pretends to be blind (he lost his nerve when he planned to blind himself with quicklime), Motes continues to preach. He succumbs to Sabbath's charms, and Emery gives him a museum's shrunken mummy which Emery believes is the "new Jesus" Motes calls for metaphorically in his preaching. Emery becomes fixated on Gonga the Gorilla, the star of a new movie in town that is promoted by an "in person" visit from the "ape"; Emery eventually steals Gonga's costume as a counterproductive means to make friends in the "unfriendly" town. Meanwhile, Motes rebuffs the offer of a partnership from an ex-radio preacher, Hoover Shoates, who sees moneymaking possibilities in Motes's ideas. When Motes refuses Shoates, the latter steals Motes's concept and dresses up a hapless resident, Solace Mayfield, to be another "prophet" in competition with Motes.

One night Motes kills the uncomprehending Mayfield by running him over with his car on a deserted road; the next day, en route to a new town to begin preaching, a police officer finds him driving without a license. Motes watches helplessly as the officer pushes his car off the highway and through a field, because, he tells Motes, "I don't like your face" (117). Having confronted his double in Mayfield, having committed murder, and having lost his car, Motes returns to the boarding house where he blinds himself with lime, enacting the self-punishment that Hawks only pretended to have undergone. He also tortures himself with rocks in his shoes and by wearing barbed wire. He is looked after in his final days by his landlady Mrs. Flood, who tends to him, scolds him about his self-punishment, and schemes to marry him. He ultimately dies in her home after an aborted attempt to leave town on foot in a rainstorm.

While a legion of O'Connor critics debate the precise significance of her writing in general and *Wise Blood* in particular, there is little disputing that these bizarre characters and dispiriting settings can be collectively regarded as a theologically informed variant of the southern Gothic made familiar by William Faulkner, and, after World War II, Carson McCullers, Tennesee Williams, and Truman Capote. The eccentric, barely human Enoch Emery takes an instinctual, uncomprehending, and literal approach to life. Sabbath Lily is a "white trash" nymphomaniac (evidenced in her recital of letters she has written to an advice columnist about "going whole hog" with boys and in her unbridled desire for Motes). There are the deceptive religious hucksters Asa Hawks and Hoover Shoates. And of course, there is Motes's own barely repressed rage, which begins as impudent rudeness and develops into murder, self-blinding, and torture. It is important to note that O'Connor, in the critic Michael Kreyling's words, displayed an "apparent obliviousness to the racial turmoil through which she lived,"[10] even as she captured the South in a time of transition. Huston's film acknowledges the character of the region's racism in an equally offhand manner; various characters utter the n-word without a second thought.

Another important aspect of the immediate postwar South that O'Connor satirizes in *Wise Blood* is the pervasiveness of consumer culture on a national scale, and its consequent degradation of religious belief, most evident in the multiple advertising signs that pervade the novel, but also in Hawks and Shoates. Their street preachings are absurdly general and vague, and their requests for money are implicitly compared with the potato peeler salesman (who describes his product as "a small miracle"), and with Gonga the film star. As the critic Jon Lance Bacon writes, "*Wise Blood* . . . [suggests] that American religion had been appropriated by the 'salesman's world.' In the world of the novel, faith itself becomes a commodity."[11]

Citing a critical consensus that took its cue from O'Connor herself, Kreyling calls *Wise Blood* "one of the most significant religious novels in American literary history" (Kreyling, "Introduction," 3). The spiritual degradation O'Connor depicted provided the context for her portrait of Hazel Motes. O'Connor's brief introduction to the 1962 edition of *Wise Blood* describes it as "a comic novel about a Christian *malgré lui*, and as such, very serious, for all comic novels that are any good must be about matters of life and death." She continues:

That belief in Christ is to some a matter of life and death has been a stumbling block for readers who would prefer to think it a matter of no great consequence. For them Hazel Motes' integrity lies in his trying with such vigor to get rid of the ragged figure who moves from tree to tree in the back of his mind [Jesus Christ]. For the author Hazel's integrity lies is in his not being able to. Does one's integrity ever lie in what he is not able to do? I think that usually it does, for free will does not mean one will, but many wills conflicting in one man. Freedom cannot be conceived simply. It is a mystery and one which a novel, even a comic novel, can only be asked to deepen.[12]

Flawed southern characters embodied O'Connor's views that "man has fallen and that he is only perfectible by God's grace, not by his own unaided efforts."[13]

Hazel Motes thus represents a negative example of Christian grace because he fails both to cast off the heritage of preaching represented by his grandfather and also to demonstrate that one can live without Christian redemption. His sleeping with the Taulkingham prostitute, Mrs. Leora Watts, his ultimately willing seduction by Sabbath Lily, his rock throwing at Emery (pushing him down to the street in the film), and even his killing of Mayfield, are all his attempts to practice what he preaches, a life devoid of the concept of sin and salvation. But his violence is actually an unintended imitation of Motes's notion of Christ, which, as Robert Brinkmeyer, Jr. has argued, is threatening and violent.[14] Motes's efforts are undercut most of all first by seeing his double, Mayfield, dressed in an identical blue suit and paraphrasing Motes's own preachings; then by his murder of Mayfield; and third by the loss of his car at the hands of the police officer. As Bacon notes, "The destruction of the product with which he has identified himself forces Hazel to consider the possibility of some reality other than the material" (Bacon, "A Fondness," 35), and in the novel Motes contemplates the landscape in which his car has been destroyed. He turns his violence upon himself, and, in so doing, he perseveres beyond Hawks's pretense and reenacts Christ's suffering as punishment for humanity's sins. Motes implicitly accepts that he cannot escape his beliefs and his legacy as a Christian.

His self-punishment has been interpreted in different ways; as Joy Gould Boyum puts it, it can be seen "as a grotesque mockery of the excesses of religious faith or as Hazel's way to salvation." (176).[15] Brinkmeyer quotes O'Connor on this point: "'I have found that violence is strangely capable of returning my characters to reality and preparing them to accept their moments of grace . . . Their heads are so hard that almost nothing else will work.'"[16] Brinkmeyer comments: "In O'Connor's fiction Christ's sword manifests itself in any number of various weapons that injure and sometimes kill her characters; and generally it is only in being injured that Christ becomes real to them" (Brinkmeyer, "'Jesus, Stab Me,'" 85).

Motes is thus shown to have "wise blood," an inheritance from his grandfather (and from Christ) of a spiritual sense that makes him both human and divine (in contrast, as Brinkmeyer notes, to Emery's intuitive knowledge that leads him downward to the earthly and the bestial via the shrunken man and Gonga the Gorilla). In the novel Emery invokes the phrase "wise blood" briefly, though the narrator describes Emery's blood as a driving force for his ritualistic actions (cleaning up his rented room without knowing why for the later arrival of the "new Jesus" before he delivers it to Motes). By contrast, Fitzgerald's screenplay elaborates upon the concept for the film's viewers. When Motes tries to shake Emery off him as they walk away from Hawks and Sabbath Lily, Emery finally gets Motes to stop when he invokes his "wise blood":

EMERY: "Standing around acting like you got wiser blood than anybody else but you ain't, cause I'm the one who has it, not you. Me."
MOTES: "What are you talkin' about?" (They stop on the street corner.)
EMERY: "'Bout I *know* things I ain't ever learned. How I can see signs and something just happens, and I got to do some things sometimes, I got to do some things sometimes I don't even want to do. And sometimes inside me I can

feel it, I can feel it pulling, and tugging at me, and pushing, and I can feel
my blood beating and I've got to do this thing right now. It's wise blood.
Ain't everybody has it. See, it's a gift. It's a gift like . . . like the gift of the
prophets. Now I ain't saying I'm no prophet. No it ain't like that, but it's like
that."

MOTES: "You're crazy boy, you're crazy and you stay away from me. I'm goin'
where I'm goin'. I got a woman see." (Hazel holds up his hand as he slowly
moves away, as if he were commanding a dog to "stay").[17]

In the novel Motes has no reply to Emery's first line. But even when the
idea of wise blood is elaborated in the film, Motes's rejection of such
insights, which explain his character better than he can, is just one of
many ironies in the novel and film.

Perhaps the greatest of these – greater than the fact that Motes has
attracted acolytes whom he cannot accept or recognize in Emery and
Mrs. Flood – is the fact that he cannot escape his Christian heritage: as
the deceptive Hawks plainly tells him, "Jesus is a fact. You can't run away
from Jesus . . . : some preacher's left his mark on you . . . Did you follow
me to take it off or to give you another one?" Motes spends most of the
film trying to prove Hawks wrong, yet he ultimately fails. And O'Connor
narrates these paradoxes with a detached, matter-of-fact tone that, when
juxtaposed with the extreme appearance and behavior of the characters,
underlines their comic dimensions.

This comic perspective, insisted upon in O'Connor's introduction to
the novel's second edition, was part of what made Huston such an unexpectedly apt choice to direct the film (a more recent, comparable instance
of surprising felicity in directorial choice might be the assignment of
Taiwanese director Ang Lee to direct a Hollywood adaptation of Jane
Austen's *Sense and Sensibility* [1998]). As critics have noted, Huston had
previously adapted a southern gothic novel in Carson McCullers's *Reflections in a Golden Eye* (1967); he had directed a rebel violently at war with
evil in Gregory Peck's Captain Ahab in *Moby Dick*; and he had luxu-
riated in the depiction of losers in *Fat City* (1972). But none of these
previous films conveyed the ironies of the characters' dilemmas with
such overwhelming force. The press kit for the film of *Wise Blood* quoted
O'Connor on this point: "The religion of the South is a do-it-yourself
religion, something which I, as a Catholic, find painful and touching and
grimly comic."[18]

Huston appreciated these qualities of the novel, and more. In an interview with Gavin Millar, he described O'Connor's "ability to combine
the ludicrous, the uproariously comic and the dreadful and terrible so
that they're together there on the screen before your eyes at the same
time. They don't go from one to the other for relief."[19] In *An Open Book*

Huston characterized the novel more concisely as "both funny and dire. From page to page you don't know whether to laugh or to be appalled" (Huston, *Open Book*, 368). No doubt he and his collaborators aimed to provoke a comparable response in their audience. Their non-Hollywood financing and location shooting in Georgia ensured that they could realize a faithful adaptation on their own terms without studio interference.

Fitzgerald's script and Huston's film

I have already alluded to the three major challenges facing the filmmakers in adapting *Wise Blood*: first, portraying the eccentric, bizarre characters that peopled the story without alienating an audience; second, suggesting the spiritual dimensions of the story and its highly symbolic or metaphorical imagery without trivializing them;[20] and third, sustaining the novel's comic detachment from these events. Black humor might provide a means of overcoming the story's surreality and its theological concerns, but it might also prove difficult to convey.

Huston and company's key strategy was to treat the action of the film in a naturalistic, matter-of-fact manner, eschewing symbolic imagery of many kinds. Boyum, in an invaluable analysis of the film as an exemplary approach to adapting metaphorical works,[21] describes the filmmakers' approach when she writes:

The director seems to have recognized (implicitly, at least) that the somewhat paradoxical problem of bringing O'Connor's metaphorical materials to the screen isn't so much in maintaining their emblematic thrust as it is in providing them with the plausibility and human acceptability (and ultimately accessibility) they lack on the printed page. Put another way, the danger in adapting a work like *Wise Blood* is that once embodied on film, O'Connor's characters might seem to us too mad, too repellent, too unbelievable to invite us to go beyond their immediate impression and search for their larger significance. (Boyum, "*Wise Blood*," 177–178)

In an interview with the O'Connor scholar Carter Martin during principal photography, screenwriter Benedict Fitzgerald indicated that the filmmakers followed the strategy Boyum describes quite consciously. He explained that while following the novel very closely, they left out many of the novel's symbolic motifs, such as the various coffins that Motes recalls seeing for his family members as he falls asleep on the train. Otherwise, Fitzgerald explained, "we might have found ourselves getting bogged down and thinking too much about the symbolic and allegorical aspects of the story." He continues: "I was trying – am trying . . . to make a clear and straightforward adaptation of the story – because the story itself has all the elements we need to suggest rather than openly point out the allegory" (Martin, "*Wise Blood*," 105). (The one symbol they did retain was Motes's car as a means of escape from Christ; the car visually manifested Motes's goals in a manner well suited to the cinema.)

Thus, by sticking to the novel's storyline as closely as possible, the filmmakers sought to create a satisfying adaptation with theological overtones. Toward the end of their interview, Martin asked Fitzgerald if he felt that "the religious nature of the film" had to be modified or handled "gingerly." Fitzgerald replied:

> Oh no, never modified; I think it is too good and too shrewd. There was some debate, of course, about exactly what is going on, and at what point there is a beginning of what we might call "grace." Other theological debates have been going on . . . particularly with the actors . . . The religious aspect of it is so much an integral part of the story, that we felt that if we dealt with the story in its strictest sense – the playing of the action, if you like – without overdoing the religious theme, we would do the trick better than if we spent too much time trying to *explain it* as a story of redemption. (Martin, "Wise Blood," 113–114)

Fitzgerald's comments refer to a principle of "concretization"[22] of the novel's details, a decision that most analysts of *Wise Blood* have praised. The South, the bizarre characters, and the novel's events unfold in a matter-of-fact manner. As a result, the story's theological overtones play out as they might with different viewers (who might or might not impose Christian symbolism, or symbolism of various kinds, on the action).

As Boyum notes, the filmmakers established the reality of the southern region through the credit sequence, their location shooting, and the cast's mix of nonprofessional, little-known, and well-known film actors. The casting and the screenplay also softened the depiction of most of the characters (Mrs. Flood is less mercenary in her marriage proposal, for example, and Emery more pathetically lonely than in the novel, as Boyum discusses [Boyum, "*Wise Blood*," 178–179]. They notably modified Motes's portrayal for the film, first by transforming his initial homecoming – a brief, two-paragraph passage in the novel – into a major scene. Also, Fitzgerald's script condensed Motes's many flashbacks in the novel to a few brief scenes to give us insight into his subjectivity. Furthermore, aside from the flashbacks, they crafted an unobtrusive visual style that emphasized Motes's driven determination and his separateness from the rest of the world. Equally significant, they relied on music to sustain the film's alternately and simultaneously melancholy and comic sensibility. I will discuss each of these aspects of the adaptation in turn; while previous critics have mentioned several of these elements, none has attended either to the film's style in most of its scenes or to its musical score.

Wise Blood firmly introduces its southern locale and religious concerns during the opening credit sequence. This shows a series of black-and-white photographs of various road signs that promise spiritual redemption: the sign in the opening shot reads, "If you repent, God has forgiveness for you in Jesus your savior." Subsequent shots wittily combine commercial advertising and religious ideas, commerce and salvation: a Baptist church on whose wall hangs a Coca-Cola sign; a Dairy Queen nighttime sign that features a call for repentance;[23] and a Confederate flag hanging next to a reproduction of Leonardo da Vinci's *The Last Supper*. All these juxtapositions encapsulate O'Connor's notion of the improvised and too often commercialized, reductive (to slogans and clichés) nature of religion in the postwar South. The extras who gather whenever Motes (or Hawks, or Shoates, for that matter) is preaching, and Mrs. Flood's question as to whether Motes's new church is "Protestant? Or something foreign?" reinforce the notion that Christianity is never far from the residents' minds. The characters are, as Huston and Benedict Fitzgerald put it, " 'Christ-bitten' people, in that almost vampiric sense" (Martin, "*Wise Blood*," 114).

These opening credit sequence signs, empty of human presence, and accompanied by Alex North's slow-paced, carefully orchestrated rendering of "The Tennessee Waltz," itself a song of loss, reinforces our sense of the simultaneously dispiriting and hopeful ethos of the region. They also show such sentiments to be so pervasive in the South that when Motes's car breaks down on the highway the first time he drives it, we are not surprised that he finds himself staring at another religious slogan ("Jesus saves") painted onto a rock by the road. The final opening credit sequence still photograph, which also bears Huston's directorial credit, shows a telephone off its hook, next to a sign reading "Call Jesus": both rest atop a cemetery tombstone that might as well be Motes's grandfather's. This image marvelously prefigures the deceased Motes family of which Hazel is an orphan and the sadness that will inform his return home and his consequent quest to overcome his past.

By portraying Motes's visit home in all its desolation, Huston is sustaining several tonal features and motifs crucial to the film's success. Most generally, the scene conveys a sense of solitude and melancholy which is established in the credits and extends to many of the characters Hazel meets – Emery, Mayfield, Mrs. Flood. As Harold Clurman wrote of the film, "Everyone is bereft of healing companionship and genuine spiritual sustenance. The atmosphere – through the characters – is, for all its grotesque features, one of sadness and benumbed compassion."[24] There are no complete families in *Wise Blood* (even the scenes of a mother and two children in a public swimming pool, cut after filming, show us a one-parent situation); the individual, be it Motes, Emery, or Mrs. Flood, is utterly alone, and the homecoming scene stresses this point in Motes's case. His homecoming certainly provides a starting point for his journey (Boyum, "*Wise Blood*," 179), but it also creates great initial sympathy for him on the viewer's part, which will be worn down by Motes's subsequent rudeness and violent determination. Laura Jehn Menides and Michael Klein ("Visualization," 232) have rightly compared the opening of *Wise Blood* – from Motes's hitchhiking a ride at an empty crossroads to his slow walk through the house – to Tom Joad's discovery of his abandoned family farm in *The Grapes of Wrath* (1940).[25] Both scenes are dramatically lit (by the legendary Gregg Toland in John Ford's film) to emphasize the homecoming character's despair before rejoining his family and embarking on a life-changing journey. Motes, of course, has no family to rejoin.

In the visual scheme of the film, lighting takes on unavoidably religious overtones as its characters promote their notion of Christianity and exhibit pretended and genuine blindness. The overwhelming darkness of the Moteses' abandoned home alludes to the pervasiveness of death in Motes's life; it is almost a substitute for the many coffins in which he recalls seeing his family members. The Motes house is the first of several dark interiors whose murkiness becomes associated later with moral ambiguity, as with the red-tinged decor and dim lights of Leora Watts's boudoir, the low-key lighting of the Hawkses' room where Motes comes to debate theology with Hawks, and the darkened central stairway and bedrooms of Mrs. Flood's house. It is, for example, in such a dreary, low-key light that Motes opens his door to the sight of Sabbath Lily wearing a dark shawl and holding the shrunken man in a parody of a *pietà* that, as Menides ("John Huston's *Wise Blood*," 210) and Boyum ("*Wise Blood*," 180) both note, the filmmakers conceived on their own.

These interiors contrast dramatically with the bulk of the film, which plays out in daylight and sunny blue skies, even when the police officer sends Motes's car across a field and into the pond. The lighting scheme of the film reaches its darkest point, however, in the nighttime scenes in which Emery steals the Gonga costume and walks through the town, while Motes follows and ultimately kills Mayfield as they stand before the headlights of Motes's car. The melancholy darkness of the Motes home is reinforced by North's music, which crucially establishes the tone and emotional meaning of individual scenes, much as O'Connor's prose does in the novel itself. Here again we hear the "dignified melodic rendition of 'The Tennessee Waltz'" (Cooper, "Literal Silences," 42) that we heard over the opening credits.

Music continues to have a powerful effect on the subsequent scene. Once outside the house, Motes pauses at (presumably) his grandfather's tombstone and briefly recalls his tent preaching, in long shot. At this point, Huston and North play the Shaker Hymn that Aaron Copland adapted to such powerful effect at a climactic moment in *Appalachian Spring*. We hear it twice more in *Wise Blood*, both toward the end of the film, first when Motes walks out into the rainstorm after blinding himself in Mrs. Flood's house. The association of this hymn with this scene suggests that Motes in attempting to leave Mrs. Flood has failed to outrun his Christian faith and the legacy of his grandfather. That sense of loss and desire for home still informs his very being, and he returns home, ironically, when he dies in Mrs. Flood's house. Hence we hear the Shaker Hymn a final time over the closing credits, as if in answer to "The Tennessee Waltz" of the opening credits.

As an orphan, Motes feels emboldened to discard his religious heritage, but the film shows us how the past powerfully affects his present life. The brief flashbacks to his childhood are filmed, like all Motes's memories, in a garish, red-tinged haze, a color-coding for emotional intensity, sin, and guilt that stands out against the norm of the film's other scenes (Boyum, "*Wise Blood*," 180) and that is picked up in the costumes and decor of Leora Watts's place and even later by Sabbath Lily. These flashbacks are the filmmakers' only ventures into Motes's subjectivity. The two flashbacks of his grandfather are also notable because they catapult Motes into action, first with the purchase of a new suit and train ticket (the cut from Motes selecting a satisfactory hat to the train at full steam conveys his determination to get on with his life), and later with the purchase of his car, itself an emblem of the postwar consumerism that pervaded America, or as Benedict Fitzgerald described it, "the great symbol of modern freedom" (Martin, "*Wise Blood*," 106). When that car comically shuts down on a highway where another road sign offers redemption through Christ, Motes thinks back to his penance for his unauthorized childhood visit to spy on a barely dressed carnival woman (he put rocks in his shoes and walked on them – an action that has deeper, subsequent consequences for his present life). As this flashback continues, we see from Motes's point of view, now more intensely because it is in a low-angle medium shot, his grandfather preaching once more, his finger pointing at the young Motes with the distortion of the wide-angle lens as he speaks of the boy's sins. The grandfather states, "This boy has been chastened and he will be redeemed," and the camera tilts down to Motes's shoes. The grandfather continues, prophetically, "Jesus will never leave him ever, Jesus will have you in the end." The grandfather's sermon appears in the novel in the first chapter as part of Motes's memories of him; there is no flashback in the novel at this point (Motes merely contemplates the road sign – the filmmakers connect the dots for viewers). His recollection inspires him to seek out Emery in order to learn where Hawks lives, so that he can challenge him and by extension defy his grandfather. These brief flashbacks, in their filming, their content, and their placement, are springboards to Motes's actions.

Hazel Motes dominates *Wise Blood* as both novel and film; few scenes take place without him.[26] During principal photography, Benedict Fitzgerald informed Martin that the brothers' inspiration for making the film lay in Motes himself: "nobody remotely like Hazel, at least to our knowledge, has been the subject of a film treatment" (Martin, "Wise Blood," 100). Yet at the same time, Motes represented to them a quintessential American character: *Wise Blood*, as Fitzgerald put it, "is a story of rebellion, which infuses it with the sort of energy which can work very well on the screen. It is also about a character with purpose, with a real mission in life – something recent American film heroes have largely been without" (Martin, "Wise Blood," 100).

Fitzgerald perhaps forgot the action heroes of the most popular films of the later 1970s, such as *Jaws* (1975) and the *Star Wars* series; he perhaps was alluding here to the impotent, overwhelmed protagonists of American cinema influenced by the European art film – characters like Hazel Motes who are haunted by their pasts, such as surveillance expert Harry Caul (Gene Hackman) in *The Conversation* (1973) or detective Jake Gittes (Jack Nicholson) in *Chinatown* (1975). Caul and Gittes try desperately to prevent certain murderous events from occurring, and they fail miserably, almost tragically; by contrast, as noted earlier, the disparity between Motes's intent and his achievements creates many kinds of comic irony in the course of the film. His determination to "do some things" collapses into random encounters (he meets the Hawkses, Emery, Leora Watts and Mrs. Flood by chance) and actions, as befitting the "negative theology" of Motes's rebellion. His very invention of the Church of Jesus Christ Without Christ is, as Fitzgerald pointed out, a spontaneous action that perhaps surprises even Motes (101). The filmmakers, interestingly, rearranged the novel's sequencing of Motes's decision to leave Taulkingham to preach elsewhere and his later murder of Mayfield; in the film Motes kills Mayfield first, then returns to the boarding house to pack, suggesting a cause-and-effect connection that, as Michael Tarantino has remarked, extends to the highway patrolman's reason for stopping Motes the next day.[27] It is not even clear that Motes understands his motivations. As Frederick Asals has observed, "O'Connor's people are among the least introspective in modern fiction, with minds at once so unaware and so absurdly assured that they have refused to acknowledge any deeper self."[28] Motes's lack of awareness generates a great deal of the comedy in the film.

Motes ends the film dead, but even before his last minutes on earth, as Boyum notes, he is, ironically, unaware that he has gained an acolyte:

Motes, who was so desperate to deny Christ, becomes, as the imagery in the final scene suggests, very much a Christ figure himself (Boyum, "*Wise Blood*," 181). If Hazel inadvertently inspires a greater spiritual consciousness in Mrs. Flood, as some O'Connor critics argue (indicated via O'Connor's dramatic shift in point of view from Motes to Mrs. Flood in the novel's final chapter (Brinkmeyer, "'Jesus, Stab Me,'" 86), he does so indirectly. From the solitary figure returning home at the start of the film who finds only darkness and emptiness there, Motes ends up at the drab first-floor bedroom at Mrs. Flood's where he is carried in dead. *Wise Blood*, through the characterization of Motes and the episodic nature of his actions, partakes of both art film and conventional Hollywood narrative film conventions, leaving viewers to draw their own conclusions. As Vernon Young points out, "Not the least striking feature of *Wise Blood* is that it's a film about preaching that doesn't preach. Your reactions are not dictated, they're your own."[29]

Motes's flashbacks and scenes with Mrs. Watts are the most stylized in the film, and previous critics have discussed them as such. Other scenes have received little critical attention, and given that most of *Wise Blood* revolves around Motes, his determination and his drive, Huston and cameraman Gerald Fisher used a moving camera to capture his restlessness as Fitzgerald's "typical American rebel hero." Fisher was a veteran British cinematographer who had worked with Joseph Losey (*Accident* [1967], *The Go-Between* [1970], *Monsieur Klein* [1976]), Tony Richardson (*Hamlet* [1969], *Ned Kelly* [1970], *A Doll's House* [1973]), and Billy Wilder ([*Fedora* 1978]). He would also shoot *Victory* for Huston in 1981. As Boyum discusses, the decision to shoot on location in Macon, Georgia, gives the film its sense of concreteness, reality, and plausibility (Boyum, "Wise Blood," 178). Fisher and Huston tailored the film's style to the characters along an axis of mobility and stasis. The camera tracks backward during the two sequences of Motes (with Dourif's angular face and sharp eyes suggesting something of the shrike's bell nose and "pecan eyes" that O'Connor writes of, his neck sticking out forward in various encounters) walking through Taulkingham, with Emery (in Shor's effective short tie, stiff upper torso, arms akimbo, man-as-ape performance) trying to keep pace with him.

The moments of contrasting camera style are equally telling. The powerlessness of characters is often recorded in this film as they recede into the background of a shot: think of Enoch running off into traffic to bring Motes the new Jesus, or when he flees the museum with the precious package in his arms: Huston is content to hold the shot as Emery's figure diminishes in the depth of the frame, the broader context of the shot (the Taulkingham streets and traffic) serving to visualize how insignificant and quixotic his exertions are. Likewise, the camera does not follow Hazel up the stairs with the lime he will use to blind himself, and his last attempt to escape, this time from his landlady Mrs. Flood, is photographed in long shot as he goes out of the door into the rainstorm. His momentum has been completely lost, and as he lies dead on Mrs. Flood's bed and she speaks to him, the camera slowly tracks around the bed then backs away from them both, even obscuring Motes's body momentarily.

In framing many of the final scenes of the film in this way, Fisher and Huston visualize O'Connor's decisive shift in point of view from Motes's to Mrs. Flood's in the final chapter of *Wise Blood*: we remain with Mrs. Flood for the final ten minutes of the film. With her, we see Motes climb the stairs, hear Sabbath Lily's screams, discover the rocks in his shoes and the blood on his sheets, and observe him leaving the boarding house, and even wait with her as she decides to call the police. This shift suggests Motes's potential impact on Mrs. Flood.

Framing and editing also convey a vivid sense of Motes's opposition to nearly everyone in his path. Two shot groupings show Emery walking alongside Motes on the streets; others show Sabbath Lily sitting beside Motes in the front seat of his car, or the physical closeness of Mrs. Watts and Sabbath Lily before they have sex with Motes; and Mrs. Flood shares the frame at times when she ministers to Motes in the final scenes. But more often, Fisher and Huston typically frame Motes's various encounters with other characters in shot/reverse shot to emphasize Motes's presence in isolated spaces and visualizing his separateness and violent opposition to others. The pattern begins in the general store scene where Motes trades his army uniform for a regular suit and answers the storekeeper's queries about his plans (not to farm, but to "do some things") evasively. It develops quite forcefully on the train to Taulkingham where Motes's exchanges with the shallow Mrs. Hitchcock are recorded in shot/countershot patterns that emphasize his rudeness and her fascination with him (and the price of his suit). It continues as he argues with the cab driver who drives him to Mrs. Watts's house about whether he is a preacher.

The pattern continues most pointedly in Motes's showdowns with Hawks. When he catches up with the "blind" preacher and his daughter in front of a meeting hall, shots of the two of them are framed with Motes at the left edge of the shot. As he and Hawks argue, reverse shots often show Motes separate or in a two-shot with Emery. Their opposition visually climaxes when Motes lights the match in front of the sleeping Hawks; when Hawks awakes and Motes confirms that he is not blind, Huston uses a shot/reverse shot pattern of extreme close-ups of their eyes on each other while slightly ominous bass piano notes play on the soundtrack.

Huston's penchant for using analytical editing, first established in *The Maltese Falcon* (1941), here proves appropriate for Motes's character and his quest. Significantly, Fisher and Huston choose a very precise framing to visualize Motes's status relative to Hawks. When he discovers where the Hawkses live, we get Motes's point of view in a long shot as Sabbath Lily escorts Hawks into Mrs. Flood's boarding house. That camera placement is repeated late in the film when Mrs. Flood escorts Motes into the same house; the formal rhyme underlines our sense that Motes has indeed transcended Hawks's example while taking his place.

Given the precision of many of these shot compositions, the intrusion of off-screen events into Motes's world is quite pronounced. When Shoates shows up with Mayfield, the camera remains on Motes as he preaches about the illusory nature of one's conscience. As he states that "'you had best get it [your conscience] out into the open and hunt it down and kill it,'" we can hear off-screen sounds of Mayfield's car pulling up, doors slamming, and Shoates riffing on the guitar as Motes finishes saying "hunt it down and kill it." Editing and off-screen sound here suggest what subsequent shots of Mayfield in his blue suit on the hood of his car affirm: that he is very much a physical embodiment of Motes, his double, and his conscience, whom Motes will hunt down and kill with his car for not being "true," and saying things he does not believe (that is, Motes's creed of the Church of Jesus Christ Without Christ), but which Motes himself actually does not believe either (Brinkmeyer, "'Jesus, Stab Me,'" 81). Another extended two-shot framing pairs Motes and Mayfield as they struggle in the headlights of Motes's car (Klein, "Visualization," 235).

The most pronounced intrusion into Motes's space, and the most comical, occurs when Shoates first sees Motes preach (the night before Shoates shows up with Mayfield). Shoates takes over when the small crowd starts to disperse while Motes is speaking. Shoates talks beside Motes's car about the little child's loss of sweetness when he or she grows up and how Motes is a prophet who can bring that sweetness out again. Motes, meanwhile, stands dumbfounded on his car hood, then kneels down to listen to Shoates's forceful spiel and his proclamations that friendship with Motes saved his life and his soul, and that the Church of Jesus Christ Without Jesus Christ has "nothing foreign about it" and it's "up to date." Motes is content to let Shoates promote this undemanding notion of faith (Bacon, "A Fondness," 43). But when Shoates starts asking for money, Motes objects violently, and Huston frames their hilarious dueling preaching in a medium-long two-shot as Motes keeps contradicting Shoates's claims – saying that they are not friends, that you do not need money to believe in a religion. Shoates quickly recovers from these rebuttals to continue making his pitch, and when he sees Motes trying to drive away he frantically wraps up by promising to return the next night to the same spot. Part of what makes this scene so hilarious is that the bulk of their dispute, their dueling preachments, unfolds in a medium-long shot long take that contains them both.

If such framings create a visual sense of irony in *Wise Blood*, the music (all of it nondiegetic except for Shoates's guitar) cues us to recognize the alternately "funny and dire" aspects of the film. I have already mentioned the Shaker Hymn that functions to underline Motes's connection to his past, his grandfather, and his return to Christ. The other melody that North uses extensively in the film, "The Tennessee Waltz," appears from the opening credit sequence onward as a major motif in the course of the film. During the credits, we hear it in a straightforward performance, in a slow-paced tempo that gradually brings in violins for more emotional power, and this version recurs immediately with Motes's exploration inside his family house, adding to our sense of loss which Motes feels. Significantly, the waltz recurs in this arrangement when Motes first sees Sabbath Lily escorting Hawks into Mrs. Flood's boarding house – interrupted by a comic, upbeat, louder version as Motes drives up to the house (and over the curb) before settling back into its "straight" arrangement as Motes gets out of the car and approaches the house. The repetition of the music here again suggests that Motes has found a new home (the one in which he will in fact die). Its recurrence as Motes follows Mayfield out on the road also creates this sense of Motes inadvertently returning to his roots.

"The Tennessee Waltz" reappears with other variations in the course of the film: we hear it in electronic echoes when Motes first approaches Leora Watts's house and peers through the window; it is slowed down to a dirge as he slowly gets up from her bed after his dreams of his guilty childhood before he buys his car; and it is arranged and performed in a more jaunty, bouncy version (virtually a fit accompaniment for a silent two-reel comedy), first when Motes first drives his car (fitfully) away from Slade's, then later when Emery first shows him the shrunken man in the museum, and third when Emery steals the shrunken man despite the presence of an elderly sleeping guard. It recurs a fourth time with this arrangement most notably when the police officer sends Motes's car running down the hill from the highway into the pond. This is an artistic choice that David Sterritt, one of the film's few critical reviewers, singled out as an example of the filmmakers' tendency to "reduce" "some of the book's most outlandish conceits" "to mere jokes." He complains that "[w]hen a policeman pointlessly destroys Hazel's precious car, for example, the effect should be hilarious and horrible at the same time. Instead, cute banjo music plunks on the soundtrack, and the episode becomes a slapstick interlude."[30] By contrast, Menides stresses that the visual elements of the shot, the car's autonomous, lengthy run across the field into a pond, emphasize more forcefully than the novel the finality of Motes's loss of the car, and the end of his efforts to create a church without Christ (Menides, "John Huston's *Wise Blood*," 211).

Wise Blood as a whole is one of the most unusual narrative films ever made by a classic Hollywood director. If the viewer does not perceive the comical aspects of the character's trials through the staging of the scenes and Fisher's and Huston's shot compositions, the music, along with the other signature elements of the film's visual style and narrative structure, ensures that we appreciate how incompetent Motes and Emery prove in pursuing their goals. As Charles Champlin wrote of North's score, it "left no doubt that this was the South of plucked strings and earthy ballads and hellfire piety, but equally the music conveyed the wry wit and the sorrow of Flannery O'Connor's bizarre chronicle of religious obsession."[31] I would argue that the music functions most prominently of all among all the film's stylistic elements, providing the extraordinary tonal combination of humor and despair that so appealed to Huston and for which O'Connor is celebrated.

Conclusion

The O'Connor critic/photographer Barbara McKenzie wrote a rare but forceful negative critique of Huston's *Wise Blood*. She found that the film's style, "if not antithetical to the dynamics of the novel, is at least not equational [*sic*] to them . . . the naturalistic style of filming has left *Wise Blood* a little too sanitized and a little less believable because of it."[32] McKenzie asserts that casting softens the characters' bizarre nature, and that the omission of O'Connor's figures of speech (such as the description of Hawks's facial scars as giving him "the expression of a grinning mandrill," quoted 35) weaken our experience of the story. She continues: "The similes, metaphors, personifications, and other figurative devices help to create the sense of distortion the reader gets from the novel. They also aid in creating a plausible psychological environment for the characters." These are unsuitable for film treatment. There is no disagreeing with McKenzie's conclusion that "[t]he inability of the many figurative and literary devices found in the novel to undergo transformation into visual images further accounts for the flattened visual effect of the screen adaptation" (36). No film could do justice to the novel in the sense she prescribes.

McKenzie writes from a traditional critical position on adaptation (influenced by George Bluestone's landmark study *Novels into Film*

[1957]) that demands that a film should remain faithful to the novel in terms of its imagery. But this view may strike some as too narrow. If, for example, Stanton's scarred face does not make Hawks look like O'Connor's "mandrill," the actor still has a paternal, threatening aspect, and his rudeness to and implied abuse of Sabbath Lily find a place in the film. Similarly, Stephen Cooper has written at length of O'Connor's imagistic metaphors that describe characters' actions via the phrase "as if." Motes on the train looks "as if he might want to jump out of it" (O'Connor, "*Wise Blood*," 3), and this use of language "suffuses the text with suggestive dimensions available only through language," as part of O'Connor's strategy for depicting her Catholic sense of religious mystery (Cooper, "Literal Silences," 44–45). But Cooper, unlike McKenzie, finds an equivalent to O'Connor's character metaphors in the film's close-ups (Cooper, "Literal Silences," 48–49).

Cooper's analysis affirms that McKenzie's is a minority view. Most reviewers and analysts of the *Wise Blood* film agree with Cooper and Boyum that the filmmakers' matter-of-fact approach to adapting the story is successful. As we have seen, this was a conscious creative strategy on their part, one that by design allows the story's theological overtones to play out as they might for different viewers. Young characterized the film as "an uncompromising act of fidelity to the Flannery O'Connor novel from which, with chilling tenacity, it was adapted."[33] John Simon writes: "The briskness with which Huston approaches his queasy subject here pays off. The simple way in which Hazel beds down with an obscenely obese whore [Mrs. Watts] or the matter-of-fact manner in which he runs over a false prophet with his car has the proper low-key dreariness from which the horror and humor shine forth all the more glaringly."[34] Boyum's persuasive argument is that the film paradoxically translates the novel's metaphorical conceits successfully by emphasizing the surface realism of the setting and characters within a narrative context pervaded by theological concerns (Boyum, "*Wise Blood*," 175–182).

In addition to its implications for the "adaptability" of symbolic novels, *Wise Blood* unexpectedly exemplifies much of Huston's other work. Motes's effort to escape Christ is compatible with the obsessive aims and unhappy outcomes – whether self-inflicted or otherwise – of the protagonists in Huston's best films: the greedy gold-diggers in *Treasure of the Sierra Madre* (1948), the diverse group of thieves in *The Asphalt Jungle* (1950), the god-battling Captain Ahab in *Moby Dick*, the overreaching adventurers in *The Man Who Would Be King* (1975), and the mediocre boxers in *Fat City*.[35] Gavin Millar characterizes the "typical Huston hero" as

a low-life adventurer, somewhere between criminal and respectable, setting out on
a near-hopeless quest with unquenchable hope, courage, and tenacity, aiming to
raise himself, by mere physical progress, into some sphere of spiritual exaltation,
perhaps kingship, perhaps even divinity. Add one rider, that the protagonist does
not always aim so to raise himself. He often has no insight into his own aspirations.
(Millar, "John Huston," 204)

As James Naremore has noted, most of Huston's good films "are quasi-
allegorical adventures about groups of exotic, eccentric people, and, as
several commentators have observed, they usually end on a note of great
ironic failure . . . Ultimately, however, Huston was less interested in
success or failure than in the moments of truth that an adventurous quest
leads up to."[36]

Those moments of truth can reveal the nature of the characters themselves. Lesley Brill argues that, in nearly all Huston's films, the director's
diverse protagonists – whatever they ostensibly seek – try "to discover, create, or recover themselves, to conceive and articulate their identities."[37]
Hazel Motes fits this pattern perfectly. Millar goes so far as to assert that:

In many ways the hero of *Wise Blood* . . . is the ultimate Huston protagonist.
He manages to do what Ahab was trying to do in *Moby Dick* – beat the devil.
Hazel, as fierce as a zealot in his thirst to prove God does not exist, beats the
powers of darkness by withdrawing from the world altogether before they can
make him do anything to compromise his mistrust of it . . . Hazel is a self-
driven derelict with no insight whatsoever into his motives or his aims – in that
respect he is mainline Huston. But for the first time in his work the Huston
misfit drives himself, comically, or tragicomically, not towards survival, but to
extinction. (Millar, "John Huston," 204)

Motes's lack of insight into himself contributes to our confusion in assess-
ing his motives and his means. He is full of determination ("I'm gonna
do some things"), but he never specifies what or how, and spontaneously
takes up the idea of his own church. He has all the markings of a driven
American protagonist, but the gap between what he says and what he
does makes him more closely resemble the hypocritical characters of an
Eric Rohmer comedy. Brill describes how Huston typically "constructs
narratives of people who struggle, who occasionally win outright, who
manage an unlikely draw . . . or who in losing still win" (Brill, *John Huston's Filmmaking*, 9–10). Brill's summation of so many Huston heroes
describes quite aptly Motes's project, goals, and outcome in *Wise Blood*,
particularly when we recall O'Connor's own description of the integrity
that Motes achieves when he fails to evade his religious heritage.

Yet sadness is a crucial component of the film's portrayal of Motes,
one that speaks to the filmmakers' and particularly Huston's compassion

for failed protagonists. It also explains the most significant change the filmmakers made from the novel to the screenplay, Motes's return home. In generalizing about Huston's heroes, Brill usefully stresses that they search for home, as part of their efforts to define themselves, and one thinks, for example, of Dix Handley's (Sterling Hayden) desire to return to his family farm in *The Asphalt Jungle* and his ultimate arrival there as he dies from gunshot wounds in a field of horses. (Brill also makes an interesting connection between the soldiers returning home in Huston's wartime documentary *Let There Be Light* [1944] and Motes's journey in *Wise Blood*). Motes's homecoming contributes to his characterization as a typical Huston hero. As Brill notes, "Loss of home and of bonds to the land frequently represents in Huston's films the loss of an innocence that his characters struggle to recover. The opening sequences of *Wise Blood* express that loss as eloquently as anything in Huston's work" (Brill, *John Huston's Filmmaking*, 79).

Finally, the compassionate yet distanced tone of *Wise Blood* – achieved, as we have seen, through the extended homecoming scene, Fisher's and Huston's careful shot framings, and North's arrangements of folk tunes – also exemplifies much of Huston's work. Brill writes of Huston's "inclination to find in the extreme and eccentric the universally human; and an empathy for weakness or futility joined with a deep respect for the pertinacity of anyone who remains upright, who survives" (Brill, *John Huston's Filmmaking*, 8).

The affinity we find between O'Connor's novel and Huston's quintessential film stories and characters are all the more striking given that, according to Huston biographer Lawrence Grobel, Huston and the Fitzgeralds had different views of the story. Dourif told Grobel that "[Huston] felt it was about how ridiculous Christianity was. But the Fitzgeralds felt it was a film about redemption. The Fitzgeralds turned out to be right. And John gave them what they wanted in some kind of backhanded way."[38] That in itself is an irony worthy of O'Connor.

NOTES

1. Peter S. Greenberg, "'Saints and Stinkers': The *Rolling Stone* Interview," *Rolling Stone* 337 (February 19, 1981). Rpt. in Robert Emmet Long, ed., *John Huston Interviews* (Jackson: University Press of Mississippi, 2001), p. 104.
2. As just one example, Lesley Brill's excellent book-length study of Huston's films (*John Huston's Filmmaking* [Cambridge: Cambridge University Press, 1997]) refers to *Wise Blood* in passing, rather than singling it out for sustained analysis.
3. See, for example, Robert Stam, "Beyond Fidelity: The Dialogics of Adaptation," in James Naremore, ed., *Film Adaptation* (New Brunswick, NJ: Rutgers University Press, 2000), pp. 54–76.

4. See Scott Hammen, *John Huston* (Boston: Twayne, 1985), p. 135.
5. Carter Martin, "*Wise Blood*: From Novel to Film," *Flannery O'Connor Bulletin* 8 (Autumn 1979), p. 99. Further quotations will be cited parenthetically in the text.
6. John Huston, *An Open Book* (New York: Knopf, 1980), p. 369. Further quotations will be cited parenthetically in the text.
7. Lawrence Grobel, *The Hustons* (New York: Avon Books, 1989), p. 714.
8. Vincent Canby, "Screen: 'Wise Blood,' Huston's 33rd Feature," *New York Times*, September 29, 1979, p. 12; Julian Fox, "*Wise Blood*," *Films and Filming* 26:3 (December 1979), p. 31; *Horizon*, 23 (June 1980), p. 70; Robert Hatch, "Films," *The Nation* 229 (March 8, 1980), p. 283; John Simon, "Christ without Christ; Nijinsky without Nijinsky," *National Review* 32 (May 2, 1980), p. 54.
9. Flannery O'Connor, *Wise Blood* (1952), in O'Connor, *Collected Works*, ed. Sally Fitzgerald (New York: Library of America, 1988), pp. 5–6. Further quotations will be cited parenthetically in the text.
10. Michael Kreyling, "Introduction," in Kreyling, ed., *New Essays on* Wise Blood (Cambridge: Cambridge University Press, 1995), p. 15.
11. Jon Lance Bacon, "A Fondness for Supermarkets: *Wise Blood* and Consumer Culture," in Michael Kreyling, ed., *New Essays*, p. 39. Further quotations will be cited parenthetically in the text.
12. Quoted in Stephen Cooper, "Literal Silences, Figurative Excess: John Huston's *Wise Blood*," *Flannery O'Connor Bulletin* 17 (1988), p. 40. Further quotations will be cited parenthetically in the text.
13. Letter to Cecil Dawkins, 8 November 58, in Sally Fitzgerald, ed., *The Habit of Being: Letters of Flannery O'Connor* (New York: Vintage Books, 1980). Quoted by Kreyling, "Introduction", p. 15.
14. Robert Brinkmeyer, Jr., "'Jesus, Stab Me in the Heart!': *Wise Blood*, Wounding, and Sacramental Aesthetics," in Michael Kreyling, ed., *New Essays*, p. 86. Further quotations will be cited parenthetically in the text.
15. Joy Gould Boyum, "*Wise Blood*: Wise Choices," in Boyum, *Double Exposure: Fiction Into Film* (New York: Universe Books, 1985), p. 176. Further quotations will be cited parenthetically in the text.
16. Sally Fitzgerald and Robert Fitzgerald, eds., *Mystery and Manners: Occasional Prose* (New York: Farrar, Straus and Giroux, 1969), p. 112. Quoted in Brinkmeyer, "'Jesus, Stab Me,'" 85–86.
17. The filmmakers' rationale for expanding Emery's comments on "wise blood" was to make Emery himself the narrator of his own otherwise quizzical actions. Benedict Fitzgerald told Carter Martin that one challenge in drafting the script was that "everything Enoch does, Flannery has very carefully prepared the reader for by telling us what goes on in his head before and even while he acts." Fitzgerald continues:

Now the question is how do you translate all that narration into a person, a dramatic person, one that an audience can recognize and understand? . . . This is how the problem was resolved: in the film, the only one who really explains anything to us about Enoch *is* Enoch. So you see, by a curious alchemical twist he suddenly becomes the narrator who also invented him. No one else can tell us what is going on inside of him except Enoch himself. It took a long time to arrive at that obvious solution – that only Enoch can explain Enoch – and by the same token, give us our only definition of what *Wise Blood* means. (See Martin, "*Wise Blood*: From Novel to Film," pp. 102–103).

18. Hammen, *John Huston*, p. 134.
19. Gavin Millar, "John Huston," *Sight and Sound* 50:3 (Summer 1981), p. 205. Further quotations will be cited parenthetically in the text.
20. Overtly religious films – be they either biopics of Christ or tales of individual spiritual journeys (such as Fred Zinnemann's *The Nun's Story* [1959]) are notoriously mixed achievements, unsatisfying in their portrayal of holy immanence, yet this is a growing field of inquiry in film and religion studies.
21. Boyum has written the best, most systematic analysis of Huston's film, which she discusses as a successful adaptation of a highly metaphorical work to film. I have noted points in the text where I agree with or have built upon Boyum's comments. Needless to say, any subsequent analysis of *Wise Blood*, including this one, is indebted to Boyum's.
22. Stam, "Beyond Fidelity," p. 68.
23. See Michael Klein's brief itemization of these in Klein, "Visualization and Signification in John Huston's *Wise Blood*: The Redemption of Reality," *Literature/Film Quarterly* 12:4 (October 1984), pp. 231–232. Further quotations will be cited parenthetically in the text.
24. Harold Clurman, "NY Film Festival," *The Nation* 229 (October 27, 1979), p. 410.
25. Laura Jehn Menides, "John Huston's *Wise Blood* and the Myth of the Sacred Quest," *Literature/Film Quarterly* 9:4 (1981), pp. 207–208. Further quotations will be cited parenthetically in the text.
26. Those scenes without Motes include Emery's theft and delivery of the shrunken "new Jesus," his Gonga encounters, and his theft of the costume; Sabbath Lily's strategizing with Hawks about seducing Motes; and Mrs. Flood's decision to call the police after Motes has walked off in the rain.
27. Michael Tarantino, "Wise Blood," *Film Quarterly* 33:4 (Summer 1980), pp. 15–16.
28. Frederick Asals, *Flannery O'Connor: The Imagination of Extremity* (Athens, GA: University of Georgia Press, 1982), p. 95.
29. Vernon Young, "Film Chronicle: Molière, Australia and These United States," *Hudson Review* 33:2 (1980), p. 255.
30. David Steritt, "Missing the Flannery O'Connor Mood," *Christian Science Monitor*, March 7, 1980, p. 19.
31. Charles Champlin, "Alex North: A Score for Reticence," *Los Angeles Times*, August 23, 1984, Section VI, p. 8.
32. Barbara McKenzie, "The Camera and *Wise Blood*," *Flannery O'Connor Bulletin* 10 (1981), pp. 31, 32. Further quotations will be cited parenthetically in the text.
33. Young, "Film Chronicles," p. 254.
34. Simon, "Christ without Christ," pp. 543–544.
35. See Gaylyn Studlar, "Shadowboxing: *Fat City* and the Malaise of Masculinity," in Studlar and David Desser, eds., *Reflections in a Male Eye: John*

Huston and the American Experience (Washington: Smithsonian Institution Press, 1994), pp. 193.

36. James Naremore, "John Huston and *The Maltese Falcon*," in Studlar and Desser, eds., *Reflections in a Male Eye*, p. 119.

37. Brill, *John Huston's Filmmaking*, p. 14. Further quotations will be cited parenthetically in the text.

38. Grobel, *The Hustons*, p. 712.

10   Genre and authorship in David Cronenberg's *Naked Lunch*

Steffen Hantke

When David Cronenberg adapted William Burroughs's (1924–1997) *Naked Lunch* (1959) for the screen in 1991, the result was a film self-consciously exploring its own status as an adaptation. Cronenberg himself calls it "an exercise in analyzing the difference between the two media . . . writing and cinema,"[1] a programmatic statement considering the film's interest in authors and their writing machines, the competition and collaboration among authors, and the origins of creativity in addiction, sexuality, personal and historical trauma, and insanity. In one scene of the film, the writer Tom Frost, played by Ian Holm and modeled on Paul Bowles, asks Bill Lee, the William Burroughs stand-in played by Peter Weller, whether it is true that he shot his wife. "How did you know?" Lee asks. "Word gets around," Frost replies. It is this reply, enigmatic and overdetermined, that provides a striking metaphor for all adaptations. Even more so, it encapsulates Cronenberg's self-conscious approach to *Naked Lunch*. When it comes to writing and filmmaking, to the process of adaptation itself, texts travel – word does indeed get around.

Apart from the larger thematic issues in *Naked Lunch*, the film also represents a crucial step in a process of authorial self-(re)fashioning in the career of its director, David Cronenberg. Apart from the director's deep personal investment in the material, which makes watching the film a strangely intimate experience, it also gives Cronenberg an opportunity to shape his public persona and position himself self-consciously as a political filmmaker. When Cronenberg makes use of this opportunity, the distinction between personal and public identity becomes blurry. Cronenberg is, after all, as much the scriptwriter of *Naked Lunch* as he is a commentator, a critic of his own work after the fact. He speaks for himself, both *through* his work and *à propos* of his work. Compacting writing and filmmaking into one coherent discourse, the cinematic text thus expands into the discourse layered around it – statements by the director and his crew in interviews and press conference, supplementary materials used in the packaging and marketing of video, DVD, and laser discs, and academic and fan discourse.

Figure 11. David Cronenberg's version of *Naked Lunch* emphasizes the novel's often cartoonish fantasy in this 1991 Naked Lunch Productions and others release.

Context: Cronenberg's career between margin and mainstream

In order to understand why Cronenberg would choose Burroughs's infamous novel *Naked Lunch* for a screen adaptation, and to understand why the film took the shape it eventually did, it is important to remember that Cronenberg was at the height of his career when he took on *Naked Lunch*, and that, judging by the earlier years of his work in the film industry, there was little to predict such later success. In other words, certain aspects of Cronenberg's adaptation reveal their full significance only in the context of Cronenberg's career. This makes it necessary, before getting into the intricacies of *Naked Lunch*, to take a brief detour through Cronenberg's early years as a director, tracing the professional developments that brought Cronenberg to Burroughs.

Little known outside a hardcore fan community during the 1970s, Cronenberg started with two horror films, *Shivers* (1975) and *Rabid* (1977), which advanced him from film school projects to professional filmmaking.[2] They were followed by *The Brood* (1979) and *Scanners* (1981), which established him as one of the new up-and-coming directors of low-budget horror films, contemporaneous with the likes of George

Romero, Wes Craven, and John Carpenter. Although Cronenberg had received funding from the Canadian government for his films, he was clearly operating outside the cinematic mainstream. This had little to do with his being Canadian. Known as a genre director of a particularly visceral and unpleasant type of horror film – one of his nicknames at the time had him pegged as "Dave 'Deprave' Cronenberg" – he had a reception by the media during those years that was often less than friendly. In an overview of reviews published mostly in British newspapers, Ian Conrich has shown that, because "Cronenberg's early low-budget horrors [were] more identifiable as part of exploitation cinema," than they were recognized as expressions of a unique artistic sensibility, they were "subjected to considerable hostility from the British press." Some critics "accused Cronenberg of reveling in gore and maximizing the special effects moments," while others charged his films with "being too unbelievable, and weak in narrative and characterization." Conrich underlines the hostility of critics by quoting from particularly acerbic, or even outright hostile reviews by Arthur Thirkell in the *Daily Mirror* and Nicholas Wapshot in *The Times*, who called Cronenberg's films "sickening," and a headline from the *Sunday Mirror* which, in reference to the infamous "exploding head" signature shot of *Scanners*, "screamed 'OFF WITH HIS HEAD!'."[3]

By the time *eXistenZ* was released in 1999, Cronenberg seemed to have had the last laugh on his detractors. In the light of the thematic and stylistic consistency of the six feature films he had made since *Videodrome* (1982), it looks as if Cronenberg prevailed by way of sheer stubborn persistence.[4] This is not to say, as Jonathan Crane reads the arc of Cronenberg's career, that, once upon a time, Cronenberg "*was* a horror film director," but now, "as Cronenberg's career has developed, his recent films cannot be so handily corralled" any longer.[5] Films such as *Dead Ringers* (1988), *M. Butterfly* (1993), *Crash* (1996), and, most recently, *Spider* (2002) may have "reconfigured" or "severely muted" the "grisly fancies and obvious hallmarks of the genre." True, *Dead Ringers* constitutes a pivotal moment in Cronenberg's turning away from spectacular special effects as reifications of "body horror." Structured around the digital effect that doubles the actor Jeremy Irons's body for his double role as Beverly and Elliot Mantle, the film nonetheless features only one single prosthetic effect of the type that earned Cronenberg the unflattering nicknames of his early years – a shot of the two bodies linked by an umbilical cord, which one of them proceeds to bite open.[6] This muting of prosthetic effects continues in *M. Butterfly* and *Spider*, which feature no prosthetic effects scenes whatsoever.[7]

During this period of Cronenberg's career, then, *Naked Lunch* poses problems for all those intent on neat generic classification. Unlike its fellow films, it is a special effects extravaganza that abandons visual moderation in favor of sophisticated puppeteering and model effects reminiscent of Cronenberg's early films. Typewriters sprout dripping penile extensions, young boys are molested by vampiric centipedic predators, and among their customers Brooklyn coffee shops count alien creatures, smoking cigarettes and dipping their tongues into glasses of undefinable liquids. The carnivalesque exuberance of these effects in *Naked Lunch* suggests that Cronenberg has most definitely not "abandoned" his interest in subject matter beyond the pale of polite filmmaking, or his willingness to articulate these interests with visual frankness.[8] But this is where the problems start, because *Naked Lunch*, though informed by aesthetic and thematic paradigms of the horror film that Cronenberg deployed in his earlier films, is also clearly not a horror film in the generic sense. If at all, it is a horror film in the same sense that some of Ingmar Bergman's films are horror films (just as Burroughs's novel is a horror text in the sense that Franz Kafka, and not Stephen King, writes horror). The problems that arise from attempts at generic classification open up Cronenberg's film to questions that reach out further toward the contextual construction of meaning, suggesting that the film's significance may arise from seeing it in the context of Cronenberg's career as a filmmaker, his adaptational practices as he approaches source material, and the construction of an authorial persona contingent on Cronenberg's ties to the horror film genre and unique vision as a cinematic *auteur*.

In the light of these questions, it appears as if *Naked Lunch* marks a period in Cronenberg's career, from the late 1980s to the mid-1990s, during which the films themselves are actually not changing all that drastically. A film such as *Naked Lunch* indicates that "mainstreaming," which critics such as Crane are bemoaning, is, in fact, an inaccurate description of what is going on. Instead, I would suggest, a paradigm shift occurred within the popular and critical reception of Cronenberg's work. This shift began to take place when "the majority of reviewers [who] could not be forced to change their aesthetic sense," were outnumbered by an even vaster majority of reviewers who were willing to embrace Cronenberg as "a committed auteur."[9] The paradigm shift – from being dismissed as an exploitation filmmaker, to being accepted within the framework of *auteur* theory – took place within a discursive field given validity by "the degree to which high culture trades on the same images, tropes, and themes that characterize low culture."[10] That is, critical discourse had mapped out a space for discourse outside the mainstream and on "the anarchic edge on the margin of bourgeois propriety" where the two extreme ends of low-budget filmmaking – avant-garde and exploitation – met. Increasingly, critics were willing to recognize that "high art has since the beginning of this century attempted to assimilate pulp culture into its regime," and vice versa.[11] Accordingly, critical opinion shifted from the perception that Cronenberg was operating within the boundaries of genre, rubbing up against these boundaries at times but no less defining himself within their limits, to the recognition that he was pursuing an idiosyncratic personal vision whose relationship to genre was one of utter indifference or, at least, of accidental convergence.

Significantly enough, this recognition also retroactively affected critical assessment of Cronenberg's earlier films. Once the critical paradigm of Cronenberg as *auteur* began to take hold, critics were amenable to reconsiderations of his earlier films. Chris Rodley, perhaps the critic with most direct access to Cronenberg, has pointed out rather succinctly that Cronenberg's reputation profited most from the opportunity that the passing of time afforded his critics to see that his films showed a consistent vision at work. "As one film followed another," Rodley argues, it

became clear that Cronenberg is an *auteur*, perhaps more in a European than a North American sense: he writes as well as directs most of his material and continues to work outside systems which threaten to wrest control in any important sense from production . . . Cronenberg continued to work on the same project, which was becoming increasingly complex, refined and highly achieved with each film he made.[12]

The market followed suit. One home video distributor, for example, started listing Cronenberg's films "under the heading 'Canadian Cinema,'" with the following catalogue note: "David Cronenberg has matured from his early B-movie period into a filmmaker whose films transcend the horror genre" (quoted in Hawkins, *Cutting Edge*, 220, n30). Packaging of recent Cronenberg films for DVD release, as with *eXistenZ* and *Spider*, now habitually features a director's commentary track – that most effective of devices to reinstate, perhaps even fetishize, individual authorship for what is essentially the product of collaborative labor. This practice was initiated by the release of *Dead Ringers* by the Criterion Collection, which prides itself on its own cut of the film employing an aspect ratio that is "David Cronenberg's preferred framing,"[13] underscoring the "strong auteurist stance" as well as the alignment with independent cinema that Joan Hawkins sees as the trademarks of Criterion's fetishization of directorial authorship (Hawkins, *Cutting Edge*, 42).

While his earlier films, up to *Videodrome*, had primarily been Canadian productions – shot in Canada, with an eye first on the Canadian market, and with funding from Canadian sources – his later films, starting with *The Dead Zone* (1983), which was produced by Dino de Laurentiis and distributed by Lorimar, received wider distribution in the United States. Cronenberg's films became a staple at international film festivals, especially with the controversy surrounding *Crash* in 1996. Having appeared in cameos and small roles in other directors' films, such as Clive Barker's *Nightbreed* (1990) and Don McKellar's *Last Night* (1998), Cronenberg further established a public persona in 1999 when he served a turn as president of the jury at the Cannes Film Festival – a form of public recognition unthinkable for the man who had been dubbed the "King of venereal horror" and "Baron of blood" in the early years of his career.[14] In 1987 his film *The Fly* even made its way into the Academy Awards (Chris Walas won for his special effects), and Cronenberg himself was to receive a Genie Award for Best Director in 2002 for *Spider*. This was after *Crash*, *Naked Lunch*, and *Dead Ringers*, respectively, had had a strong showing at the Genie Awards in the years of their release.[15] Often compared with David Lynch, or younger Japanese directors such as Miike Takeshi, he had shed the label of genre director and secured the status of serious *auteur*. In other words, after roughly twenty years of thematically and stylistically consistent film work, word had gotten around: David Cronenberg had arrived.

The adaptation: premises and approach

Cronenberg's adaptation sets out from a startling and somewhat paradoxical premise – the categorical impossibility of adapting Burroughs's novel. Producer Jeremy Thomas comes flat out stating that it was considered "impossible to make a film of [the novel]" (DVD). Weller, as Bill Lee, muses, "To do the book absolute visual justice, you'd probably have to animate it" (commentary track). Cronenberg himself describes the experience of reading *Naked Lunch* in a documentary by Rodley on the making of the film: "As a book, you can kind of dip into it. You don't read it wall to wall; you dip into it. It's like the Bible, it's a little bit here, a little bit there, with cross-references . . . or perhaps [like] the I Ching."[16] Other sources in the same documentary confirm the absence of narrative cohesiveness in the base text as a problem for cinematic adaptation. The Beat historian Barry Miles, for example, calls the novel "a collection of routines," which Burroughs devised after he had moved from New York to Tangiers in 1953, while Burroughs himself explains how Jack Kerouac and Alan Ginsberg helped him to assemble the disorganized manuscript of the book, and how the arbitrary arrangements of manuscript sections at the printer's turned out to determine the novel's ultimate shape. Taken together, all these sources collaborate in evoking an image of Burroughs's text that foregrounds its fragmentation and discontinuity, its radical departure from nineteenth-century realist narrative, and its high modernist hermeticism. However, this emphasis on the book's difficulty is perhaps less a matter of historical accuracy than one of a deeply ideological reconstruction of the text from the point of view of its cinematic adaptation. According to Miles, Burroughs started experimenting with cut-up and montage techniques only after the publication of *Naked Lunch*.

Apart from these problems of narrative cohesion, Cronenberg goes on to outline two other aspects of Burroughs's novel that contributed to its reputation as impossible to adapt. First, "the scope of it," as he puts it, would make a film version of the novel "the mother of all epics"; that is, production costs would be prohibitive. In an age when directors such as James Cameron or Wolfgang Petersen clock in at $200 million a film, however, this seems a minor consideration. But Cronenberg is talking about budgeting an *auteurist* project, not a Hollywood blockbuster.[17] Why not then conceive of the film as a high-profile epic? After all, Lynch gave it a shot with adapting Frank Herbert's *Dune* (1984), the critical and commercial outcome of which, on second thoughts, might answer this question. But Cronenberg does not foresee a lukewarm reception of *Naked Lunch* if it were conceived on a grand scale. Far worse, a faithful adaptation of Burroughs's novel would be, as he himself puts it, "banned in every country in the world, of course" (*Making Naked Lunch*). Despite the introduction of the NC-17 rating for the North American film industry, gay pornography is still off limits for mainstream cinema – and this is what Burroughs's novel would be if it were put on the screen. Its subject matter, as well as its pervasive moral and political tone, would pose insurmountable obstacles for any adaptation within the boundaries of mainstream filmmaking and the North American ratings system.

No matter whether these problems in adapting Burroughs to the screen are actually as daunting as Cronenberg and his collaborators make them out to be, their prevalence in the discourse surrounding the film lend Cronenberg's endeavor an aura of artistic mystique and personal risk. Regarding the problem of obscenity, Cronenberg is aware of the possibility that social changes since the time of the novel's publication may have created a very different political and moral climate for the popular and critical reception of the film. Whereas Burroughs had to fear the Christian right's accusation that he went too far, Cronenberg may have to worry that feminist and queer studies would accuse him of not going far enough or of simply going in the wrong direction (*Making Naked Lunch*). The possibility that social change may have diminished the novel's potential for subversion and provocation does not, however, keep the discourse from bracketing the trope of personal risk. Rodley's documentary shows us Cronenberg as he discusses the fatwa against Salman Rushdie as an exemplary case of the artist as an outsider who, at great personal risk, challenges the status quo.

Similarly, the issue of textual fragmentation, and the degree to which it makes a cinematic adaptation of Burroughs's novel impossible, is, if not dismissed, then transformed into an opportunity for Cronenberg to extend his authorial control over Burroughs's text. The more the novel is in need of reshaping in order to function as film, the more the scriptwriter asserts control over the novelist. To position Burroughs's text as unfilmable, as Cronenberg does, renders it open, porous, susceptible to penetration by another artistic sensibility. This is a complex rhetorical maneuver, which strategically blurs the boundary between Burroughs and his writing. On the most superficial level, the film was marketed as a collaboration of Cronenberg and Burroughs. Both appeared together in press conferences, discussing the film and answering journalists' questions about the collaborative process. The tagline used in advertising the film in television commercials read, "David Cronenberg and William Burroughs invite you to lunch." At first glance, this appears as an attempt, on behalf of the film's distributor, to cash in on the notoriety of Burroughs's novel, perhaps even on the notoriety of its author, whose face and, perhaps even more so, voice had become a recognizable trademark at this late point in his life – "that kind of metallic, nasal Midwestern twang that Burroughs had and that he's very famous for" (*Making Naked Lunch*).[18] After all, this is the motivation behind many cinematic adaptations; at a time when the average production cost of feature films has skyrocketed, distributors are inclined to minimize financial risk by capitalizing on the prior success of text that has already proven itself and established a reputation in the marketplace. Literary adaptations come premarketed, with their own commercial buzz, and with free advertising.

However, this would seem an odd rationale in the case of *Naked Lunch*. Although the book has a broad reputation, it was published more than forty years ago, and no specific recent event or trend had been launching it back into public consciousness by the time Cronenberg's adaptation came along. Its actual readership had always been too small to justify such financial maneuvering; and even among its readers its status had been that of many "cult novels" like it – that it is widely known, but rarely read.[19] *Naked Lunch* might be famous, but apart from scores of unread copies of the book on the shelves of the fans, it has never been a bestseller.

It might have had an impact on American culture, but only indirectly, through mediation and rumor. It is one of those books about which word gets around. The book's notoriety derives from what I would call, in reference to Walter Benjamin,[20] its aura, more so than from concrete encounters of large audiences with the text, driven by deep emotional investment and resulting in lasting emotional impact. Consequently, it fails to provide a solid foundation for a commercial advertising strategy. The constant highlighting of Cronenberg and Burroughs as joint authors of the film must, therefore, have had other reasons.

It is obvious that Cronenberg is interested primarily in the aura of Burroughs's novel – that experience that Benjamin described as "a unique phenomenon of a distance however close it may be," and which he linked explicitly to "the cult value of the work of art" by way of its appearing forbidding, daunting, or altogether unapproachable.[21] Although this aura may be evoked during textual production, as a deliberate aesthetic effect, it applies mostly to the process of textual consumption – though, in the case of adaptations, both production and consumption collapse into one and the same moment, as the reading of the base text is identical with the production of the adaptation. Auratic readings would then be characterized, for example, but relative indifference to textual detail and by a paradoxical simultaneity of awe and intimacy. This oddly disorienting *distance at proximity* may very well be one crucial aspect of all "cult books" – not so much that readers pore over them obsessively, but that they experience textual intimacy through contextual or intertextual absorption of the text. An adaptation of such a text faces the challenge of capturing its spirit – a task as elusive and elliptical as the notion of "distance at proximity" – rather than faithfully reproduce certain key elements.

Every one of Cronenberg's viewers will immediately confirm that fidelity to Burroughs's novel, in the strict empirical sense, was not on the director's mind. This becomes strikingly obvious in the way Cronenberg's screenplay folds Burroughs himself into the text of his own novel, insinuating rich analogies between author and text and reenchanting the process of textual production. Offering the character of Bill Lee as a stand-in for Burroughs, Cronenberg stages the viewer's audience into the film together with actor Peter Weller's first appearance as Bill Lee on screen – as, in his own words, "an iconic Burroughsian moment" (commentary track, DVD). Weller was cast, Cronenberg explains, not so much because he looked exactly like Burroughs ("an actor who looked like Burroughs to a certain extent . . . and yet I didn't want to go to the extent of parody or impersonation"), but because he "had the feel of him" (commentary track, DVD).[22]

As the opening shot reduces Bill Lee to the shadow of Burroughs's trademark fedora falling onto a door, the visual simplification is geared toward the audience's instant recognition and the confirmation of a pre-existing iconography. This approach also resurfaces in what Cronenberg refers to as the film's attempt to capture the *Zeitgeist* of the 1950s – through the music of Ornette Coleman on the soundtrack, the pastiche of Saul Bass in the opening credits, and the warm glow and saturated pastels that cinematographer Peter Suschitzky uses throughout the film as an *hommage* to such Technicolor and Eastmancolor masterpieces of 1950s cinema as Hitchcock's *Vertigo* (1958) or Douglas Sirk's *All That Heaven Allows* (1955). In all these details Cronenberg's practice is highly attuned to the auratic aspect of *Naked Lunch* as a base text, approaching it as unapproachable, creating distance at proximity, as Benjamin would have it, and folding the novel and its author into one single text.[23]

Cronenberg's auratic approach to Burroughs's novel is closely linked to his own biography as a filmmaker. Obviously, Cronenberg identifies with Burroughs as an outsider, a radical individualist, and an artist pursuing a vision at high personal risk. For this act of creative self-fashioning to work, it is sufficient that the audience has only a cursory knowledge of the novel and its author. While this identification with Burroughs's artistic persona may be a matter of deep personal concern for Cronenberg, it also lends itself to the advertising for the film, which plays heavily on iconic identification of Cronenberg with Burroughs. Notoriety is a key concept in this advertising, as television advertisements for the film quote some of Burroughs's more outraged contemporary reviewers. One film clip that features prominently in these advertisements shows Bill Lee (Peter Weller), as he catches his wife Joan (Judy Davis) shooting up bug powder in her breast, tell her wryly, "I thought you were done with weird." This is a densely overdetermined line of dialogue. Simultaneously, it serves as a promise to the audience about what to expect from the film, and as a description of David Cronenberg having transformed himself from the "Baron of blood" into the jury president at the Cannes Film Festival. It appeases horror fans who might have been disappointed at the absence of gory trademark effects in *Dead Ringers*, announcing that Cronenberg has returned to his generic roots. For critics such as Jonathan Crane, who see Cronenberg's *auteurist* ambitions lamentably compromised by mainstreaming, the term "weird" promises a return of the *auteur* to his unique, unclassifiable style. These three meanings are by no means mutually exclusive or contradictory; rather, they amplify each other as they converge in a variation on the trope of the outsider couched in terms of paracinematic polygenericity (or nongenericity, depending on one's preference).

As the discourse mobilizes tropes of Cronenberg's own notoriety, Burroughs remains in the picture. In Rodley's documentary, Cronenberg explains how he joined his own sensibility to that of Burroughs, creating "a third thing" in between the two of them that was neither one man's nor the other's exclusive product or property. He explains this process as "the two of [them] fusing in the telepod in *The Fly*, and [he himself is] possibly the fly, and Burroughs is Seth Brundle; he's bigger" (*Making Naked Lunch*). This comment sounds very much like Cronenberg, in another passage from the documentary, saying that he received his "blessing from the Pope," having asked Burroughs for permission to depart from the novel in crucial respects. Both instances suggest that Cronenberg wants to associate himself with Burroughs by subjugating himself to the figure of greater cultural authority, acknowledging this difference and confirming it by paying his respect to the superior figure.

But like every Oedipal scenario, Cronenberg's bow to Burroughs tacitly implies a narrative trajectory. At a closer look, it is exactly the language that Cronenberg employs that lends ambivalence to his identification with Burroughs. The reference to the telepod from *The Fly* is, after all, a reference to one of Cronenberg's own films. It suggests that the terms on which the collaboration between the two authors is ultimately being negotiated are those of Cronenberg and not Burroughs. Over the formative years of his career, Cronenberg forged his reputation by working exclusively with original screenplays (*Shivers, Rabid, Videodrome, Scanners*), but both the film that landed him outside his native Canada (*The Dead Zone*) and the film that established him as a commercially viable director (*The Fly*) were adaptations – the former garnering only moderate commercial and critical success, the latter being a hit. The risks involved in making the wrong decision in this respect are obvious. Frequently, directors with a strong authorial signature have avoided taking on original texts for adaptation that are too strong, too present in the audience's mind. Hitchcock is the prime example of a director steering clear of the struggle with a potentially overpowering original text, selecting, for the most part, material from relatively unknown authors (Victor Canning's *The Rainbird Pattern* [1972] for *Family Plot* [1976] or Winston Graham's *Marnie* [1961]), a source text so short that a substantial reshaping had to take place at the screenwriting stage (Daphne du Maurier's "The Birds" [1952]), or popular fiction lacking the high modernist imprint of a unique individual style (John Buchan's *The Thirty-Nine Steps* [1915]).

Perhaps Cronenberg learned his lesson from adapting Stephen King's *The Dead Zone*. Critical reception was lukewarm, perhaps because the film managed neither to satisfy the fans of King, who had already emerged as a high-profile author with a substantial popular following, nor to show signs of a pronounced authorial style on Cronenberg's part. The coldness of the film that many critics remarked upon fell short of the human interest that King manages to sustain for his characters, while the absence of Cronenberg's trademark "body horror" elements, following the lead of King's novel, made the film something less than a "David Cronenberg film." *The Dead Zone* was watered-down Cronenberg *and* watered-down King. It represents a draw between the authorial personae of adaptor and adaptee; a clear win on either side of this struggle would satisfy at least one segment of the audience.

Conclusion: Cronenberg as horror *auteur*

Naked Lunch leaves little doubt about the outcome of the Oedipal struggle. Despite the persistent evocation of Burroughs, *Naked Lunch* carries its director's auteurial signature. The film reproduces many of the themes and visual tropes that run through Cronenberg's earlier films – an abiding interest in bodily abjection, and in the nature of creativity and the psychosocial role of the artist, and an exploration of layered ontologies. Like other Cronenberg films from the same period, it "continues the auteur's fascination with protagonists seeking to redefine their corporeal and existential realities" an "ongoing concern with 'masculinity in crisis' . . . frequently dramatized through an impossible vision of male interiority" the "literalization of organs emerging outside the bounds of organic pragmatism" and "an invasive social order – especially its medical and media technologies"; and it features an "insidious corporate takeover or . . . the dangerous vision of a solitary, venomous imagination" (Crane, "A Body Apart," 51).[24]

In the final instance, *Naked Lunch* represents an attempt on the part of Cronenberg to situate himself within the discursive space that Hawkins has called "paracinema" (Hawkins, *Cutting Edge*, pp. 3–9). In this respect, it is in keeping with other Cronenberg films from the same period that are marked by a degree of self-conscious introspection and by attempts to reflect back on his own practices as a filmmaker.[25] As with the Eisenhower era we see in *Naked Lunch*, one might consider the displacement of the plot into Britain in the 1950s in *Spider* as attempts by Cronenberg to revisit his Canadian childhood. An early variation of this attempt might be the scenes from the childhood of the Mantle twins in *Dead Ringers*, in which Cronenberg reflects very specifically on period and setting in examining the origins of a creativity that operates outside the cultural conventions of its time. As David Thomson has noted, Cronenberg tends to incorporate "his response to all the controversy" that his films create among viewers and critics "in which he seems ready to educate us in how to watch him."[26] Xavier Mendik concurs: "The requirement for a 'reflexive' theory of the director's cinema is made all the more important by the fact that Cronenberg is so clearly a filmmaker who actively *engages* with the theory that surrounds his work."[27] As I have tried to demonstrate, *auteur* and genre theory are such crucial contextual factors. By discursive alignment with Burroughs, Cronenberg may be confronting some of the contradictions that, more so at this stage of his career than at any time previously, plague his work – the contradiction between his high modernist ambitions and his working within commercial cinema, and the contradiction between his *auteurist* persona and the fact that many of his deeply personal concerns stubbornly tend to express themselves within the genre vocabulary of horror film. Some critics have used the term "horror *auteur*," which, in its oxymoronic montage of the idiosyncratic and the conventional, tries to account for directors like Cronenberg, more so perhaps than for some of the other directors (Dario Argento, Wes Craven, George Romero) to whom it has been applied. Cronenberg's vision sits uncomfortably, but no less purposefully, between the two categories. But comfort has never been something Cronenberg has promised his audience.

NOTES

1. Commentary track to *Naked Lunch*, David Cronenberg and Peter Weller, Criterion Collection, 2003. Further quotations will be cited parenthetically in the text.
2. Previously Cronenberg had made a few short films, starting around 1966, and had done some work for television during the first half of the 1970s.
3. Ian Conrich, "An Aesthetic Sense: Cronenberg and Neo-horror Film Culture," in Michael Grant, ed., *The Modern Fantastic: The Films of David Cronenberg* (Trowbridge: Flicks Books, 2000), pp. 36, 37.
4. These intermediate films are *The Dead Zone* (1983), based on the novel by Stephen King; *The Fly* (1986), based on a story by George Langelaan, as well as on Kurt Neuman's 1958 film with Vincent Price and Patricia Owens; *Dead Ringers* (1988), based on the novel *Twins* by Bari Wood; *Naked Lunch* (1991), based on William Burroughs's novel; *M. Butterfly* (1993), based on the play by David Hwang; and *Crash* (1996), based on J. G. Ballard's novel.
5. Jonathan Crane, 'A Body Apart: Cronenberg and Genre," in Michael Grant, ed., *The Modern Fantastic: The Films of David Cronenberg* (Trowbridge: Flicks Books, 2000), p. 50; italics added.
6. The shot appears, bracketed within the diegesis, so to speak, as part of a nightmare sequence, and is visually reminiscent of another Cronenberg signature shot at the end of *The Brood* (Nola Carveth, played by Samantha Eggar, severing the umbilical cord to her offspring with her teeth).
7. *Crash* remains, somewhat undecided, in the middle, since there are a few prosthetic effects – as, for example, in the vaginal suture at the back of the

Rosanna Arquette character's leg – which, in their visualization, amount to little more than sophisticated make-up.

8. Crane, "A Body," p. 50.
9. Conrich, "An Aesthetic Sense," p. 39.
10. Joan Hawkins, *Cutting Edge: Art-Horror and the Horrific Avant-Garde* (Minneapolis and London: University of Minnesota Press, 2000), p. 3. Further quotations will be cited parenthetically in the text.
11. Clive Bloom, *Cult Fiction: Popular Reading and Cult Theory* (New York: St. Martin's Press, 1996), p. 16.
12. Chris Rodley, *Cronenberg on Cronenberg* (London and Boston: Faber and Faber, 1992), pp. xv–xvi.
13. Criterion Collection, David Cronenberg, *Naked Lunch*, home page, May 18, 2004; ww.eriterionco.com/asp/release.asp?id=220. In its product description the Criterion website goes on: "This new high-definition digital transfer was created on a Spirit Datacine from a 35mm interpositive and was approved by David Cronenberg."
14. Marco Rambaldi, "Biography for David Cronenberg," Internet Movie Database, March 19, 2004; www.indb.com/name/rm0000343/bio.
15. For detailed information on the Genie Awards and on Cronenberg's record, see www.academy.ca/hist/history.cfm?rtype=1&curstep=4&nname=David+Cronenberg.
16. *Making Naked Lunch*, directed by Chris Rodley, *The South Bank Show*, ITV, April 12, 1992. Further quotations will be cited parenthetically in the text. This documentary is also included in the extras with which Criterion has loaded up its double-disc edition of the film.
17. According to Cronenberg himself, the film was budgeted roughly at $17 million (*Making Naked Lunch*). It went on to gross $2,541,541 in the United States (www.imdb.com/title/tt0102511/business).
18. He had made appearances, for example, in Laurie Anderson's film *Home of the Brave* (2004) and in Gus Van Sant's *Drugstore Cowboy* (1989). For a complete list of Burroughs's film appearances, see www.imdb.com/name/nm0123221/.
19. The same can be said for J. G. Ballard's *Crash*, which undercut the titillating elements of its content with the deadening affectlessness and repetition of its style and structure. One might speculate that Cronenberg's attraction to this type of base text for the purpose of adaptation is based on its relative inaccessibility, more so than its potential for scandal.
20. Walter, Benjamin, "The Work of Art in the Age of Mechanical Reproduction," in Benjamin, *Illuminations: Essays and Reflections*, ed. Hannah Arendt (New York: Schocken, 1968), pp. 217–222.
21. Ibid., p. 243.
22. Cronenberg provides a similar rationale for the creation of characters, like that of Yves Cloquet, played by Julian Sands, that do not appear in the novel, or in any of Burroughs's novels – Cronenberg calls Cloquet "a Burroughsian type character" (commentary track).
23. To some extent, Burroughs himself prefigures such readings of his work through his own cultivation of a public persona – the perpetual suit and tie and fedora – and the use of the Bill Lee character in his work.
24. Walter Chaw, "Cronenberg Re-examines Cronenberg," *The Film Freak Central Interview*, March 4, 2004; Linda Ruth Williams, "The Inside-Out of

Masculinity: David Cronenberg's Visceral Pleasures," in Michale Aaron, ed., *The Body's Perilous Pleasures: Dangerous Desires and Contemporary Culture* (Edinburgh: Edinburgh University Press, 1999), p. 32; Elisabeth Bronfen, "A Womb of One's Own, or the Strange Case of David Cronenberg," in Bronfen, *The Knotted Subject: Hysteria and its Discontents* (Princeton, NJ: Princeton University, 1998), p. 402.

25. I have argued the same case elsewhere in regard to *eXistenZ* and its multi-layered examination of the earlier *Videodrome*. The essay is currently under review by *Literature/Film Quarterly*.

26. David Thomson, "David Cronenberg," in *The New Biographical Dictionary of Film* (New York: Knopf, 2002), p. 190.

27. Xavier Mendik, "Logic, Creativity, and (Critical) Misinterpretations: An Interview with David Cronenberg," in Michael Grant, ed., *The Modern Fantastic*, p. 169

11 Screening Raymond Carver: Robert Altman's *Short Cuts*

Robert Kolker

This may be an oversimplification, but there are two kinds of adaptations from fiction to film that occur in general film production. The first and most common is the process by which a studio, an agent, or even a director or star buys a novel that would make good fodder for a film. "Fodder" is an appropriate word, because novels were and, in many cases, remain material to be chewed up and digested in order to fill the enormous appetite for stories that filmmaking lives on. Two functions are served: the material is there for the writers to get to work on, and whatever cachet may lie in the original fiction might be carried over to help sell the film. The resulting film may bear some, little, or no relation to its literary source, and is usually judged on that premise.

But there is a second kind of adaptation, rare and even more rarely successful, where a filmmaker wants to realize a narrative of written fiction in film because that work carries such meaning and emotional drive that the pressure to do it in cinematic form is great. The problem with this gets to the very root of fiction-to-film translations. A great work of fiction has already achieved a completeness of form that makes it all but impossible, except perhaps for the most talented filmmaker, to visualize it in the form appropriate to his medium – to make a new narrative in a different expressive form from that of the "original." This, of course, brings up all the complexities of how meaning is created. If, as I believe, meaning is a creation of form, then the greatest cinematic adaptation *must* be different from the original because of the different formal means of expressing it. Add to this an axiom that says that only bad novels make good films, precisely because they are unfinished, open to another medium to reformulate them. But a good novel, which is the kind most likely to grab the intellect and emotion of a filmmaker, may not make the translation despite the filmmaker's desires, precisely because of its completeness.

Mario Puzo's *The Godfather* (1972) was a perfect example of an ordinary work of fiction that allowed itself to be rethought, reseen, even reimagined in the hands of a young filmmaker who was asked by the producers to make it and who co-wrote the script with Puzo. Nikos

Figure 12. Miscommunication and disconnection characterize all the relationships in *Short Cuts*, a 1993 Avenue Picture Productions and others release.

Kazantzakis's *The Last Temptation of Christ* (1955) is an example of a complex work that obsessed Martin Scorsese until he finally made a religiously controversial but cinematically not overwhelming film in 1988. There are not many films that transcend a strong literary base to become complex works of cinema while retaining a connection to their source. Eric von Stroheim's *Greed* (1924), his adaptation of Frank Norris's *McTeague* (1899) and Orson Welles's 1962 adaptation of Franz Kafka's *The Trial* (1925) come to mind. The reason is simply that these filmmakers absorb the original and refashion it in their own cinematic terms.

Words and images are different. This is a truism long known to film scholars, but perhaps understood by relatively few filmmakers because their greater interest in words and "story" rather than in *mise-en-scène* keeps them from understanding the fact that plot transfer, even dialogue transfer, is not the same as a complete rethinking of the literary source and a moral commitment. As Abraham Polonsky said, concerning a literary original and its cinematic remake, "Adapting a book to a film is fundamentally a moral crisis . . . Assuming the intention is serious, the book is not chosen to be translated for non-readers but because still embedded in the conception is a whole unrealized life whose language is a motion of images."[1]

A world realized in images is the mark of an adaptation that is imaginatively alive, busily rethinking and reworking its source, reseeing it, giving it visual as opposed to verbal existence. To get to our primary example, I want to work backward, almost perversely so. In 1999 a young director, Paul Thomas Anderson, made his third feature, *Magnolia*. It is a film of many characters who live in Southern California and whose disparate and desperate lives cross in coincidental ways. The potential gentleness of the film is pumped by Anderson to an almost intolerable melodrama that ends not merely with reconciliation, but with, inevitably, death, and improbably (and amusingly) frogs raining down from heaven.

The film is a deeply compromised, bad-faith imitation of Robert Altman's *Short Cuts*, made in 1993. *Short Cuts* is Altman's cinematic *summa*. From the credit sequence of helicopters over Los Angels, preparing to spray for Medfly – an insect plague that struck California late in the twentieth century – that are reminiscent of the images of helicopters that opened *M.A.S.H*, more than twenty years earlier, through its multiple characters and narratives, it is clear that the filmmaker was thinking about all his work, making *Short Cuts* a career summary of one of America's most prolific directors.

What is it summing up? Altman's best work is an ongoing process of representing an American cultural and political milieu that he sees as ridiculous at best, barren and cruel at worst. It is an ironic and sometimes misanthropic process that often takes pleasure in exposing meanness while at the same time exercising an intellectual rigor that permits the films to investigate the destructive assumptions underlying the ideological givens that meanness represents. At their most acute, Altman's films, with their unrelenting zooms to, from, and through characters, their fractured narratives and coincidental crossings and linkings of characters, invites our gaze into spaces that we usually go to the movies to avoid. His films that concentrate on women (such as the early *That Cold Day in the Park* [1969], *Images* [1971], *Three Women* [1977], and *Kansas City* [1996]) are excellent examples of this, for they insist on complexity of point of view, and a difficult, complex notion of mutual victimization. They look at gender as a cultural phenomenon, heir to all of culture's ideological contradictions. *Short Cuts* carries the process as far as Altman can probably take it. He has zoomed out from the subject itself, examining not women in particular, but gender as a whole. At the same time, he zooms in on particular groups and a geographical space. Instead of the marginalized, only partly sane – or driven-insane – figures that inhabit *Three Women*, or the upper-middle-class inhabitants of *A Wedding* (1978), he focuses on a broad sample of lower-middle-class and working-class white couples, all of them constricted economically and/or emotionally, some diminished as well by their short-sightedness, their oppressions, their mute despair, their gender panic. The setting is contemporary Los Angeles. Not the West Los Angeles and Hollywood of *The Player* (1992) or the demi-monde of *The Long Goodbye* (1973), but the suburban sprawl of gangly neighborhoods, every other house up for sale, where nature – whether the Medfly or earthquakes – threatens some kind of retribution against the gender warfare going on beneath every roof.

In *Magnolia* Anderson did not understand the complex irony and misanthropy of his source and turned it into a melodrama of machismo, old age, and that inescapable Hollywood cliché, redemption. Neither did Paul Haggis in the most recent redemption-filled melodrama of chance encounters in L.A. to come from *Short Cuts*, *Crash* (2004). Without understanding that his source was the equivalent to a formally complete work of fiction, he attempted to redo it from a perspective that diminished rather than reinterpreted it. Of course, this comparison could be construed as merely an Altman admirer's pique, but there is a point. Anderson bases a film on another film and the result is a bad move and a mediocre movie. Altman bases his film on a literary source, and the result is one of the most remarkable transformations, or more accurately, as we'll see, retransformations in film.

Short Cuts is based on a number of short stories by Raymond Carver (1938–1998), whose work, in construction at least, is as different from Altman's cinematic practice as Anderson's is from Altman's. The spareness of Carver's verbal language and narrative, even the oddness of metaphor and event that captures emotion on a kind of sidebar of relevance run counter to Altman's large, colorful canvases, filled with people coming and going, usually in the wrong direction. Carver's is a fiction of isolation and occulted epiphany; of people alone, desperate without knowing so, and with barely a hint of redemption. But Carver and Altman share a dark, even misanthropic, view of human behavior, and especially of gender relationships. The lower-middle-class inhabitants of Carver's stories offer Altman a somewhat different perspective on class from the one he usually takes, and the very spareness, even meanness, of their narrative lives suggests a way for Altman to approach his characters from somewhat different angles than he is used to.

Especially interesting to our notion of formal incompleteness inherent in a work of fiction that makes it amenable to filming is the fact that ongoing literary research is tending to prove that Carver is less an author and more a construction. I am not simply talking from the Foucauldian or Barthesian point of view, but from a peculiar editorial reality. Carver's editor, Gordon Lish, it seems, created the Carver we know. He restructured and even rewrote many of his works. The brevity and lack of sentimentality that we so admire in Carver is possibly not

Carver, but Lish. For Altman, reconceiving Carver in his own cinematic terms was very much like Lish reconceiving Carver. So multiple transformations take place, such that in a peculiar sense, *Short Cuts* is an adaptation of an adaptation and of literary sources that are hard to pin down.[2]

Despite all this, in his transformations Altman found a way to maintain and reconfigure the sense of isolation and incompleteness inherent in the Carver most of us think we know, processing them into his favorite structure of large interlocking narratives, where characters' paths cross in unexpected ways and the poverty of their lives keep affecting one another, even without their being aware of it. *Short Cuts* creates an interlocking web of narrative not only by having the characters appear within and affecting each other's stories, but through often ironic internal references: parallel physical movements or gestures, television sets showing images that imitate or mock the characters' actions, counterpointing and associating them across the narrative field. He turns the sense of isolation and gender panic that is explicit in his own work and inherent in Carver's into a global statement. He knits Carver's isolated figures and their barely completed narratives into a geography of gender pain, porous borders, and interlocking sadness and cruelty.

It is intriguing to see how Altman worked with his fictional source. "A Small, Good Thing" (1983) is Carver's story about a couple whose son suffers a hit-and-run accident and dies. The couple are harassed by the baker who made the son's birthday cake, and, in their despair, they confront him. He suddenly (in Carver's version of the story) shows a constricted expression of sorrow and remorse. The son's doctor at the hospital is Dr. Francis, a rather blank, bland figure, described as "a handsome, big-shouldered man with a tanned face," wearing a three-piece suit. After the child's death, Dr. Francis takes the couple into the doctor's lounge. As if to fill the scene with another figure merely to indicate the ordinary ongoingness of the world in the face of the couple's despair, Carver observes:

There was a doctor sitting in a chair with his legs hooked over the back of another chair, watching an early-morning TV show. He was wearing a green delivery-room outfit, loose green pants and a green blouse, and a green cap that covered his hair. He looked at Howard's and Ann and then looked at Dr. Francis. He got to his feet and turned off the set and went out of the room.[3]

He is not heard from again, at least until Altman's film, where he becomes the doctor treating Howard's and Ann's son, Casey. He is dressed as he is in the novel and can be imagined – as Altman does imagine him – walking out of that narrative into one of his own, birthed by Carver's story, taking on a larger life in *Short Cuts*, becoming Ralph

Wyman, not only the doctor treating Casey, but also the seething husband whose wife's one-time sexual indiscretion is cause for his continual anger. These characters originate in Carver's "Will You Please Be Quiet, Please?" (1976). In the film Ralph's wife, Marian, is a painter of grotesque laughing or screaming figures. She is a direct descendant of Willie in *Three Women* and June Gudmundsdottir in *The Player*, bringing their characters into the film through her painting. In fact, with this character Altman closes the relationship of painter, painting, and subject that figures in a number of his works (one of which, the 1970 *Vincent and Theo*, is about van Gogh). Marian's work is a clear expression of her and Ralph's anger and discomfort with each other; hysteria and rage blossom from the images and merge with the character.

The film ends with a drunken party in which Ralph and Marian are joined by Stuart and Claire. These two emerge from Carver's "So Much Water So Close to Home" (1977), the main event of which becomes one focal point of the film: the discovery of a dead woman in a lake by a group of fishermen who then completely ignore her. In the film Claire had met Marian at a concert given by another character in the film, a cellist, who will commit suicide, the daughter of a jazz singer whose songs of pain and anger constitute the film's soundtrack. These characters are roughly pulled from the story "Vitamins" (1983). In the course of the party, they put on clown make-up (Claire works as a clown for children's shows). They play *Jeopardy* (Alex Trebeck happened to show up at that concert where the two women first met, one of those celebrity appearances that Altman loves). They talk, and Marian remembers her art schoolteacher – the one with whom she had the affair that tortures Ralph – who killed himself. He taught her the primitive use of painting to express emotion. At the end of her speech, Altman cuts to Ralph, in clown get-up, distorting his mouth in a scream and squeezing the neck of a balloon so that it emits a grotesque squeal of his repressed pain – looking like the figure in one of Marian's paintings.

Cries of pain emerge subtly throughout *Short Cuts* in various guises, through suicide, aggression, inappropriate actions, expressions of repressed sexual anger. They are perhaps more explicit cries than any Carver character would utter, but not melodramatic ones. They are seen and must be interpreted, because of the complex weave into which Altman puts them. Women are almost always the objects of these destructive acts, more so than in Carver. Before the party, Ralph forces Marian to retell the story of her affair, he seated amidt the paintings in her studio, as if he were one of them. In close-up, one of Marian's portraits of a man's head with a manic grin is placed next to him. Ralph asks Marian why her figures are always naked, "Why does naked make it art"? Marian, having walked out, comes back to the room and stands next to a naked female, who is smiling in happiness. She spills her drink and removes her skirt. From the waist down she, like her paintings, is now naked. This moment of intimacy – Marian cannot comprehend Ralph's ruthless pain over her past indiscretion – pushes Ralph to even greater anger and aggressive language: "Marian, look at me. You don't have any panties on. What do you think you are, one of your goddamn paintings?" She dresses and, admits to having intercourse with her teacher, and Ralph goes back to his sad anger.

Marian's nakedness (it is Ralph who gets naked, and in a different context, in Carver) makes her directly vulnerable, particularly to the viewer's gaze. This kind of imagery brought some accusations of sexism against the film. But actually the opposite of sexism is happening. Altman *is* asking us to look at Marian naked, and she is very attractive. But in the context of Ralph's anger, her own repressing of the memory of the affair, and the paintings that surround her, we are offered a cinematic and narrative space to consider why we enjoy our own voyeurism and why the naked body is not merely attractive, but the potential target of anger to the one who looks. In fiction the narrative space must be imagined; in film it must be visually articulated, turned into a signifier of the character's state. Marian is clearly unembarrassed by her appearance before her husband; he clearly is enraged. The viewer is ricocheted between his point of view, the larger context of what he is doing to Marian and their marriage, and – given all that has already happened in the film – what the female body sometimes means to the male gaze: arousal and the desire to take revenge on arousal's object. The point has been made absolutely clear in the episode, referred to earlier, of the fishermen who discover a naked woman's body in their lake, pee on it, then leave it in the water until they are ready to go home.

The structure of that incident, the intercutting of the men engaged manfully in their sport and camaraderie with shots of the woman's body, silent, face down under the water – recalling so many of Altman's characters who die in water – causes a kind of lyrical juxtaposition between callousness and its victim. It is this kind of juxtaposition that Carver avoids in his intent to keep the characters and their meager lives separate from each other. He and his editor did, after all, write short stories, not novels. Altman makes films in which every character affects another, becomes connected, often with pain. When one of the fishermen, Stuart – who is with his wife Claire at Ralph's and Marian's party later in the film – comes home, early in the morning, he immediately begins making love to her, despite her protests about his fishy hands, a comment that Stuart cannot possibly let go without making a vulgar analogy. The sequence is intercut with some other narrative moments in which various other characters talk about aberrant sex or sex as aberration. After their lovemaking, Stuart tells Claire about the body in the water. As she listens, lying next to him in the bed, the camera zooms slowly to her. This is one of the longest shots in the film, and it occurs as a kind of pivot for the viewer's own recognition, a turn further toward the female consciousness that reacts to the brutality around it. Obviously this is a technique not possible in prose, and in "So Much Water So Close to Home" the closest Carver gets to it is by writing the story in the first person from Claire's point of view. The reader sees as much as (and more than) she does. In the film, in which first person does not work, the simple, lingering zoom at Claire allows us to comprehend the compassion she feels for the dead woman that was unavailable to the men. She gets out of bed and takes a bath, as if to share some of the victim's experience while cleansing herself of a shared guilt (she learns that the victim was raped and smothered). She later drives to Bakersfield for her funeral. In one of the film's most intriguing moves, she mimes signing the guest book; she writes her presence absently, like the dead woman herself, leaving no trace of her presence at the scene. Like most of the women in the film, she has been written out and written off, in one episode written on, by the men.

The main traces throughout the film are not of women's presences as active, self-protective, but as objects of assault and rage, their personalities quashed. These traces move from the inane to the violent. Stuart and the fishermen visit Doreen's diner and make her bend over to get things for them so that they can ogle her backside. The characters emerge from "They're Not Your Husband (1983)." In the story the husband is openly complicit with the oglers. Altman is a bit more subtle. Her husband sits by, saying nothing. The rage is ours. Elsewhere, the rage is overt, as the weatherman, Stormy Weathers, rips his ex-wife's house to shreds. There is rage transferred, in Gene the cop, who cheats on his wife and steals his child's dog (roughly emerging from Carver's "Jerry and Molly and Sam" [1983]); and in the smarmy make-up man, Bill, getting a "chubby" as he pretends to beat his wife while making up her face with wounds, literally writing his hatred on her with marks of violence, and then taking pictures of her. A funny, chilling, and quite Altmanesque moment occurs when the fishermen go to a photo kiosk to get their pictures of the drowned woman at the same moment that Bill and his friends get the pictures of the mock beating of Bill's wife. The photos are mixed up, and each group looks at the other's images with horror then quickly transfer them and go their separate ways. A metaphor for the film, the lunatic act of horror over sublimated real violence, echoes Altman's shuffling of Carver's stories – and making up his own from them.

Women destroy themselves in this film – as in the suicide of the cellist, Zoe Trainer – or are driven by economics into being sexual objects. The sequences between Jerry and Lois are particularly grueling and lead to the cataclysm that ends the film. The characters emerge greatly expanded from "Tell the Women We're Going (1983)," and Altman places them just above Earl and Doreen on the economic scale. Jerry is a pool cleaner and Lois supplements her husband's income by doing phone sex. Every time Altman returns to this couple, the rage builds. Altman's attitude toward Lois is ambiguous. She does a job that is especially degrading, but she seems unaffected by it – too much so, because she is able to carry on dirty phone talk while feeding her child, but seems unwilling to express sexuality at all to her husband. After all, she has to do it for a living. In scene after scene – again something impossible in Carver's short, self-contained verbal fiction – Altman zooms in on Jerry's expressions of hurt, confusion, and, finally anger. It pushes him to murder. He and his friend Bill – the make-up artist – pick up a girl while picnicking with their families in Griffith Park. They go off for a walk, and Jerry hits the girl with a rock. An earthquake occurs.

The murder is inevitable and the earthquake metaphoric, as if nature were reacting to the welling up of gender violence and hatred in the film's characters. It is a major expansion that clarifies Carver's almost withholding simplicity against Altman's need to make a wider statement. "Tell the Women We're Going" ends: "He never knew what Jerry wanted. But it started and ended with a rock. Jerry used the same rock on both girls, first the girl called Sharon and then on the one that was supposed to be Bill's."[4]

Typically abrupt. Altman extends it and makes nature itself rebel against the murder of yet another woman. This is not the silliness of Anderson's rain of frogs, but one more expected Los Angeles disaster that coincidentally coincides with and somehow expresses the outrage toward a woman's murder. Yet it is not final, not the "big one," and hardly the apocalypse. Altman is not a director of large closures. It turns out to be a small quake – the television announces to the partygoers that only one person has been killed, the girl murdered by Jerry – and therefore unimportant. It even makes room for some small compensatory gestures. The bullying baker, when confronted by Howard and Ann, offers them baked goods and protection from the quake (the "sentimental" version that Carver wrote for his story). Earl and Doreen stand under the lintel of their trailer, hoping that this quake is the big one, satisfied that it is not, reaching a momentary accommodation in their affection for each other. Gene, the cop – having previously relented and taken the dog he left in another neighborhood away from its new owners and back to his children – stands bravely in his backyard, barking safety orders to his neighbors through an LAPD bullhorn. The drunken couples – Stuart, Claire, Ralph, and Marian – continue their angry, retributive revelries – the macho Stuart in a wig, Ralph in clown whiteface. All the fragments drawn from the Carver story are observed; they come together, then drift some more. The camera slowly pans away from them, over the Los Angeles cityscape and then, as in *The Long Goodbye*, to a map of the city. On the soundtrack Annie Ross (the jazz singer who plays Tess, a depressed, alcoholic jazz singer, mother of Zoe) sings "Prisoner of Life."

Short Cuts, like its fictional analogues, is a kind of prison house. Its characters move through proscribed physical and emotional spaces, come in contact with one another, accidentally, as relations, as friends or strangers, all the while living out a singularity of despair, bad luck, or anger. The bright light and color of Los Angeles surround them, but they remain dark and obsessed. They move, but are frozen in their depression and anger, in their economic and cultural blight. And this suggests something else, a painter and his work that triangulate against the writer and the filmmaker, one whose content is very much homologous to Carver, and whose form somewhat echoes Altman. The light of Edward Hopper's paintings is not of Southern California, but it has the same bright pitilessness as the light that Altman throws on his characters. Hopper's work has influenced the lighting of many, many films. Individual Hopper paintings – most especially *Night Hawks*, that far shot of a diner at night – have been directly copied by a number of filmmakers. But Altman, perhaps unconsciously, has captured, without imitation, the loss and diminishment of personality that so many of Hopper's paintings connote: lives negated by depression and loneliness. The poet Mark Strand writes:

Within the question of how much the scenes in Hopper are influenced by an imprisoning, or at least a limiting, dark is the issue of our temporal arrangements – what do we do with time and what does time do to us? . . . Hopper's people . . . are like characters whose parts have deserted them and now, trapped in the space of their waiting, must keep themselves company, with no clear place to go, no future.[5]

In *Short Cuts* the characters barely have themselves as company, but continually seek out others to visit their own discomfort on them. In the hospital, as Howard and Ann agonize over their dying child, hit by Doreen's car, Howard's estranged father comes to visit and unloads upon him the story of a wretched affair he had with his wife's sister many years ago. The inappropriateness of his actions, and those of all the characters, is barely tolerable. Pain is always inflicted. Movement is always brought to an end by all of them. They look to each other and see only their own pain. Class, culture, environment, the ennui of economic and intellectual entrapment create the impossible turmoil of self-hatred, gender hatred, and finally, a panic that occurs at the recognition of entrapment. The characters often do move. They get nowhere, and they hurt others on the way.

Strand writes about Hopper that his paintings

are short, isolated moments of figuration that suggest the tone of what will follow just as they carry forward the tone of what preceded them. The tone but not the content. The implication but not the evidence. They are saturated with sugges-tion. The more theatrical or staged they are, the more they urge us to wonder what will happen next; the more lifelike, the more they urge us to construct a narrative of what came before. They engage us when the idea of passage cannot be far from our minds . . . Our time with the painting must include – if we are self-aware – what the painting reveals about the nature of continuousness. Hop-per's paintings are not vacancies in a rich ongoingness. They are all that can be gleaned from a vacancy that is shaded not so much by the events of life lived as by the time before life and time after. The shadow of dark hangs over them, making whatever narratives we construct around them seem sentimental and beside the point.[6]

Again, the comment applies well to Carver, or whatever "Carver" wrote the stories, and slips over to Altman, too. Carver supplies the isolated moments "saturated with suggestion." Altman gives the continuousness, the ongoingness that is in the shadows of the vacancies. He gives us nar-rative, more narrative than Carver. After all, he makes films – in this case a three-hour film – not paintings or short stories. But his films, with very few exceptions, do not allow us to construct another sentimental narrative around them, and they always reveal that the nature of con-tinuousness – of continuity – may be the sham that hides the fact that connection without betrayal or despair is rare. When we move, we cause hurt. It is the mark of being human, like aloneness. And like Hopper, like any creative imagination that sees into the form of the work and asks the viewer or reader to see as well, Altman allows us in on the process. The despair and vacancies, the revelation of our propensities toward passivity, a willingness to be oppressed by manufactured images that are accepted as historical realities, the ease with which we descend into emotional or physical violence: the images manufactured by Altman to inscribe these subjects refuse to dominate the viewer as Carver's stories and Hopper's paintings themselves refuse to do. The open narrative construction – the flow, the sense of process and accident that so many of his films achieve – attempts to take apart the very subject they create, expose their manufacture, and affirm the fact that it is the viewer who must make sense of them. Make us, as Strand hopes, self-aware. Two distinct voices seem to be speaking these filmic, literary, and painterly discourses. One announces the inevitability of defeat and despair through the hopeless yielding to domination. The other enunciates a freedom of perception, and therefore a control over what is seen, understood, and interpreted.

NOTES

This essay is expanded from material in Robert Kolker, *A Cinema of Loneliness: Penn, Stone, Kubrick, Scorsese, and Altman*. 3rd edn (New York: Oxford University Press, 2000). Used by permission of Oxford University Press.

1. Abraham Polonsky, in Andrew Sarris, ed., *Interviews With Film Directors* (New York: Avon Books, 1967), p. 392. Originally published in *Film Quarterly* 15 (Spring 1962).
2. David Wyatt revealed the recent research on Carver, which can be found in Günter Leypoldt, "Reconsidering Raymond Carver's 'Development': The Revisions of 'So Much Water So Close to Home,'" *Contemporary Literature* 43:2 (2002), pp. 317–341. Leypoldt argues that there is a continuity from the original to the edited versions of the stories.
3. Raymond Carver, "A Small, Good Thing," in Carver, *Cathedral* (New York: Alfred Knopf, 1983), pp. 65–66, 80.
4. *Short Cuts: Selected Stories by Raymond Carver* (New York: Vintage Books, 1993), p. 154.
5. Mark Strand, *Hopper* (Hopewell, NJ: The Ecco Press, 1993), p. 25.
6. Ibid., p. 2

12   *The Color Purple*: translating the African American novel for Hollywood

Allen Woll

When it was announced that Alice Walker's (b. 1944) Pulitzer Prize-winning third novel *The Color Purple* (1982) was to be filmed in 1985, there was reason for considerable optimism about the result. Hollywood's top moneymaking director Steven Spielberg had decided to direct the film with Walker's approval. Quincy Jones had joined the company as a producer, and young talents Whoopi Goldberg, Oprah Winfrey, and Margaret Avery had signed for the major roles of Celie, Sofia, and Shug.

As the year's Academy Award nominations were announced, it seemed that *The Color Purple* might sweep the board. Nominated for eleven Oscars, including Best Picture, Best Director, and three acting awards (Goldberg, Winfrey, and Avery), the film faltered at the presentation, winning none of the honors. The big winner that year was *Out of Africa* (directed by Sidney Pollack and starring Robert Redford and Meryl Streep), which won many of the awards for which *The Color Purple* had been nominated. *The Color Purple* won some secondary awards (a Golden Globe for Goldberg), but it finished out of the running for the most prestigious ones.

While *The Color Purple* earned respectable grosses during its first six months of release (approximately $94 million), it was also greeted with considerable criticism during this period. Many would later argue that the harsh reception of the film, particularly from the African-American community, hurt both its earnings and its award potential, and left a lingering bad taste among the various participants in the film. Alice Walker, herself, revisited her experiences during the making of the film in a 1996 work, *The Same River Twice – Honoring the Difficult*. This memoir includes journal entries and articles from newspapers, as well as the unfilmed Walker 1984 script (*Watch for Me in the Sunset*) for *The Color Purple*. The memoir reveals the mixed feelings that Walker experienced during the filming of her work. On the one hand, she felt that her work was protected by some of the top talents of Hollywood; on the other hand, she was surprised by the vitriolic criticism of her and her work after the film premiered.

191

Figure 13. An innocent Celie (Whoopi Goldberg) receives instruction about being a proper woman from her husband's mistress, Shug (Margaret Avery) in *The Color Purple*, a 1985 Amblin Entertainment/Guber-Peters/Warner Brothers release.

A reader of *The Same River Twice* might be surprised by the harshness of the criticism of the film of *The Color Purple*, but one should remember that all the talents involved in the making of the film have matured considerably in the past two decades. The Walker we know now was not the same Walker when the film was made, nor was Spielberg the Spielberg we know today. Whoopi was not Whoopi, but merely a promising comic talent, and Oprah had just begun to host a talk show in Chicago. Looking back with the vantage of hindsight at what seems a promising juncture of talent at the time tends to obscure how new many of the talents were to the making of a film of a major American novel.

The Color Purple seemed an unlikely choice for mainstream Hollywood fare, since it deals with issues that Hollywood had tended to ignore. It also seemed a difficult candidate for film, since all the novel's action was included in the main character's (Celie's) letters to God and to her long-absent sister Nettie, as well as Nettie's letters to Celie, who had been raped by her father, has her two children taken from her, and is then given in marriage to the malevolent Mr. __ (henceforth Mr.), who finds her a disappointing third choice for marriage. He would have preferred the glamorous nightclub singer Shug or even Nettie. Mr. later sends Nettie from the farm, and she eventually migrates to Africa, but Mr. ensures that Celie never receives the letters her sister sends. Celie eventually meets Shug and finds herself attracted to her in the same way that her husband had been. Shug ultimately provides Celie with the strength to escape from Mr.'s domination and make a life for herself. As the novel ends, Celie is reunited with both her sister and her long-lost children, whom Nettie had raised in her African sojourn.

Spielberg essentially "auditioned" for the role of director. Walker recalled the night that Spielberg arrived at her home in February 1984, ushered in by Quincy Jones:

Quincy first, in an enormous limousine that had difficulty turning into my lane . . . Quincy, beautifully dressed and hair done just so. And Steven, who arrived later, casually and (partly) in someone else's clothes. Quincy had talked so positively about him I was almost dreading his appearance – but then, after a moment of I don't know what, uneasiness, he came in and sat down and started right in showing how closely he had read the book. And making really intelligent comments. And Quincy beamed.[1]

After a lengthy discussion they agreed to the project and the arrangement that Walker would work on the screenplay and confer on the film.

"Audition" seems an odd word for a director as successful as Spielberg, one who had almost coined the concept of the "summer blockbuster" with his hit film *Jaws*, which had filled cinemas in 1975. Spielberg had quite a track record by the time he met Walker. After a directing career for television (segments of *Night Gallery*, *Columbo*, and *Marcus Welby*, *M.D.*, as well as made-for-television films), he moved to the big screen with *The Sugarland Express* (1974) and *Jaws*. He revealed his interest in science fiction with *Close Encounters of the Third Kind* (1977) and *E. T., the Extra-Terrestrial* (1982), and recreated the movie genres he recalled from his youth, such as the movie serials which were echoed in the Indiana Jones series (*Raiders of the Lost Ark* [1981] and *Indiana Jones and the Temple of Doom* [1984]), completed before *The Color Purple*. All his films were financially successful audience pleasers with the sole exception of *1941* (1979), a World War II comedy that was long on talent but short on humor. By the time that Spielberg associate (and ultimately a producer of the Walker film) Kathleen Kennedy brought him the novel *The Color Purple* for his consideration, he had emerged as one of the most financially successful directors in modern Hollywood.

Nonetheless, Spielberg seemed an odd and controversial choice at the time. Nothing in his previous film work revealed any ability to work with a novel as complex as *The Color Purple*. His films of the previous decade are notable for the fluidity of his direction, but also for Spielberg's lack of interest in any issues of importance to society. Yet, after filming Spielberg confessed to an interviewer for the *New York Times* that:

> for a long time I'd been wanting to become involved with something that had more to do with character development. I really wanted to challenge myself with something that was not stereotypically a Spielberg movie . . . I wanted to work in the same arena as directors like Sidney Lumet and Sydney Pollack – and Paddy Chayevsky, in terms of what he'd done as a playwright and a writer.[2]

These were lofty ambitions for someone whose films tended to have special effects and chase sequences dominate over character. While individual acting turns might be remembered, such as Roy Scheider, Robert Shaw, and Richard Dreyfuss in *Jaws*, the performances often appeared secondary to the spectacle. Furthermore, looking at all Spielberg's blockbusters before 1985, the relative absence of African-Americans is striking. Those of his films that consider contemporary American life seem to be located in a blissful suburbia, where daily life is interrupted only by stranded aliens or flying saucers. Could someone who had virtually ignored the African-American experience during fifteen years of filmmaking be the ideal candidate to adapt *The Color Purple* for the big screen?

Walker had not seen many of Spielberg's films, and "was unprepared to argue with those who thought that, had [she] seen them, [she] would have avoided what was, in their opinion, [her] dreadful mistake of having allowed him to film [her] book." Nonetheless, she had been taken to see *E.T.* and had enjoyed Spielberg's depiction of the alien who was trapped on earth. Was it Spielberg's sympathy for the outsider that had attracted her interest?

While Walker had not been familiar with the totality of Spielberg's work, she had, of course, been quite familiar with the way Hollywood had depicted African-Americans during the past several decades. Was Spielberg and his company a part of that tradition? Walker recalled one of her "memorable moments in moviemaking" in *The Same River Twice*: "The day Steven referred to *Gone With the Wind* as "the greatest movie ever made" and said that his favorite character was Prissy (150). The 1939 film had quite a different meaning for Walker:

> I believe movies are the most powerful medium for change on earth. They are also a powerful medium for institutionalizing complacency, oppression, and reaction. Steven's feeling about *Gone With the Wind* was so different from mine that when he said he considered it "the greatest movie ever made" I felt the only appropriate response would be to faint. I slept little for several nights after his comment, as I thought of all I would have to relay to him, busy as he was directing our film,

to make him understand what a nightmare *Gone With the Wind* was to me. It is a film in which the sufferings of millions of black people over hundreds of years of enslavement is trivialized to the point of laughter. It is a film in which one spoiled white woman's summer of picking cotton is deemed more important than the work, under the lash, of twenty generations of my ancestors. (282)

It was not just *Gone With the Wind* that disturbed Walker; it was the fact that "Hollywood had a terrible track record in depicting black people."[3] From the first years of Hollywood filmmaking, screenwriters and directors had often depicted African-American characters in a stereotypical fashion. D. W. Griffith's classic *Birth of a Nation* (1915) was arguably the cinematic masterpiece of the silent era, but this tale of the Civil War and Reconstruction South painted the Ku Klux Klan as the film's heroes, and the African-American characters (many of them white actors in blackface make-up) as cowardly or violent figures who had to be tamed if order were to be restored to the defeated South. While this film was praised by President Woodrow Wilson as "history written with lightning," it managed to paint African-American characters in horrid stereotypes. While the film garnered critical praise and ample box-office takings, it became a *cause célèbre* for the nascent NAACP (National Association for the Advancement of Colored People) as it greeted the film with large-scale demonstrations in major cities.

Despite the protest against Griffith's film, the problem with stereotypes lingered in Hollywood for decades. Donald Bogle's classic work *Toms, Coons, Mulattoes, Mammies, & Bucks: An Interpretive History of Blacks in American Films* (2001) argues that these stereotypes lingered for decades. Worse still, some of the most talented African-American actors were trapped by these stereotypes in their film portrayals, thus limiting the scope and range of their film performances. The first African-American performer to win an Oscar for a film performance was Hattie McDaniel for her role as Mammy in *Gone With the Wind* in 1939 – it would be the sole such honor for an African-American actor for the next twenty-five years (when Sidney Poitier would win for *Lilies of the Field*). In this fashion, African-American performers would have to struggle with decades of demeaning tradition when presenting screen characterizations.

The second dilemma of Hollywood tradition was that few African-Americans were potent figures behind the screen during most of Hollywood history. While D. W. Griffith's silent films dominated the age, African-American filmmakers were few and far between. Some names are recognized from the silent era – such as Oscar Micheaux – but his independent films were primarily low-budget efforts distributed primarily to African-American audiences. With the solidification of the studio system and its domination over the motion picture production business, African-American writers, directors, and producers were relegated to the sidelines. The only African-Americans who had any degree of power within the new studio system were the actors, and they had little control over the direction of their on-screen roles. Some performers noted that they could reject stereotypical roles, but then they would not be able to act on screen. With the absence of African-American talent behind the screen, there were few people who could agitate for improved roles for African-American performers.

Matters improved somewhat in the decade or so before *The Color Purple*. With such financially successful independent films as *Sweet Sweetback's Baadasssss Song* directed by Melvin Van Peebles in 1971, Hollywood recognized a large untapped African-American audience. Often dubbed "blaxploitation films," these Hollywood productions, such as Gordon Parks's *Shaft* (1971), brought African-American directors, writers, and performers into the Hollywood mainstream. While this trend would ultimately play itself out, it helped to open the doors to new and influential behind-the-scenes talent in Hollywood.

Nevertheless, when Hollywood came calling on Alice Walker, there should have been some slight trepidation about where this collaboration would lead. Trepidation surely, but also some hope. A recent adaptation of Charles Fuller's play *A Soldier's Story* had been released by Columbia in 1984 with an outstanding roster of African-American talent (including Adolph Caesar, who would also appear in *The Color Purple*), and had received critical acclaim. Similarly, with Quincy Jones as a producer and composer on *The Color Purple*, Walker would be assured that there would be African-American participation behind as well as on the screen. Jones also remained a staunch supporter of Spielberg as the right person to direct the film, introducing him to Walker and bringing him to her home.

Walker's adaptation used the major themes and characters of the novel, and it was more complex in structure than the film. More characters made their way into her screenplay than appeared in the final version, and scenes retained the complexity of the novel. Furthermore, her screenplay was heavily descriptive, providing information about the story's various locations, the characters' appearance and their dress, that was not apparent in the novel. Rather than being a strictly chronological narrative, the script presents a series of flashbacks as Celie reflects on "her colorful, beautifully appliquéd quilt" for visions of her complex past.

The filmed version of the novel simplified the storyline, conflated characters and scenes, and, in general, enforced a chronological narrative on what had initially been a series of letters, first addressed to God, and later between sisters Celie and Nettie. Alternative writers found the project a daunting one, and Walker and Spielberg ultimately chose Menno Meyjes, a young Dutch writer who had lived in America since 1972. He had worked on a screenplay about the Children's Crusade of 1212 (when thousands of children from France and Germany sailed to the Holy land but were captured en route by pirates and sold into slavery), released in 1987 as *Lionheart*, which had caused Spielberg to notice him. Meyjes worked closely with Spielberg on the script, and Walker approved the final product, giving him additional advice on language and settings. Walker remained on set during the filming of *The Color Purple*, and she continued to make suggestions on the shape of the final film, but not all her ideas were accepted (Walker, *The Same River Twice*, 178–179).

Walker was also influential in making recommendations for the casting of the film, though her preferences were not always honored. Nonetheless, the casting choices make her and casting director Reuben Cannon seem almost prescient. The two major performers – Goldberg and Winfrey – had read the novel and were eager to appear in the film. Goldberg had even written to Walker of her desire. Yet, while these two women are superstars now, they were barely known to the public in the months before filming. Goldberg is often described as a multitalented "performance artist" in *The Same River Twice*, reflecting her background as a San Francisco mimic who created a stable of eccentric characters in *The Spook Show* which Mike Nichols later directed in a Broadway version. Walker saw her perform in Los Angeles: "I liked her right away. I like people who refuse to be victims, and delight in showing everyone else how this is done. She was wonderful, dreadlocking with an irrepressible, sly gleam in her eye. She makes it really clear there's no use actually trying to fit into this madness" (Walker, *The Same River Twice*, 48).

Winfrey, at the time, was at the beginning of her career as a Chicago-based talk show host. Jones was visiting Chicago during the planning of the production, and happened to notice Winfrey's show while in his hotel room. Impressed by her performance, he brought her to Cannon's attention and she was selected for the role of Sofia. Tina Turner seemed the early favorite for Shug, but when she rejected the role, Margaret Avery signed on for the film.

Walker's public response to the completed film was cautious. She had been warned by executive producer Peter Guber that she might be shocked when she saw it and it was almost a decade before she could contemplate her experience with the film – the highs and some surprising lows. Her initial reaction recorded in a journal revealed her disappointments:

One basic way I feel about the film – after one viewing – is terrible. It looks slick, sanitized, and apolitical to me. Some of the words coming out of Shug and Celie's mouths are ludicrous. The film looks like a cartoon. There are anachronisms. Would Shug's father be driving a horse and buggy in the '30s for instance? In short, on first viewing I noticed only the flaws. (Walker, *The Same River Twice*, 285).

Yet she confessed that there was much to like about the film:

the parting scene between Celie and Nettie, and the scene where Nettie defends herself against Mister. Nettie, in fact, is quite wonderful . . . The kissing scene between Celie and Shug. The whole section where Shug and Celie find the letters and begin to read them. Especially the scene where Celie smells the dried flower petal. Shug in the jookjoint, first song . . . The scenes in the church are all fine . . . The music is wonderful. [Walker, however, hated the opening strains of the film, which she felt made it sound more like *Oklahoma* than *The Color Purple*]. Although Nettie in Africa is teaching reading and writing, not music. The ending is moving. But I wanted Mister up on the porch too! [Walker had made this suggestion during the filming but it had been rejected.] (Walker, *The Same River Twice*, 285)

While *The Color Purple* received a respectable showing of Oscar nominations, the film met with considerable criticism from African-American opinion makers. Walker recalled the praise that greeted the film, yet she was dismayed by the fact that she had to cross lines of protesters to attend it. The first picketline she crossed in her life was a benefit showing for *The Color Purple* by the Black Women's Forum headed by Congresswoman Maxine Waters, and a similar protest erupted on the evening of the Oscar presentations (Walker, *The Same River Twice*, 285).

The complaints concerned both the film and Walker herself. The film, protesters claimed, revealed a hatred of men, and of African-American men in particular, and it was especially destructive of the African-American family. One column particularly stung Walker:

I'm quoting others because I did not see the movie – and never intend to. If the NAACP had produced it, I would not go to see it. One black man walked out of the Chicago premiere, confronted a black actor in the film, and asked him how a black man could take part in such a degrading movie. The Coalition Against Black Exploitation said it degraded black men, children, and families. A white Los Angeles newspaper said "all that's missing . . . is a shot of Uncle Remus . . ." Willis Edwards, president of the Hollywood NAACP, said it was "stereotypical" and demeaning. Furthermore, the Los Angeles opening was picketed by a host of harsh critics. (Walker, *The Same River Twice*, 223–225)

Brown went on to attack Celie's and Shug's lesbian relationship in an age when the mainstream mass media avoided gay issues: "And lesbian affairs will never replace the passion and beauty of a free black man and black woman. In *Purple* emotional and sexual salvation for women is found in other women. That's not the real world, as some black women, out of frustration, seem to want to believe" (Walker, *The Same River Twice*, 285). Walker was stung by these complaints, but there are elements of truth in the criticism expressed against the Spielberg film. These same criticisms do not necessarily ring true for the novel. The men in the film are either unrelentingly grim, or in some cases, unintentionally comic characters. Walker's novel ends with reconciliation, as Mr. reveals a certain fondness for Celie: "Took me long enough to notice you such good company, he say. And he laugh. [Celie responds:] He ain't Shug, but he begin to be somebody I can talk to."[4] As Celie is reunited with her children and her sister at the novel's end, Mr. is a part of Celie's world and extended family. In the film Mr. remains unrepentant throughout most of the action, and while he does provide the assistance that allows Nettie to return to America, he remains an outsider. He watches the reconciliation from a distant field, a mere observer of the reunion of Celie's family. Had Walker's original plotline been salvaged (which she had recommended), the harshness of Mr.'s character would have been muted. Danny Glover, who has evolved into an avuncular screen character in the *Lethal Weapon* films, gives an arresting performance, which (until the last few minutes of the film) is a portrait in venom. Spielberg did film a six-minute sequence to be used late in the film for Celie's forgiveness, but he decided to cut it, arguing that the film was not Mr.'s story but Celie's, and this plot exposition was unnecessary. He felt that the several brief reaction shots showing a smiling Mr. contemplating Celie's reunion with Nettie conveyed his regrets to his wife about his previous cruel treatment of her, but such an interpretation is ambiguous at best.

In a similar vein, the novel's Harpo, Mr.'s son and husband of the strong-willed Sofia, often seems a comic stereotype. Although admittedly somewhat lazy, his main comic characteristic is that he is so inept that whenever he tries to build a dwelling he falls though the roof of the building. Otherwise, he is portrayed as a carbon copy of his father, whose only road to domestic bliss is beating his wife until she obeys his every whim. This leads to his break-up with Sofia and the destruction of her life as well. Yet the son, like his father, also learns the error of his ways by the novel's end and joins the extended family, not only with his first wife Sofia, but also with his second paramour, Mary Agnes. While Harpo (Willard Pugh) and Sofia (Oprah Winfrey) become a part of Celie's extended family in the film, the context of the reconciliation is rendered more fully in the novel.

Critics lambasted the film for its portrayal of a lesbian relationship between Celie and Shug, arguing that it undermined the black family.

This sequence of the film is also quite different from the novel, which is explicit. In the film gay issues are addressed obliquely, if at all, and Spielberg acknowledged that he would not be the appropriate director to film the scenes from the novel as Walker had written them. Instead, he invoked color (vivid reds) and lighting to heighten the emotions of the scene. There is, indeed, a remarkably chaste kiss or two, but, in general, the lovemaking between the two women evolves into a scene that allows Celie to recognize her inner beauty and strength. The deflowering comes as Shug encourages Celie to move her hands away from her own face and smile – and discover her own body. Celie begins to smile for the first time in the film, and she takes her first independent steps away from the tyrannical Mr. Once the scene is completed, the theme becomes secondary throughout the rest of the film, and would have been unnoticeable to most audiences. Nonetheless, for audiences in 1985, merely broaching lesbian issues was quite remarkable compared with the mainstream film fare of the age.

These issues were all brought to the fore as Walker crossed the picket-lines at the Academy Awards celebration, and her film received no Oscars:

It wasn't that I did not know a single soul making decisions on behalf of the Academy, but my instinct was that they were seriously out-of-balance white men of a certain age, material ease, and social mobility, who would not care for what *The Color Purple* was about, or even, after a lifetime in Hollywood, know . . . For me, not getting an award for *The Color Purple*, especially after so many nominations, felt very clean. *Out of Africa* [the big winner] is reactionary and racist. It glamorizes the rape of Africa and attempts to make colonialists look like saviors . . . It patronizes black people shockingly, and its sly, gratuitous denigration of the black woman is insufferable. But it is a worldview the Academy understood, and upheld. (Walker, *The Same River Twice*, 285)

Not until 2002 would an African-American woman win a Best Actress award – Halle Berry for *Monster's Ball* (2001).

While the controversy that greeted *The Color Purple* on its premiere may seem somewhat out of proportion today, many have argued that it slowed the mainstream acceptance of African-American actors and directors in Hollywood. In a similar fashion, screen adaptations of novels by African-American writers slowed as well.

Nonetheless, *The Color Purple* has been viewed more favorably in recent years. On the occasion of the DVD release of the film in 2003, four documentaries that discussed the transformation of novel into film provided an official history of the journey. These amounts of *The Color Purple* by Laurent Bouzereau (who provided behind-the-scenes works for other Spielberg films as well) tended to obscure some of the controversy which Walker had noted in *The Same River Twice* in 1996, and, by the same token, elevate the work to "classic" status in the opinion of all those who worked on the original film. While the conflict was not wholly eliminated, the issues are painted as minor bumps in the road that were resolved in the completed film.

Modern audiences have the opportunity to judge the controversy for themselves as they view the film. What endures is the high quality of the performances. Winfrey, whom most now know as the popular talk show host, gives a tenacious performance as Sofia, which should not surprise anyone. Glover, who has evolved as an easy-going and likeable actor, is perfectly chilling as Mr. – a role unlike many of his later performances. The irrepressible Goldberg in the lead is somewhat harder to admire. An actress who is known for her joy and spirit must repress her emotions during most of the first half of the film. It is difficult to believe that she would endure the behavior of Glover's Mr. Nonetheless, when Shug Avery encourages Celie to stand up for herself, Goldberg's talents emerge, with a more believable performance in the second half of the film.

There is no question, however, that the film's merits are considerable. Spielberg's version of *The Color Purple* not only marked the first time that a controversial, politically tendentious novel written by an African-American had been brought to the screen; it is also, artistically speaking, something of a triumph, an ambitious and largely successful attempt to dramatize and screen a story originally conveyed in a form that rendered filming difficult, if not impossible.

NOTES

1. Alice Walker, *The Same River Twice – Honoring the Difficult: A Meditation on Life, Spirit, Art, and the Making of the Film The Color Purple Ten Years Later* (New York: Charles Scribner's Sons, 1996), pp. 17–18. Further quotations will be cited parenthetically in the text.
2. Glenn Collins, "New Departures for Two Major Directors," *New York Times*, December 15, 1985, Section 2, p. 1.
3. *Conversations with the Ancestors: The Color Purple from Book to Screen*, directed by Laurent Bouzereau (DVD), Warner Home Video, 2003.
4. Alice Walker, *The Color Purple* (New York: Harcourt Books, 2003), p. 276.

13   The specter of history: filming memory in *Beloved*

Marc C. Conner

Toni Morrison's (b. 1931) 1987 novel, *Beloved*, grapples with ghosts in the most literal sense: haunting figures from the past that assume bodily form and come back to the earthly realm to exact retribution. The central character, Sethe, tries to explain to her surviving daughter, Denver, the persistence of the past: "Some things go. Pass on. Some things just stay. I used to think it was my rememory. You know. Some things you forget. Other things you never do. But it's not. Places. Places are still there." This richly evocative moment suggests many of the essential elements in the novel: the illusory nature of time, the complexity of memory, and the inability of the past ever to die – certain traumatic events take on an existence independent of memory. This is the novel's definition of a ghost. As Denver responds to Sethe's account: "[T]hat must mean that nothing ever dies." And Sethe assures her that "Nothing ever does."[1]

Sethe has escaped from slavery with her four young children. But when the slave catchers track her down, she kills her two-year-old daughter rather than allow her to be taken back to the plantation. The novel begins sixteen years later, with her two sons having fled, and Sethe living with Denver in a house haunted by the ghost of the baby. An old friend from Sethe's plantation days, Paul D, arrives, and sets in motion the appearance of the ghost. Yet Morrison seeks to present not merely the ghosts that haunt individuals, but the specter of history. Through the story of one haunted family, the novel evokes the ghost of slavery that clings to Western consciousness. Its famous dedication – "Sixty Million and more" – gestures toward the innumerable victims of centuries of slavery, from Africa to the Middle Passage to the plantations of the American South. Morrison seeks to give voice to voicelessness, to express the laments of those whose cries were never heard. This is a formidable narrative task: how does one render the voices of anonymous millions in a convincing, understandable fashion? Or render events that were never witnessed, that could not be transcribed or reported? Or conjure the voices of victims, particularly women, across generations and even across worlds? And of

Figure 14. Sethe (Oprah Winfrey) leads her family's fight during Reconstruction to overcome the lingering effects of slavery in *Beloved*, a 1998
Harpo Films/Touchstone Pictures/Clinica Estetica release.

course, how does one display on the page the body, thoughts, and words
of a ghost?

Film, a craft of images, certainly offers many opportunities for expressing the implications and meanings of *Beloved*. If we view adaptation as an
effort to interpret and express literature in the terms of another form of
art – what Robert Stam describes as "the trope of adaptation as
translation"[2] – then the possibilities are vast. As Brian McFarlane argues,
such an approach emphasizes adaptation as "an example of convergence
among the arts."[3] Yet image alone may fall short of the historical, transhis-
torical, and imaginative meanings conjured by the novel. Spearheading
the project of turning Morrison's novel into a film was Oprah Winfrey,
who first contacted Morrison about writing a film treatment in 1987 after
having read the novel.[4] Winfrey's considerable cultural capital made the
project possible, from her ability to write Morrison a check for "whatever
she asks" for the movie rights to her heroic efforts to promote the film.
Yet Winfrey's cultural status may well be one of the reasons for the film's
box-office disaster, and her role in the production and overall conception
of the film and novel may have limited the film's ability to realize the
possibilities of Morrison's text.

Beloved represents a signal event in the history of African-American cinema. Never before has so much money, high-profile talent, and industry power been poured into an African-American film. Production costs exceeded $53 million, and advertising costs were estimated at $30 million.[5] The closest comparison would be the Steven Spielberg-directed *The Color Purple* (1985). But the *Beloved* project set out with a different aim from that of *The Color Purple*. As one reviewer remarked, this film "doesn't sanitize its tale of African-American loss and survival – the way Steven Spielberg's *The Color Purple* did – but delves deeply, heartbreakingly into an American tragedy."[6] The *Beloved* project aimed to present as complex, uncompromising, and challenging a portrayal of African-American history and culture as possible. Director Jonathan Demme maintained what he called a "slavish" fidelity to the novel's details, from language to dress to architecture to depictions of food.[7] In particular, the film offers the same complexity in its representations of gender and sexuality as that found in the strongest novels in the African-American tradition. Indeed, the film's treatment of black male sexuality represents a landmark in the history of African-American film.

With the opening shot the film calls attention to the complexity of the title figure, which is both singular and plural, referring to the murdered daughter of Sethe who returns from the grave, but also to the unnumbered victims of slavery whom the novel seeks to gather and heal. The film opens with a slow zoom into a crooked gravestone in a snow-filled cemetery, as gradually we see the name on the stone: "BELOVED." When Beloved appears several scenes later, she matches the description that opens the fifth chapter of the novel: "a fully dressed woman walked out of the water" (50). Dressed in black, Beloved staggers against a tree then lies there asleep for a full day and night. She next appears in front of Sethe's house, leaning against the remains of a tree, crucifixion-like, when Sethe, Paul D, and Denver return from the Carnival.

Thandie Newton, playing Beloved, emphasizes the birth imagery and newborn qualities that Morrison's novel suggests. The novel states that Beloved's "lungs [hurt] most of all," that "the weight of her eyelids" and "her neck" were more than she could bear, that she "had what sounded like asthma," and "had new skin, lineless and smooth" (50). Newton gasps and wheezes, her eyes are half-lidded, her head bobs and drops on her neck, and her movements are jerky and uncoordinated, like a toddler learning to walk. When Sethe presses her for her name, she responds in a croaking, raspy voice, spelling the letters from the tombstone: "B-e-l-o-v-e-d." Denver mothers this apparent child – feeding her, washing her soiled sheets, helping her to walk and talk. Kimberly Elise as Denver expresses superbly her joy at being able to care for somebody, thereby relieving her own overwhelming loneliness. In some shots Denver suggests an almost erotic longing for Beloved. But Beloved soon reveals that she has come for Sethe, not Denver. When Denver asks Beloved where she comes from, Beloved answers only, "[T]he dark place . . . I'm small in there." Denver asks her never to leave, and Beloved cries with chilling glee, "This is where I am!" Yet when Denver asks her not to tell Sethe who she really is, Beloved shouts, "Don't never tell me what to do!" "But I'm on your side," Denver responds, but Beloved tells her, "She the one I need." Elise's face moves from pain through jealousy to the first hint of fear over what this girl's strange love may do to her mother.

The "dark place" is one of the few suggestions in the film about Beloved's breadth of representation. The novel makes clear that Beloved has experienced, in some fashion, the dread of the slave ships on the Middle Passage from Africa to America. In her central monologue Beloved's thoughts describe this experience: "[T]he man on my face is dead," "the men without skin bring us their morning water to drink," and "those able to die are in a pile" – "they fall into the sea which is the color of the bread" (210–211). Beloved could not have experienced this herself, but she seems to have lived it through the lives of her foremothers. Thus Beloved recalls, or embodies, female ancestors – Sethe's mother, who survived the Middle Passage, and her grandmother, who did not. In the novel Beloved muses, "The woman is there with the face I want, the face that is mine," thinking of Sethe's mother, and then, "[T]he woman with my face is in the sea," recalling Sethe's mother watching her own mother commit suicide by leaping into the sea ("they do not push the woman with my face through, she goes in" [210–212]). Crucially, Beloved's insistent questions recall these forgotten memories to Sethe's consciousness. Beloved comes partly to reunite, through present recollection, the matrilineal line of four generations, stretching from America to Africa.

Morrison renders this extraordinary collapsing of both self and time through an unmediated flow of words from Beloved's mind that conjures the multiple selves and times that she embodies. One might well wonder, how could a film capture all of this? One of the solutions of Demme and his screenwriting team was not to try.[8] Aside from Beloved's one evocation of the "dark place," the only other clue to Beloved's complexity of identities comes at the film's end. Here Denver, pressed by Paul D to say whether she thinks Beloved were "sure 'nough your sister," responds, "At times. At other times . . . I think she was more." Although this signals some of the scope of Beloved's identity, it is not sufficient without the allusions to the Middle Passage and to the matrilineal line that Beloved embodies. We lose the sense that Beloved is more than the ghost of Sethe's murdered daughter, that she comes not merely to exact revenge for her own murder, but to restore the entire range of mother-daughter relations severed by slavery.

However, the film does connect Sethe to her African heritage, specifically through the actions of Beloved. In a crucial scene of recollection, Beloved asks Sethe, "Your woman she never fix up your hair?," shifting Sethe's thoughts toward her own mother. Through flashback, Sethe envisions her mother's hanging, and the woman Nan telling Sethe that although her mother was taken many times by whites and had several children by them, she kept only Sethe, because she loved only Sethe's father. Nan speaks to Sethe in the African dialect while the fires of the lynching illuminate their faces. Young Sethe watches her mother die while Nan communicates this essential information that preserves the mother-daughter bond (in the novel Nan tells this to Sethe after the lynchings, when the bodies are piled and virtually unidentifiable).[9] This recollection is the first burst of rememory in the novel brought about by Beloved, as Sethe suddenly realizes that "she was remembering something she had forgotten she knew . . . What Nan told her she had forgotten, along with the language she told it in. The same language her ma'am spoke, and which would never come back." Prompted by Beloved's questions, Sethe "was picking meaning out of a code she no longer understood" (61–62).

This scene also suggests the crucial link between Beloved and storytelling. Beloved's refrain throughout the film is "Tell me" – "Tell me 'bout your woman," "Tell me 'bout your diamonds" – generally delivered from a kneeling position, looking up into Sethe's face as if the hunger for words and food were identical. Beloved longs for *story*, for the transmission from mother to daughter of the memories that confirm the existence of the female ancestors, such as Sethe's mother's death, and the words of Nan. Although the novel provides several of Sethe's important story-memories, the film omits most of these scenes. Instead, early in the film, while Sethe and Paul D sleep, a whole series of Sweet Home memories – Sethe's husband Halle at the butter churn, Paul D's collar of iron – are projected in newsreel-style black-and-white flashes onto the wall above them. While this effect is visually shocking, it has no narrative connection to the immediate story on the screen, and so is difficult to comprehend. This sequence is one instance of the film's failure to account for the historical complexity of the novel.

The one memory that the film does treat extensively is Sethe's escape from slavery. In this lengthy sequence we see the astonishing suffering and heroism of Sethe in her passage northward, and particularly the depth of sacrifice that she undergoes for the sake of her children. The sequence begins with a quick shot of young Sethe, played with moving intensity by Lisa Gay Hamilton, running through woods, then lying on the ground. She is exhausted, very pregnant, and bloody from the whipping she received. She moans, from mingled pain and labor, and at that moment Amy Denver appears. Sethe looks at her with dread, but also a hint of relief that she is a woman. Amy is also running, and the image of two running women recalls Sethe's earlier line to Paul D: "[F]eel how it feels to be a coloredwoman roaming the roads with anything God made liable to jump on you." The Amy character, in a fascinating, thoughtful performance by Kessia Kordelle, displays a feral, twitching delight at stumbling upon Sethe. Amy's face is flushed and feverish; she turns her head in abrupt glances as if fearing what might be approaching, but also gazes at the world with childlike wonder, suggesting that she, too, has escaped into the free world for the first time.[10] She aids Sethe with a combination of female sympathy and a child's delight at having something to care for – like Denver's delight at being able to tend Beloved.

The sequence is awash with the mingled green-and-yellow of overexposed sky, as Amy and Sethe walk together through the Kentucky wilderness to the Ohio River. The visual effect of seeing these two young women, close in age (Amy seems older than her likely age of fourteen or fifteen in the novel; Sethe is nineteen at this point), one black and one white, wandering in the wild, is striking. Amy opens up Sethe's shirt and treats her wounds; she tends Sethe's feet; and, as hinted in the novel, she serves as Sethe's guide, which emerges powerfully when they come upon the Ohio River. Sethe looks in amazement at this symbol of freedom and seemingly uncrossable barrier. The camera pans to the river and focuses on a steamboat, conjuring in a brilliant image the entire literary tradition of crossing the river to freedom, linking Morrison's story with such complex archetypes as *Uncle Tom's Cabin* (1852) and *Huckleberry Finn* (1885). As soon as Sethe steps into the river, her waters break. While Sethe screams, Amy pulls the baby out of her through the mingling of river water and birth water, and into the open air in a scene of astonishing intensity. The musical accompaniment – an *a cappella* chant of female voices, which emerges at various points of significance throughout the film – commences as soon as the two young women see the Ohio River, and punctuates this powerful event of female camaraderie, as two stranger women give birth to another daughter in the very midst of danger, threat, and violence.[11]

After the birth, an exhausted Sethe lies on the riverbank and receives the newborn from Amy. Amy looks at the baby and says softly, "She ain't even gonna know who I am. You better tell her who brung her into this world." Staring at the new life she has helped to birth, Amy's face is a study in mixed emotions – wonder, envy, regret – and seems a foreboding of her doom. Kordelle's portrayal of Amy suggests that she has not long to live, that her mad flight cannot possibly bring her to a place of safety and peace – the "Boston velvet" for which she longs. This powerful and poignant sequence emphasizes the creative female bonds that do not transcend, yet are not limited by, racial difference. In the most horrific of circumstances, in which mere survival seems miraculous, new life is brought into the world through female agency and solidarity.

That the child born at the end of this sequence is Denver implies that Beloved is not the focal point of the matrilineal heritage. Yet Beloved's eruption into the world reestablishes matrilineal bonds. Her presence and her requests for story provoke Sethe's rememory, particularly the recollections of her mother and of Denver's birth. Yet Beloved's "love" is – like her mother's, perhaps – too "thick," as Paul D states. Her need for love is voracious, and ultimately she does not restore mother-daughter bonds, but rather rends them. As the film approaches its climax, Sethe is dying while Beloved, now pregnant, is an emblem of fecundity, of disordered and overly abundant life. The women of the community bring about the eventual restoration of order. Alerted by Denver to the reemergence of the baby ghost as a full-grown, threatening woman, the older women gather in front of 124, Sethe's home, and send up a chant that exorcises Beloved and empties the house, and perhaps the world, of her haunting presence.

This moment is the climax of the novel. The film creates a prefatory scene in which the women discuss what is happening to Sethe, and the leader of the group, Ella, proclaims, "[N]obody got *that* comin'. . . The children can't just up and kill the Mama!" The women come to the house in support of Sethe, and of the travails of motherhood more generally, and hence in opposition to Beloved's rupture of the mother-daughter bond. Crucially, the chant in the novel calls up a power that is literally unrepresentable – what I have described elsewhere as "a communication that transcends the coherence of language":[12] "They stopped praying and took a step back to the beginning. In the beginning there were no words. In the beginning was the sound, and they all knew what that sound sounded like . . . the voices of women searched for the right combination, the key, the code, the sound that broke the back of words" (259, 261). Again, this poses a powerful challenge for language, but an even greater challenge for film. How might one give image to that which cannot be rendered into an image? Unfortunately, the film reduces the scope of the scene to an all-too-human confrontation, and this marks its greatest failure to express the breadth of Morrison's subject.

As Denver prepares to leave for her new job, she lingers in the doorway of Beloved's room, and Elise conveys Denver's unavoidable choice between her mother and her sister. With a last look of mingled regret and loathing, Denver turns from Beloved and goes onto the porch. A moment later, the group of women gather in the road, holding Bibles, testaments, branch-woven crosses, rattles; and then Ella shouts, and the rest of the women respond with moans, screams, and cries of "Jesus." After several seconds, this modulates into a spiritual. The music enters the house, bringing Sethe and Beloved onto the porch, holding hands. The choice to employ a spiritual, in place of a supralinguistic cry, severely limits what is at work in this scene. Beloved now stands for straightforward demonic possession, and the women are the voice of communal Christianity, exorcising the devilish spirit. While this may well be part of the confrontation here, one senses that a conventional Christian response to the challenge of Beloved is inadequate.

Newton's interpretation of Beloved here is just short of disastrous. Although from the start she emphasizes Beloved's newborn qualities, she never shows Beloved's *development*. We might imagine that Beloved progresses from the temperament of a child to something closer to her eighteen years, particularly as she enters into sexuality and becomes pregnant. The performance could certainly express Beloved's gradual maturation, providing a more intriguing breadth of emotion in this crucial final scene. But when Beloved appears on the porch, Newton leers absurdly, growls, and barks at the women, and when Sethe lets go of her hand, she screams in what comes across as another temper tantrum from this pampered child.[13] When the time comes for Beloved to vanish, she literally does, in a cheap comic "poof" that hardly matches the sophisticated effects throughout the film. This climactic confrontation is radically reduced, suggesting that Demme was simply defeated by its implications.[14]

The most effective part of the scene occurs at the end, when Denver looks back to the now-empty porch with mingled relief and sorrow. Elise's performance is the revelation of the film, and she carries its narrative burden; for she is the only character who grows, who offers the narrative arc that the film as a whole lacks: "the film tries to replicate Morrison's dense, elliptical, incantatory construction. The danger it faces is stasis. Sethe doesn't travel the usual arc of change we're used to seeing in screen narratives. She is essentially standing her ground."[15] The collapsing or outright omission of many crucial scenes from the past causes much of this near stasis, limiting the action to the present, which is not where the real drama of the novel occurs (the novel's drama consists precisely in its revelations from the past).

Initially, Elise's character is overshadowed by Newton's attention-grabbing portrayal of Beloved, and also by the central narrative of Sethe

and Paul D. But when Paul D is driven from the increasingly claustropho-
bic house, Denver reaches outside of the house into the larger world. To
do this, she must openly oppose Beloved, who wants only to live within
a cocoon-like world with Sethe. The moment of rupture comes with the
changing of the seasons, as winter moves into spring. The camera shifts
from ice thawing, to ladybugs hatching, to tree blossoms, then to the outside of the house, now in ruins, the front door open, the garden untended.
As the camera enters the house, we hear Beloved's cry for "Mama." Sethe
awakens, looks for food, and upon finding one egg and a handful of flour
looks up with an expression of utter helplessness – the first time we have
seen such a look on this indomitable woman's face. We then shift to Denver, getting out of her bed and walking slowly to Beloved's room. Beloved
is wrapped in a multicolored quilt, and Denver eyes her and states, in a
low, even tone, "You leave that quilt alone. That's Grandma's quilt."
Beloved rips the quilt into two pieces, horrifying Denver, but by declar-
ing her hostility even to Baby Suggs, the spiritual mother of the entire
novel, Beloved shows her ultimate hostility to mother-daughter bonds.
Denver realizes that this shredding is precisely what Beloved portends for
Sethe.

   Over the next several scenes, Denver emerges as the heir to the matrilineal line, confirmed by her sudden vision of Baby Suggs. "You mean I
never told you 'bout your Daddy?," Baby Suggs asks. "Didn't I tell you?,"
she continues, and then tells Denver pieces of her past. This repeats the
effort of the mother figures to "tell" the daughters, to convey the crucial
skills and links necessary to survive. Baby Suggs comes to aid Denver. "Is
that why you scared to go down them steps and out the yard by yourself?"
she asks. "You got to go out yonder, *by yourself.* Go on out the yard – *go
on!*" Denver then leaves the house, walks out of the yard, and makes her
way into the community. When the women realize that Denver and her
family are starving, they respond with pity and female solidarity. They
leave a basket of food for Denver, and when she opens it, one of Demme's
trademark butterflies rises, suggesting the metamorphosis occurring. For
the community bears some of the guilt for Sethe's crime – a point that
is made powerfully in the novel (152, 177), but left out of the film. In
a crucial scene Denver goes to the Bodwin home to seek work. Janey,
their African-American housekeeper, opens the door and breaks into a
smile, exclaiming, "You Baby Suggs's kin!" The matrilineal descent that
Denver now claims as her own gains her entry into the larger female community. Now the women will gather and exorcise Beloved, for now the
ghost threatens one of their own – threatens them.

   The focus on Denver follows a major concern of Morrison's late work:
the figure of the young girl who embodies the hope and promise of the

generations to come. But *Beloved* also offers a new element in Morrison's fiction that Demme's film elaborates with brilliance: the revision of black male sexuality. In the figure of Paul D, Morrison depicts a combination of tenderness and heroism, grace and valor, healing and resistance that the film takes up, in what may well be its most radical contribution to the African-American film tradition.

Demme provides an early scene that is only referred to in the novel: the flight of Sethe's two sons from the house. This vision of the male figures leaving the home is both one of the dominant tropes of the African-American tradition (one thinks of the absent or fleeing fathers in Frederick Douglass's *Narrative of the Life of Frederick Douglass* (1845), Richard Wright's *Native Son* (1940), and James Baldwin's *Go Tell It on the Mountain* (1953), to name only a few prominent examples) and also one of the most challenging cultural crises in contemporary American culture.[16] But this stereotype is countered with the first appearance of Paul D walking down the road, *toward the house*, bringing the sense of the past that Sethe has lost. (In the novel he does not arrive walking – Sethe finds him sitting on her porch – but Demme emphasizes his physical act of returning.) His arrival prompts her to tell some of the story of her outrage – the taking of her milk, the whipping, and her pain about Halle's failure to meet her. When Paul D tells her the truth of Halle's madness and likely death, he asserts the limits that black manhood can endure: "A man ain't a goddam ax. Things get to him. Things he can't chop down because they're inside!" Although Paul D is a figure of remarkable endurance, the most admirable qualities he proffers are sympathy and fidelity. Demme portrays him as the black man who returns and wants to restore the home and the family: "Me and you, Sethe," Paul D says early in the film, "we could make a life!" Paul D wrestles with the ghost and casts it out of the house for a time, but he is not adequate to defeat Beloved when she reappears as flesh – the women must accomplish this final banishment. Yet Paul D plays an intimate part in this action.

When Beloved enters into her erotic stage, she chooses Paul D as the agent of her sexual initiation. As occurs frequently in Demme's shots, this scene opens without a human character in view. The camera moves along moon-drenched ground to the cold house where Paul D has been "moved" by Beloved's conjuring. The light and shadows ripple, like water moving in the moonlight, suggesting some sense of the Middle Passage trauma. Beloved's taking of Paul D is figured explicitly as a rape: he resists her overtures and tries to turn away from her, and when she forces herself upon him he cries out repeatedly, "No! No!" The scene has no sense of eroticism but is awash with violence and dread, as emphasized by the same pulsing red light that affronts Paul D when he first enters 124.

Again the light ripples, reminding us of the waters from which Beloved emerges. The music to this scene is also crucial: not the spiritual chants of the choric female voices that always accompany the scenes of healing and regeneration, but rather a harsh, percussive African drumming, particularly the striking of sticks, reminding the viewer of the African origins of Beloved's need for vengeance.

Paul D's portrayal as sexual victim contrasts starkly with his sexuality in the lovemaking scenes with Sethe. In these scenes he is gentle, his touch soft; he handles Sethe's breasts with sympathy, sorrow, and a wish to ease her burden. There is also at times a playfulness to their sexuality, a sense of youth being restored. All of this signals a marked contrast to the dominant images of American cinema, where, as Jacquie Jones argues, the black man's sexuality functions as "an indictment of his feral nature, spiritual deficiency and lack of allegiance to the group, the society, by failing to create or maintain ties with other individuals." The result suggests "the psychic inferiority of the Black male. Further, by removing the Black male's capacity for intimacy in this society, the audience is never able to conceive of the Black male character as completely human." Restricted from portrayals of full human intimacy, the films leave only "models of violence and other forms of antisocial behaviors" for the black male.[17] Demme and Glover present the black male as a figure of intimacy, fidelity, tenderness, and devotion. This stands as a signal achievement in the film.[18]

At the novel's end Paul D again returns to Sethe and aids her in realizing her best thing, her own self. Here his full character emerges as a figure of grace. When Sethe looks up from her sickbed, she sees "the thing in him, the blessedness, that has made him the kind of man who can walk in a house and make the women cry. Because with him, in his presence, they could" (272). Paul D thinks of Sixo's words of love about the Thirty-Mile Woman: "She is a friend of my mind. She gather me, man. The pieces I am, she gather them and give them back to me in all the right order. It's good, you know, when you got a woman who is a friend of your mind" (272–273). This first conclusion of the novel suggests the reconciliation between Sethe and Paul D, the successful maturation of Denver, and a model for a mature sexuality between man and woman that is humanity's best effort to ensure continuity, survival, even love.

Yet the corresponding scene in the film falls disappointingly short of this sense. Glover plays Paul D in a lighthearted, joking manner. There is no effort by Demme to situate Paul D's emotions in the context of his years of wandering, no sense that here he sees his last, best chance to establish a place of home. Winfrey's muted, groaning "Me?" at the end, more whimper than recognition, is essentially uncertain, suggesting neither affirmation nor negation. The lack of chemistry between the two principals here is particularly apparent, though we see it also in their intimacy scenes, especially with Winfrey, who looks indulgently bored in these shots. Winfrey's overall performance in the film is certainly competent and credible. Morrison herself praised Winfrey's acting, saying, "[A]s soon as I saw her, I smiled to myself, because I did not think of the brand name. She inhabited the role."[19] But overall Winfrey does not capture the full range of Sethe's character, as is most evident in the challenging scenes of intimacy, passion, and also doubt. As one reviewer states, "[T]here's a dimension missing here – the crack in Sethe's iron resolve, an invading terror of self-loathing – that a more experienced professional would have conveyed."[20] Ultimately, Winfrey's conception of the novel seems reductive. In speaking of the film, she states, "[W]hat I'm trying to tell people every day is to open the door and let the past in. You won't be swallowed by the past, you will be healed by the light that pours in."[21] Such advice, while perhaps apt for Winfrey's talk show, seems rather absurd in the face of Sethe's trauma. One wonders how Sethe would respond to the suggestion just to "open the door and let the past in." As a result, the closing scene greatly diminishes Paul D's character and what he offers in the film, and misses an opportunity to develop the radical revision of black masculinity that Glover's performance has suggested.

The final scene is left, however, to Beah Richards and her brilliant conception of Baby Suggs. Baby Suggs gives one sermon about one-third into the novel, but Demme splits this into two sequences, one at the midpoint of the film, and one at the conclusion. Cinematographer Tak Fujimoto employs the same green-and-yellow, overexposed sky technique that he uses in the Amy Denver-Young Sethe scene, thereby unifying the events in guiding Sethe toward healing. This visual effect lends a surreal, even timeless quality, as if the sermons are still going on somewhere under the trees. Certainly, that is how Demme presents the first sermon, when Sethe, Beloved, and Denver walk into the forest and suddenly Baby Suggs appears on the praying rock in the clearing. Her vivid dress, a blend of gold and orange, stands out against the subdued colors that dominate the house scenes. She cries out, "Let the children come," lines that, in the midst of this film about the devastation visited upon children, resonate as a spoken gesture of grace and healing. The children crowd about her, and she tells them, "Let the mothers hear you laugh," and the children laugh boisterously, joyfully. Then she calls out – as the chorus of female voices begins – "Let the grown men come," and tells them, "Let your wives and your children see you dance." Then slowly, building up speed and intensity, the men begin a rhythmic, athletic, graceful circular dance, each man dancing a different step, but all in concert as they move around the central figure of Baby Suggs. Finally, she calls to the women, "Women, I want you to weep. Just weep. For the livin', for the dead." In the midst of this circle of laughter, dancing, and weeping, she looks at Sethe, and raises her hand as if to wave. The camera then returns to Sethe, who smiles slightly, then returns to the now-empty clearing. The scene captures the rememory process that Sethe had described earlier: this past sermon recurs *now*, made momentarily present through Sethe's recollection.

Demme concludes this sermon at the film's very end. After Sethe's final groan of "Me?," her face dissolves into the face of Baby Suggs, back at the clearing. As if the sermon has not paused, Baby Suggs continues in midsentence: ". . . and the beat, beat of your heart!" The female singers grow louder, as she exhorts the congregation to love their hearts even more than their lungs, the womb, even the private parts – these are all signs and sources of life, but the heart, she repeats, "is the prize." As the camera circles her face – putting the viewer into the positions of the congregation – Baby Suggs laughs, cries, kisses the children, touches the men and women, and finally shouts, "Hallelujah!" This is the final word of the film, as the scene then shifts to a high shot of the house – now repaired, the garden cleared, all ghosts gone – and the one word, "Beloved," appears.

In the novel, however, after Sethe's reunion with Paul D, Morrison proffers a second ending that returns to Beloved and suggests her destruction: "In the place where long grass opens, the girl who waited to be loved and cry shame erupts into her separate parts, to make it easy for the chewing laughter to swallow her all away" (274). To end with Baby Suggs, instead of with the vanishing figure of Beloved, is a bold interpretive choice: the film closes with the central female ancestor shouting "Hallelujah" in the midst of a communal gathering emphasizing rememory over the "disremembered" of the novel. This choice gives this often bleak film an uplifting, affirming voice at the end that suggests a hopeful survival for the characters involved. This mood is certainly powerful in the novel, which many critics have seen as offering a positive hope at the end, but a devastating grimness persists as well, and the film may lose some of that. Yet the film's triumph consists in its emphasis on matrilineal heritage. Thus to close with the face and voice of Baby Suggs confirms its central teaching: if survival and restoration are possible, they will be found in the ancient properties and remarkable endurance of wise women.

NOTES

1. Toni Morrison, *Beloved* (New York: Alfred A. Knopf, 1987), pp. 35–36. Further quotations will be cited parenthetically in the text.
2. Robert Stam, "Beyond Fidelity: The Dialogics of Adaptation," in James Naremore, ed., *Film Adaptation* (New Brunswick, NJ: Rutgers University Press, 2000), p. 62.
3. Brian McFarlane, *Novel to Film: An Introduction to the Theory of Adaptation* (Oxford: Clarendon Press, 1996), p. 10.
4. Oprah Winfrey, *Journey to Beloved* (New York: Hyperion, 1998), pp. 17–18.
5. Bernard Weinraub, "'Beloved' Tests Racial Themes at Box Office," *New York Times*, late edition, October 13, 1998, p. E1.
6. Edward Guthmann, "Ghosts of Slavery," *San Francisco Chronicle*, final edition, October 16, 1998, p. C1. For critiques of Spielberg's project as revising Walker's more radical portrayal of African-American female identity, see Jacqueline Bobo, "Reading Through the Text: The Black Woman as Audience," in, Manthia Diawara, ed., *Black American Cinema* (New York: Routledge, 1993), pp. 273–275, and Bobo, "Sifting Through the Controversy: Reading *The Color Purple*," *Callaloo: A Journal of Afro-American and African Arts and Letters* 12:2 (Spring 1989), pp. 332–342. See also Allen Woll's essay in this volume.
7. Richard Corliss, "Bewitching 'Beloved,'" *Time*, October 5, 1998, p. 76.
8. The screenwriting process began with Akosu Busia, who, according to Demme, "tried to put too much of the book in" (Jeff Strickler, "Bewitched, Bothered, and 'Beloved,'" *Minneapolis Star Tribune*, October 11, 1998, p. 1F). Demme then enlisted Richard LaGravenese (screenwriter for *The Bridges of Madison County* [1995]) and Adam Brooks (*French Kiss* [1995]). On the whole, the screenplay adds little to the film, and one might suspect that these backgrounds in sentimental and romantic comedy were not quite appropriate for adapting *Beloved*. Morrison refused Winfrey's invitation to contribute to the screenplay.
9. In the film Sethe's mother is wearing a mouthguard at her hanging, a brilliant touch that implies she has used her teeth to attack her captors. This addition also serves as a visual echo of Beloved's claim (in the novel) that she would "bite the circle around her neck bite it away" (p. 211) in her recollection of the Middle Passage. This detail reinforces the identification between Beloved and Sethe's mother.
10. The novel implies that Amy has fled some sort of indentured service or even borderline slavery (p. 33).
11. The musical score by Rachel Portmann, featuring work from Oumou Sangarre, Dianne McIntyre, and research by Bernice Johnson Reagon, as well as two songs written by Morrison herself, is one of the triumphs of the film.
12. Marc C. Conner, "From the Sublime to the Beautiful: The Aesthetic Progression of Toni Morrison," in Marc C. Conner, ed., *The Aesthetics of Toni Morrison: Speaking the Unspeakable* (Jackson: University Press of Mississippi, 2000), p. 69.
13. Newton's performance drew near-universal criticism from reviewers, though some sympathized with the difficulty of playing a metaphor. One critic

commented, "Newton is forced to play a literary/poetic conceit rather than a person." Calling it "a fearless performance," he concludes that "it defeats her, but it's a fascinating struggle to watch" (Steve Murray, "Stars Shine, but 'Beloved' Fails to Put Poetry in Motion," *Atlanta Journal and Constitution,* October 16, 1998, p. 1P).

14. The cameo appearance of Jason Robards as Mr. Bowdin does not help. Such a famous persona on the screen snatches the viewer's attention, and the camera lingers on Bowdin's reaction to Beloved, at the cost of focusing on the women, Sethe, and especially Denver. This sudden shift from African-American female labor to a white, male face is jarring in every way.

15. Jay Carr, "'Beloved' Has Flaws," *Boston Globe,* city edition, October 16, 1998, p. C1.

16. Charles Johnson and John McCluskey, Jr. note that "fifty-seven percent of black children live with only one parent" and that "among black women, 70.3 percent are unmarried when their first child is born, and find themselves raising their children in fatherless homes" (Johnson and McCluskey, eds., *Black Men Speaking* [Bloomington: Indiana University Press, 1997], p. xi).

17. Jacquie Jones, "The Construction of Black Sexuality," in Diawara, ed., *Black American Cinema,* p. 250.

18. This accords with Morrison's novel, and indeed with most of her portrayals of black men. Although Morrison is often included in the "Alice Walker Criticism" – "those black women writers who have chosen Black men as a target" (Mel Watkins, "Sexism, Racism and Black Women Writers," *New York Times Book Review,* June 15, 1986, p. 36) – Morrison's men are often spectacularly admirable: Ajax, Son, Guitar, Paul D, and Joe Trace are rendered with a sympathy and admiration that hardly fits what Spike Lee describes, referring to Hollywood's treatment of African-American characters in general, as black men as "one-dimensional animals" (Bobo, "Sifting Through," p. 337).

19. Corliss, "Bewitching 'Beloved,'" p. 76.

20. Guthmann, "Ghosts of Slavery."

21. Joanna Connors, "Oprah's 'Beloved,'" *Cleveland Plain Dealer,* October 11, 1998, p. 11.

14 Filming the spiritual landscape of James Jones's *The Thin Red Line*

R. Barton Palmer

One of their number

On January 1, 1943, as a member of F Company, 27th Infantry Regiment of the 25th Infantry Division, Army private James Jones (1921–1977) landed on the island of Guadalcanal, which had been successfully invaded and partially occupied by the 1st Marine Division some months before. The Marines had suffered nearly 2,400 casualties in the bitter fight to take this outpost in the Solomons, from which the Japanese controlled the sea-lanes into northern Australia. The remaining Marine effectives were almost all suffering from malaria and other tropical diseases when they were withdrawn from a jungle battlefield that offered an obstacle almost as hostile to American arms as the enemy. The task facing the 25th (along with the Americal Division and units of the 2nd Marines) was to secure the rest of the island, whose airbase could then be used to project American power further into the ring of island fortresses that marked the forward advance of the Japanese offensive in the South Pacific.

The American command did not know at the time that the Japanese, hard pressed on land and in the surrounding waters, had determined to evacuate the majority of their troops, leaving behind only selected units, composed of men suffering desperately from disease and lack of food. These would fight a bitter rearguard action to the death in order to shield their retreating comrades. Japanese resistance was nowhere stronger than on the so-called Galloping Horse, a 900-foot hill the reduction of whose hidden machine-gun and mortar emplacements was the task assigned to the 27th on January 10. A massive artillery barrage preceded the frontal assault, which was slowed by both the difficulty in reducing well-sited enemy positions and a shortage of water. Perhaps the signal event of the attack occurred when a machine-gun nest that had pinned down the advance was daringly silenced by five volunteers, whose officer, Captain Charles W. Davis, eventually received the Congressional Medal of Honor for his bravery and initiative.

Figure 15. Witt (Jim Caviezel) encounters the childlike innocence of Melanesian culture in Terrence Malick's unusual war film, *The Thin Red Line*, a 1998 Fox 2000 release.

At one point during the day's action, Jones was relieving himself when he suddenly found himself facing a lone Japanese soldier, desperately ill and perhaps crazed, who tried to run him through with a bayonet. Jones killed the man with his bare hands and experienced such a profound revulsion that he swore never to take another life. That resolution was never really tested. On January 12 Jones was hit in the face and head by mortar fragments. Although he recovered from this disabling wound in an area hospital, by the time he rejoined his company the campaign for the island had finished. A recurrent ankle injury then led to his being shipped back to America for treatment. After his return, Jones went absent several times and began to suffer from what would now be termed posttraumatic stress disorder. As punishment, the Army intended to assign him to a "hard-case" outfit and ship him back overseas, but, after some negotiation about his mental problems, Jones received an honorable medical discharge in 1944, a year before the Japanese surrender.

In *The Thin Red Line* (1962), written almost two decades later, Jones would offer a thinly fictionalized version of the fighting on Guadalcanal in which he participated. The attack on the Galloping Horse (renamed the Dancing Elephant) constitutes the centerpiece of the novel's plot.

The author's other experiences, including the painful facial wound, are all included in one form or another, though, tellingly, there is no main character modeled on the author. Like the other two volumes of his World War II trilogy, *From Here to Eternity* (1951) and *Whistle* (which appeared posthumously in 1978), *The Thin Red Line* is both deeply autobiographical and historically accurate, an unforgettable and vivid retelling of the battle that, in the hackneyed phrase, "turned the tide of the war" in the Pacific.

Several distinguished novelistic or journalistic accounts of the campaign were published at the time or later, including William Manchester's *Goodbye, Darkness: A Memoir of the Pacific War* (1980), Richard Tregaskis's *Guadalcanal Diary* (1943), and John Hersey's *Into the Valley: A Skirmish of the Marines* (1943). Norman Mailer's much-celebrated *The Naked and the Dead* (1948), though it draws on the later campaign in the Philippines in which the author served, covers some of the same thematic ground with a similarly unflinching realism. *The Thin Red Line*, however, is the only one of these fictional recreations that, in the words of the critic Peter G. Jones, manages both to stage "an imaginative sequence of combat actions . . . with great competence" and to offer the reader a deep sense of "psychological veracity."[1] With a carefully developed serial focus on a number of characters, who are viewed by the extradiegetic narrator from the inside, Jones is able to present "startlingly various insights into the possibilities of individual motivation." On one level, these portraits possess a truth to life whose great power even Mailer was forced, albeit somewhat grudgingly, to acknowledge. Jones's novel, he declared, paints "so broad and true a picture of combat that it could be used as a textbook at the Infantry School."[2]

With its double emphasis on the external world of group action, where force and chance reduce men to little more than disposable instruments, as well as on the solitary, unique consciousness, which is never reducible to general rules or shared experiences, Jones's novel is an impressive formal achievement. As Mailer and others have recognized, it is comparable in the American tradition only to Stephen Crane's *The Red Badge of Courage* (1895), which achieves a similarly layered effect through an ironic juxtaposition of the hero's romantic ideas of glory and courage with the brutally impersonal facts of modern industrialized warfare. For Peter G. Jones, surveying the war fiction produced since Crane, *The Thin Red Line*'s signal virtue is its realism, its amazing fidelity to lived inner and outer experience: "As a fictional account of combat it is unsurpassed."[3]

Yet there are strong indications that it was not Jones's intention to produce a version of the campaign that would simply memorialize it in appropriate detail as a *rite de passage* for his generation. In accord with the author's limited involvement in a battle that lasted for months on sea and land, the novel provides little in the way of an overview. The strategic importance of the struggle for control over Guadalcanal merits only brief and indirect mention; a reader ignorant of the larger issues involved in the Pacific war would learn nothing on this subject from the book. *The Thin Red Line*, to put this another way, is hardly objective or, perhaps better, "historical" in the global sense that the accounts of Manchester and Tregaskis certainly strive to be. These authors take pains to connect individual to national experience and thereby firmly fix the collective meaning of what has been suffered and accomplished. Jones may be, however, the better "realist" in these matters. He adopts throughout the viewpoints of ordinary soldiers, who are generally kept in the dark about strategic and even tactical considerations; they might well take little interest in them even were they better informed, or so a fellow veteran of the war suggests.[4] Furthermore, the novelist does not pretend to be a spokesman, even for those who shared much the same experiences.

At the end of *The Thin Red Line*, the noncharacter narrator (a figure who "was there" but in no particularized diegetic guise) predicts his own summoning into being in terms that suggest that the resulting account – that is, the book the reader is now holding – may indeed lack any sense of authenticity, even for those who were there on the island: "One day one of their number would write a book about all this, but none of them would believe it, because none of them would remember it that way."[5] Throughout the story, the narrator disposes of a selective omniscience, entering the minds of different characters and voicing their thoughts and feelings with perfect knowledge. But in concluding, he speaks to the limited access to the truth that the implied author enjoyed. Jones's understanding of "what happened" on Guadalcanal is thus as irreducibly personal as those of his fellows, even though in the fiction he pretends to speak authoritatively for them.

Yet the paradoxicality of this concluding proviso, it seems, reflects not only the necessarily subjective nature of individual experience. The novel also defies the usual ways in which the experience of war is "universalized." Jones has his characters respond in unexpected ways, including sexual arousal, to the sanctioned killing that is war. Furthermore, Jones otherwise partially eschews the verifiability and facticity of ordinary historical novels, such as *War and Peace* (1865–69) or *Gone With the Wind* (1936), where the background and setting are not fictionalized, even though the characters at the center of the plot, though eminently plausible as period types, are purely imaginary. In the "Special Note" that prefaces the novel, Jones goes so far as to deny the truth to life of the events he intends to present, even though, as I have outlined, these are fairly accurate accounts of what Jones and other members of "F" Company of the 27th suffered and accomplished:

> Anyone who has studied or served in the Guadalcanal campaign will immediately recognize that no such terrain as that described here exists on the island. "The Dancing Elephant," "The Giant Boiled Shrimp," the hills around "Boola Boola Village," as well as the village itself, are figments of fictional imagination, and so are the battles herein described as taking place on this terrain . . . It might have been possible to create a whole, entirely fictional island for the setting of this book. (ix)

By "entirely fictional," Jones apparently means that the island battle, though not specifically identified as that for Guadalcanal, could have been developed more abstractly, as an imagined, yet typically "true," campaign of the Pacific war, more or less the course that Mailer pursued in *The Naked and the Dead*. But Jones, though he had Mailer's example before him, chose not to do so because, as he affirms, "what Guadalcanal stood for to Americans in 1942–1943 was a very special thing." So "to have used a completely made up island would have been to lose all the special qualities which the name Guadalcanal evoked for my generation" (ix).

Jones intends, in other words, for *The Thin Red Line* both to reference the battle that offered America its first land victory in the war against the Japanese and to refuse to be bound by the historical details of the campaign. Even though he is not forthcoming about the book's basis in fact, Jones wants the reader to believe that he has "taken the liberty of distorting" what actually happened and has laid down "smack in the middle of [the island] a whole slab of nonexistent territory" (ix). *The Thin Red Line* thus becomes a multifaceted drama unfolding on that partially abstracted piece of ground (the nonexistent made part of the existent) that the novel creates (coopts?) for its setting. And that ground is primarily psychological in the sense that the narrative deals with a collectively individual journey of self-discovery that plays out over an expanse of culturally significant, and yet abstracted, space.

This journey does not lack for the heroic (which is more analyzed than glorified). But it is defined as well by mental destinations of a different order, including depravity and madness. Jones would find that the battle turned him toward something like pacifism, even as it filled him with a sense of thrill that vacillated between disgust and enthusiasm. For him, as for Mailer, however, the war never entirely lost its Kiplingesque glamor (in fact, a line from Kipling's *Tommy* [1890], "the thin red line of 'eroes," furnishes him with the book's title). "O, shades of splendid endeavor" was how later, in his nostalgic homage to the American GI, Jones would choose to describe the memory of his few weeks on the island.[6] There he had experienced a kind of combat different from the later struggles in the Pacific, operations that were often conducted on a mammoth scale. Guadalcanal was a battle, he remembered, "fought at an earlier period of the war, when the numbers of men and materiel engaged were smaller, less trained and less organized." So "there was an air of adventure and sense of individual exploit about it . . . it was still pretty primitive, Guadalcanal" (39). It was a place, in other words, where the heroic was still possible and the lone rifleman could still make a difference.

The Hollywood Renaissance *redivivus?*

As had been the case with his two previous bestsellers, *From Here to Eternity* (1951) and *Some Came Running* (1958), the screen rights to Jones's novel were sold soon after publication in 1962 to Hollywood. Fred Zinnemann's screen version of *From Here to Eternity* (1953) turned out to be one of the most acclaimed films of the decade. This story of prewar Army life in Hawaii won the Academy Award for Best Picture, making its producers a great deal of money in the process. Hollywood did not have the same luck with its second Jones property, which deals with the experience of veterans returning to a small Midwestern city. *Some Came Running* (Vincente Minnelli, 1958), despite being given the prestige picture treatment, was a substantial disappointment. Strong performances by Frank Sinatra, Dean Martin, and Shirley MacLaine impressed audiences more than the somewhat puerile melodrama of the plot, from which Jones's extensive philosophical framework had been largely excised.

By the early 1960s, the classic period of the war film genre was fast coming to an end, and the bidding was not strong for Jones's fictional version of the fight for Guadalcanal. None of the big studios showed much interest. After being sold to the independent producer Philip Yordan for a fraction of what the other two novels had received, *The Thin Red Line* was brought to the screen with a very limited budget by the director Andrew Marton, who was nearing the end of a lengthy but undistinguished Hollywood career, mostly as a second unit director (*55 Days at Peking* [1963], *The Longest Day* [1962]). In the postwar era Marton showed his aptitude for military subjects with an occasional "B" picture, most notably *Prisoner of War* (1954), in which Ronald Reagan starred as one of a group of Americans held by the North Koreans and Red Chinese. But he was best known in the business as the director of the very successful 1950s television series *Sea Hunt*, which offered exciting underwater action, at whose staging Marton proved to be quite skilled. The script for *The Thin*

Red Line was written by Bernard Gordon, another minor industry player who spent his career, which was compromised by a blacklisting for Communist sympathies, mostly on "B" pictures. Yordan insisted on adding a lengthy dream sequence, only tangentially related to the plot, whose main purpose seemed to be creating a role for the producer's wife, Merlyn.

With only two actors of minor note (Keir Dullea and Jack Warden) at their disposal, Yordan and Marton turned out a black-and-white programmer solidly in the mold of the war film genre. Released in 1964, the film did minimal business and received mixed, but mostly negative, reviews because of what were thought to be significant flaws in the script. Jones was informed of the problems encountered during production with the screenplay. The original screenwriter, Jon Manchip Whit, a novelist and World War II veteran himself, had quit the project and asked for his name to be withdrawn from the credits because of Yordan's interference. But Jones had lost interest in Hollywood after the scorn heaped by many reviewers upon Minnelli's *Some Came Running*. Satisfied with the rights money, the novelist made no effort to intervene. The film thus came and went without much notice being taken of it. It certainly did nothing to enhance Jones's literary standing or that of his novel.

When Terrence Malick's adaptation of *The Thin Red Line* appeared in 1999, it betrayed no connection to its little-known antecedent, of which it was in no meaningful sense a remake. No doubt, in the thirty-five years that separated the two films, Jones's reputation, which was at its nadir in the early 1960s, had substantially improved. In the view of the critic George Garrett, in the decade following his death in 1977, Jones had "earned for himself an enduring place in the history of American literature, chiefly as the author of the trilogy of war novels."[7] Yet the release of Malick's film was an event that took place within American film, rather than literary, culture. Reviewers often made no more than passing reference to the writer who had penned the original novel. That one of the most acclaimed books about the war that defined American history in the twentieth century had been brought again to the screen, this time as a major production, went virtually unnoticed.

Most film versions of prestige literary sources, of course, are "made known" as such. As the film theorist Dudley Andrew observes, "[E]very representational film adapts a prior conception" (that is, some script or written source). The "adapted film," however, is a special case because the overt connection between the two versions, written and cinematic, "delimits representation by insisting on the cultural model of the text." A film adaptation is thus defined in some important sense by "its appropriation of meaning from a prior text."[8] Yet this process can be occulted, with the result that the film is then understood as "originary." Whether an adaptation is received as such depends not just on the marketing decision to identity its recycling of a valued literary property. Other institutional and cultural factors are often involved, whose effect can be to disable or sidetrack such a reading.

Perhaps the most important of these is the industrial context that obtains at the time of release. Malick's film began its run several months after the exhibition of one of the most acclaimed films ever to take World War II as its subject: Steven Spielberg's *Saving Private Ryan* (1998). It was not surprising, as we shall see, that the decade witnessed a revival of screen treatments of the war. Yet it was certainly an accident of institutional history that Spielberg's film was released just before Malick's, whose reception it significantly affected. A largely unfavorable comparison with *Saving Private Ryan* overshadowed the amazement and sense of pleasure that many film enthusiasts and Hollywood insiders felt at the appearance of a new work of an unrepentant *auteur* from the cinematic past. Much celebrated for two important independent productions of the notorious 1970s, *Badlands* (1973) and *Days of Heaven* (1978), Malick had finally broken two decades of silence and inactivity. Perhaps this withdrawal from a career in which he was fast becoming an important figure was Malick's comment on the profound turn to political and artistic conservatism made during the Reagan era by the American film industry and the culture that supported it.

In the late 1990s, however, the director reengaged with filmmaking, involving himself with a project that seemed to promise popular appeal even as it offered him the chance to indulge his particular cinematic obsessions. His earlier films had shown him to be a practitioner of what John Orr terms "the American cinema of poetry," which is always "inseparable from the mythologies of the American dream" even as it remains resolutely "material" because of its double investment in both landscape and history.[9] Its story unfolding in a part of the world that Americans at the time thought a tropical Eden, fabled for its beautiful weather and exotic flora and fauna, Jones's novel deals with a central event in national history, making it suitable for a poetic treatment of this kind. World War II also offered the director an ideal backdrop for examining the moral themes central to his portrayal of characters who find themselves estranged by violence from the natural spaces they occupy, thereby recapitulating a central Western myth, the expulsion from paradise.

Malick's new project seemed to many a signal that a new age of commercially successful independent filmmaking might be in the offing. He might help to fulfill the long-abandoned promise of the hallowed tradition that had become known to scholars as the "Hollywood Renaissance." After all, another director-star of that era was also soon to emerge from a long artistic hibernation. Stanley Kubrick's *Eyes Wide Shut* (released later in 1999) similarly raised high hopes for a more general return of the American cinema to intellectual engagement, historical consciousness, and formal experimentation. Both films, however, met with not only a mixed critical response, but also discouraging results at the box office. This failure of a revivified American art film movement to take root in late 1990s film culture was clearly anticipated by the critical and popular success achieved by *Saving Private Ryan*, which was a self-conscious throwback to both the studio era and its celebration of World War II as the "Good War."

The cultural moment was certainly right to revisit the war and the kind of screen fiction that had once celebrated both American feats of arms and also the unquestioned rightness of the attempt to "make the world safe for democracy." A decades-long disposition to forget the enormity of national (and global) suffering, sacrifice, and effort was replaced during the 1990s by a culture of remembrance. The most obvious evidence of this altered atmosphere was to be seen in the belated plans to install a Washington, DC memorial to World War II veterans and in a flurry of museum building. The United States Holocaust Memorial Museum in Washington, DC was dedicated with much fanfare in 1993 (to be soon followed by similar projects around the country), while the National D-Day Museum in New Orleans was founded in 1991 by the historian Stephen F. Ambrose, who was then engaged in compiling several volumes on the war in Europe that proved to be runaway bestsellers.

The film industry was not far behind. Spielberg's *Schindler's List* (1993) had discovered an event within the larger, barely imaginable horror of the Holocaust to glorify and memorialize, pleasing critics and audiences alike. *Saving Private Ryan* was also intended as a celluloid monument, this time to the achievements of what, in an equally popular oral history published that same year, the journalist Tom Brokaw jingoistically christened "the greatest generation any society has ever produced."[10] Immensely successful with both domestic and foreign audiences, the film furthered the reverential recovery of the neglected past that had reached its peak in 1995 with the fiftieth anniversary ceremonies of the ending of World War II, held at numerous hallowed sites of sacrifice and triumph, including, and especially, the very same military cemetery overlooking the Normandy landing beaches whose moving depiction opens and closes the present frame of the story told in *Saving Private Ryan*.[11]

In Spielberg's fiction this contemporary moment involves both a physical return (the aged veteran visiting the battlefield on which he fought) and the man's extended reminiscence, in which the truth of his war is revealed to the viewer, if not to his accompanying and mostly uncomprehending family. This authenticating rhetorical move marks the film as substantially different from the entertainment fantasies that had become the production staple of Hollywood in the late 1990s. As the marketing campaign emphasized, Spielberg's film was based not on a literary property, but on a script specially prepared for the project that fictionalized the "true story" of a soldier from the 101st Airborne Division who, having parachuted into Normandy, was brought back from the line and returned home to his mother after his three brothers were killed in combat.

Like the HBO series *Band of Brothers* that Spielberg and Tom Hanks would subsequently collaborate on, *Saving Private Ryan* was self-consciously historical, with meticulously orchestrated visual and oral effects meant to evoke the actual, sensorially overwhelming experience of modern warfare, which had never before been presented so realistically.[12] An immense and much ballyhooed effort was also made to recreate the realia of the period. Military history buffs could find little in the film, from German weapons (including an impressive variety of armored vehicles) to American unit badges, that was not absolutely authentic. And yet *Saving Private Ryan* is as nostalgic as it is historical, balancing its investment in making the viewer feel the horror and confusion of modern combat with a clear demonstration *in parvo* of the German enemy's formidable perfidiousness.

Here is none of the "epic equity" found in many post-1945 screen versions of the European war, such as Darryl F. Zanuck's *The Longest Day* (1962), in which a number of "good" Germans appear. Interested, as always, in the genres of the studio period, Spielberg intended to revive the classic Hollywood World War II combat genre; the film was to recreate not only history, but also the representational form that, for three decades, had given it an acceptable shape. His film offered viewers of a new generation the emotional and ideological satisfactions of a time-honored commercial form, whose basic, exhortatory parameters had been established in large part through the industry's wartime cooperation with Washington, DC's Office of War Information. The aim of the domestic propaganda effort, as John W. Dower shows, was to establish the enemy as "the slave world, whose histories were swollen with lust for conquest, whose leaders were madmen, and whose people were a subservient mass, a 'human herd.'"[13] Spielberg's Germans are bestial "others" in this sense, to be justifiably slaughtered. His war, in Dwight D. Eisenhower's phrase, is a "crusade in Europe" dedicated to destroying an overpowering evil and restoring a blighted continent to moral and political wellbeing.

Saving Private Ryan's main theme is admittedly unconventional, involving a mission not to kill the enemy or take some objective, but to remove from harm's way a sole surviving son. An interesting moral question about war is thereby raised. Is the saving of one life, suddenly deemed precious, worth the expenditure of lives not so deemed? The narrative eventually answers in the affirmative, but, halfway through, it takes a significant detour from this struggle to save life to the more traditional task of defeating the enemy. Rescuers and the rescued alike, learning that an enemy force is coming that might threaten the landing beaches, delay their return to the coast in order to serve a larger good. They join with a small force of others in an attempt, successful but highly costly, to prevent a German armored column from advancing over the bridge they tenuously hold.

Finally embracing a mission that is true to generic form, *Saving Private Ryan* depicts how a demonized enemy is defeated at great cost by a gang of heroes in spite of themselves. These ordinary Americans rise to the occasion of sacrificing themselves for a sacred national purpose, making the world safe for a new generation whose accomplishments must "earn" the blood, pain, and spent treasure that have made them possible. As Martin Flanagan suggests, "Spielberg's movie had stoked perceptions of the conflict as an honorable one . . . finally concluding that the value of an entire way of life is maintained through such symbolic individual cases."[14] Much the same might be said of any classic war film, from *Back to Bataan* (1945) to *Sands of Iwo Jima* (1949) and even the first screen version of Jones's novel.

At the end of the 1990s, *Saving Private Ryan* and *The Thin Red Line* competed, if unintentionally, to draw some important meaning from the American experience in World War II. The confrontation between film styles and artistic purposes that had dominated the end of the 1970s was renewed. Some twenty years before, the so-called "movie brats" such as Spielberg and George Lucas had proved able to muscle out from industrial prominence the European-influenced *auteurs* of the Hollywood Renaissance, who self-destructed (Francis Coppola, Michael Cimino), lost creative energy (Arthur Penn), found funding difficult in the face of box-office failure (Robert Altman), or simply faded from the scene (Hal Ashby, Peter Bogdanovich). Spielberg's devotion to the classic Hollywood commercial model, as well as to its conservative ideological and formal traditions, had given him, after more than two decades of success, a prominence in the industry by the time of *Saving Private Ryan*'s release that few directors in this country had ever attained.

Nothing is sheltered from fate

Malick's *The Thin Red Line* was widely interpreted as opposing the Spielbergian model, not only artistically (certainly true enough), but also politically (a proposition that needs careful nuancing). It has been claimed, for example, that the director, supposed to be reflecting the anti-war atmosphere of the 1970s and in some sense remaking Francis Ford Coppola's (in)famous *Apocalypse Now* (1979), therein promotes the view that "all violence is regrettable." Yet this is a reading that is difficult to sustain for either the film or the novel, which are hardly antiwar.[15] For Jones (in both *The Thin Red Line* and *From Here to Eternity*), the war is an unquestionable fact of national life, something to be faced and endured by the professional soldier. It is to be neither regretted nor idealized. Like Jones, Malick neither endorses nor contests the ideological premise of the war film genre, which is the Augustinian view that the killing and destruction that war entails, while always morally unfortunate and marked by sorrow, loss, and suffering, are nevertheless justified by the collective need either to defend life or to extirpate evil.

But (and here he is especially faithful to the novel) Malick rejects, or at least tellingly redefines, the narrow narrative and thematic conventions of the war film genre. These include the identification of the narrative as recounting a "historical" event that is fictionalized in order the better to reveal its political and moral truth; the understanding that the war is defined by the metaphysical or at least the moral opposition of good to evil; the narrative's emphasis on the decisive encounter, in which inevitable victory confirms that righteousness is on "our side"; the plot's organization around an Everyman hero who leads a unit that reflects the diversity of American society; a refusal to confront the impersonal and mass nature of modern conflict through, instead, a focus on a small group of suitably differentiated individuals, for whom sympathy can be readily developed; and, finally, the discovery that camaraderie is a positive element of wartime experience, as the individuals who make up the unit are brought to acknowledge that the collective goals of preserving the group and completing the mission are more important than saving their own lives.

The Thin Red Line departs substantially from this model. Malick's film makes little more than a gesture toward the history that is the Guadalcanal campaign. Although it shows a mission (the hillside assault) being accomplished and with no little heroism, the narrative does not hinge on that event, but ends instead with the profoundly anticlimactic sense that victory, signified by the withdrawal of Charlie Company from the island, has somehow been secured off-screen. The Japanese enemy is not presented as a horde of buck-toothed savages whose bestiality justifies their slaughter. Instead, Malick views them as companions in misfortune to the American soldiers. Their suffering and death becomes a spectacle both empty of triumph and also difficult to endure. The film demonstrates, in the phrase of Simone Weil, that "nothing is sheltered from fate," especially not the apparent victors, "for the strong man is never absolutely strong, nor the weak man absolutely weak." In a striking moment, a mutilated Japanese corpse addresses us with such a message from its final resting place in the mud, reminding Private Witt, who is transfixed by the grisly spectacle of a face separated from its body, that such virtues as he might possess will not prevent his similar annihilation, for the corpse affirms that he, too, was "loved by all." And so, following Weil's admonition, Malick demonstrates that we are "never to admire might, or hate the enemy, or despise sufferers."[16]

It is thus hardly surprising that no sympathetic heroic leader, with whose virtue and strength the viewer identifies, emerges to focalize the narrative and equate righteousness with might. The regimental field commander, Colonel Tall (Nick Nolte), is a man who has been passed over many times for promotion from colonel; he is eager only to boost his career now that "his war" has finally come, small compensation for a life spent in self-denial and bootlicking. In contrast, the company captain, a civilian lawyer turned soldier named Staros (Elias Koteas), turns out to be too "tender-hearted," never fully committed to the bitter reality that success depends on his willingness to send the men he loves to their deaths. None of the other officers, or enlisted men, provides the consistent providential, charismatic leadership on which the war film genre depends. To be sure, *The Thin Red Line* promotes the value of comradeship and self-sacrifice, but not in the service of justifying the war, balancing the cost in lives against a larger good, as does *Saving Private Ryan*. The film's most heroic moment, not derived from the novel, is also its most unconventional, as Private Witt (Jim Caviezel) sacrifices himself by leading the Japanese away from his company, who are trapped in a vulnerable position and might easily be wiped out. No mission beyond the preservation of their lives is thereby accomplished. If not true to the letter of Jones's fiction, this episode accurately reflects the novelist's often expressed views of human purpose and ethical development. In a general sense, the film, by rewriting the novel, is more deeply faithful to it, or so I shall argue.

What puzzled viewers most about *The Thin Red Line*, even those who were prepared for some formal unconventionality, was that Malick had not produced a film that conformed to the ideological premises of the genre, which had just been reestablished by Spielberg. Tom Whalen, for example, objected to Malick's "maudlin metaphysics," opining that the film's poetic voiceovers, which foreground the spiritual and philosophical questions raised by (the) war, could surely have no place in a "war film," as if films that take human conflict as their subject cannot offer alternatives to the action-oriented, nationalistic model invented by

Hollywood.[17] *The Thin Red Line*, however, drew fire not only from those who preferred their generic pleasures unadulterated by a new intellectual perspective, but also from those whose partisanship of an alternative cinema was beyond question. The leftist film scholar Colin MacCabe, for example, complained unfairly that Malick shows "no interest in the Second World War," presumably because the director does not take pains to establish the political "meaning" of the battle for Guadalcanal, which, because this is an "independent" film, he should then presumably go on to ironize, as does Altman to the Korean War in *M.A.S.H.* (1970). But few human endeavors, we might agree, are more complicated and less reducible to some narrow understanding than war, which surely, even from the point of view of a naive realism, may be granted its multifarious psychological and spiritual dimensions.

It is true enough, as MacCabe says, that the film's soldiers are engaged in "a conflict which is as old as time, which is simply a modern version of the Trojan War."[18] But an unabashed and uncynical interest in the transcendent aspects of human experience does not preclude a meaningful, even critical engagement with the historical (or the legendary), as readers of Homer might bear witness. Malick's war certainly not only takes place in the twentieth-century Pacific, but, like that of his Greek predecessor, also participates in an enduring and unavoidable existential reality. The film goes beyond (yet also includes) the novel's recreation of the historically grounded "feel of combat," for which Jones was often praised (the phrase is Mailer's in *Cannibals and Christians*, 113). Importantly, Mailer's only complaint about the book is that Jones's account is "too technical" and thus lacks the encounter with the "mystical" and the spiritual that so distinguishes the earlier *From Here to Eternity* (112). Malick provides the story with this added dimension, adopting the transcendental approach to human experience that Jones took more obviously (if sometimes ponderously) in his other fiction, particularly *Some Came Running*.[19] The inner life, understood as a neverending search for meaning and understanding, is a central element in the other two novels that constitute his war trilogy.

Jones has been much celebrated as a man's man in the Hemingway tradition. After all, he wrote a macho paean to the dangerous pleasures of scuba diving, *Go to the Widow-Maker* (1967), of which Papa would certainly have approved. Similarly, in his war trilogy, Jones is undoubtedly committed to the unflinching portrayal of the conflict between men of honor and the nurturing but oppressive institution that is the army, whose interpersonal tensions are tellingly revealed by the proving ground of combat. But it is also true that, like Ralph Waldo Emerson rather than Hemingway, the novelist was actually more interested in the larger theme of portraying "spiritual growth through reincarnation and karma," in the phrase of Steven R. Carter, who convincingly places Jones within an American tradition of enthusiasm for non-Western spiritualism. Borrowing eclectically from "transcendentalism, Orientalism, Platonism, and theosophy," Jones created a philosophical system (given its fullest expression in *From Here to Eternity*) "in which each soul is forced to discern its similarity to all other souls on earth – and its isolation from them."

Only "a series of distressing and humiliating experiences designed to break the ego," such as occur in war, were in his view strong enough to "provoke the realization that everyone is treated the same way." Proceeding from this acknowledgment that all share equally in the human condition, this process of spiritual growth could ultimately lead an individual soul to "a state of compassionate understanding in which it feels sorry about the pain in everyone's life without wishing to change or eliminate that pain."[20] For Jones's soldiers, this means accepting the inevitability of one's own death, as well as the deaths of others. Such a reconciliation to ultimate reality weakens the claims of the ego and defamiliarizes the habits of modern civilized life, which are predicated on the denial of mortality, for these are irrelevant in a landscape where an ironic version of the golden rule holds sway. In that landscape, despair may prevail, as Malick emphasizes in the film. Watching his men die around him, Sergeant McCron screams out, "We're just dirt," in a recasting of a commonly mouthed biblical observation about human destiny whose full meaning has just become vividly clear. Which is to say that Jones is more interested in the phenomenology of death in war than in any political meaning it might be said to possess. Somewhat paradoxically, his version of Jones's spirituality is more material, a point requiring further discussion below.

To be sure, the full Jonesian emergence through struggle against authority to the understanding of selfhood that provides spiritual peace, most famously experienced by Robert E. Lee Prewitt in *From Here to Eternity*, does not find a place in *The Thin Red Line*. But in his later novel, Jones shows great skill in portraying various aspects of the destruction of the ego that military service effects. The film emphasizes how some resist this process of "uncivilizing." Most notably, private Bell (Ben Chaplin), until her betrayal, remains emotionally attached to his wife and therefore to a life he no longer possesses. Others, such as Private Dale (Arie Verveen), who pulls out gold teeth from Japanese corpses, find themselves reduced to the animal state of isolation and anomie, passing beyond the "thin red line" that separates the sane from the mad, a phrase from an old proverb, according to Jones, that gives the book's title another kind of resonance. Because death can come to anyone in an instant, war is also the great leveler. Survival in modern combat, as Jones stresses again and again, is determined strictly by chance, while victory is measured by actuarial calculations of losses inflicted and sustained.

The novel eschews the spiritual ascent, satisfying itself with Private Doll's strictly psychological evolution into the perfect soldier. Doll develops a mental shield of invulnerability that enables him to attack the enemy without worrying about losing his life. It is no accident that Marton's film, accommodating the narrative as fully as possible to the classic war film genre, makes Private Doll (Keir Dullea) the main character. At first desperate to find some edge to help him to survive, Doll becomes a reckless hero whose bravery enables the assault on the hill to succeed, a feat that endorses the American association of accomplishment with individual exertion. The young man's reckless lack of self-regard costs the life of Sergeant Welsh (Jack Warden), who violates his own code of looking out for number one to take a bullet meant for his protégé, giving dramatic expression to the archly generic theme of self-sacrifice. But Malick's version, we might say, "out-Joneses" Jones, making more explicit the connections that the novelist intended it to have with the other two volumes of the trilogy. Both these novels offer the transfiguring deaths of principal characters, each of them rebels against authority. *The Thin Red Line* does not, but that asymmetry is corrected in Malick's film.

A minor character in the novel, Private Witt is transformed from an ignorant and intolerant nonconformist into a visionary whose refusal to be limited to officially sanctioned experience gives him a glimpse of "another world," which is exemplified by the native village of Solomon Islanders that he goes absent to visit before the battle begins, in an episode that is not in the novel. Although he is a deserter, Malick's Witt is no coward or pacifist. He seeks only the private space he needs to understand the war, and especially the prospect of his own death, which he hopes to face with equanimity. Witt does not shrink from the history that catches up with him. Loyal to his comrades, he shares their experiences, including the killing, though he will not allow himself to be brutalized by the savagery and suffering of combat.

Witt, as his name suggests, is a reduced form of Prewitt. Essentially the same character, now named Prell, is the main character in *Whistle*. Sergeant Warden in *Eternity* becomes Sergeant Welsh in *The Thin Red Line*, and Sergeant Winch in *Whistle*. A soldier of exceptional talent and courage, Prewitt is too idealistic to survive in a world of inauthentic emotions and senseless misfortune. Sergeant Warden is Prewitt's brother in arms, determined both to mold the recalcitrant young man into an ideal soldier and to save him from his own perhaps perverse sense of personal honor. Warden takes refuge in an unremitting cynicism (especially about officers) that distances him from an institution that he nonetheless loves deeply, an emotional attachment he shares with Prewitt. Once again bringing the film into closer alignment with the other two narratives in the trilogy, Malick emphasizes Witt's attachment to Welsh (Sean Penn), who becomes a character of greater sympathy and spiritual depth, much like Warden.

Witt is the more prominent character in the film, with his expanding sense of human brotherhood emphasized at the expense of Welsh's bitter rejection of redeeming national purpose and the spiritual side of human nature. Witt's meditations on war and death in the native village reflect the transformation that Prewitt experiences when confined in the stockade, where he meets a fellow soldier who instructs him about spiritual growth. This is one of the novel's richest episodes, inviting, like Witt's visit to the native village, an allegorical reading. If the stockade, place of enlightenment, confinement, and correction, exemplifies military life, then the native village, a place colonized and yet uncivilized, located in the midst of a gloriously beautiful landscape where modern war will be waged, perhaps stands for the two sides of human nature (the primitive and the "civilized") that are alienated in modern times from one another. Human beings, one of the soldiers observes in the voiceover that accompanies the shots of the village, once constituted a "family," but, having gone their separate ways, they are now trying to rob each other of "light and life." In a vision of how the world once was, the islanders' homeland is the setting for a war that neither touches them, nor alters the rhythms of their Stone Age existence. But spiritual growth challenges, if it cannot overcome, that separation. Stepping outside the modern offers a glimpse of, if never a full participation in, a more inclusive, perhaps more authentic human reality, imbuing Witt with a stronger sense of fellowship that transcends, even as it includes, his loyalty to Charlie Company.

Malick deeply enriches the ways in which *The Thin Red Line* recapitulates the major themes of Jones's war trilogy. Paradoxically perhaps, the director's most important departures from the literal text make his film more faithful to the novelist's overall vision of men at war, including especially the supplying of the story with a sense of transcendental experience. Witt conquers his own fear of extinction and grows ever more deeply into a "compassionate understanding" of others, his fellow soldiers in Charlie Company as well as the captured Japanese, whom he will not dehumanize. Witt accepts the necessity of killing the enemy when they face him as soldiers, but, after they become his prisoners, he respects their humanity and understands their plight as simply another version of his own. He interrogates the imperatives of modern dissociation and nihilism, especially Welsh's assertion that in a totalizing modern society "a man himself is nothing." Welsh believes that there "ain't no world but this one."

Witt opens himself both to the nature he discovers and to the experience of war, which is revealed as simply a more authentic version of life itself. He becomes convinced that there is more to existence than those grand narratives that occult all sense of individual agency, such as Welsh's socialist view that the war is only about "property." This is why he is eager to comprehend the incomprehensible (dis)connection between the peacefulness of islander culture and the seemingly senseless war that is the reflex of the civilization into which he had been born. After the hillside assault, he returns to the village, finding himself even more of an outsider than before, estranged from the people he once moved easily among, who now find him an object of fear.

Like Prewitt, Witt has to face contradiction, finding himself expelled from "paradise," first by the patrol boat that returns him to the troop ship and, after his second visit, by his refusal to abandon his comrades and desert a second time. In both instances he returns to the war. Prewitt does the same. He honors the promise he made to his dying mother not to kill. A talented boxer, he unwittingly kills one of his opponents and resolves not to box again thereafter, despite pressure from his commanding officer. Ironically, that resolution sets in motion events that force Prewitt to commit murder, even if it is in order to right a moral wrong. Wounded physically as well as psychologically, he must flee the barracks to his lover, who lives in town, only to rejoin his comrades at night when war breaks out. Mistaken for a Japanese saboteur, he is shot and killed by them as he makes his way to trenches dug near the coast of Oahu in the days after the Pearl Harbor attack.

Neither Prewitt nor Malick's Witt, though both are deserters, can escape being connected to their comrades. Solidarity is the cardinal precept of the soldiers' code, and both characters are preeminently moralists, concerned above all with upholding personal honor and the right in a world that puzzles more than it enlightens. Malick notes in the screenplay that "the idea of service to humanity, of comradeship, of the solidarity of men, is slowly perishing from the world, but in Witt it still runs strong."[21] Much the same could be said of Prewitt, Jones's first sketch of this character and in all likelihood the model for Malick's refashioning of Witt.

The war is also at the heart of nature

Malick makes Witt a more fully Jonesian hero than the novelist himself was willing to do, focusing on his evolution from anxiety and uncertainty at the prospect of approaching death to an acceptance of annihilation if it will mean deliverance for his comrades. At this moment, Witt searches for understanding and, perhaps, some kind of metaphysical reassurance.

Surrounded by Japanese soldiers, he provokes his own death by drawing his weapon in acknowledgment of the inevitable. He first looks toward the heavens, perhaps for a sign. Yet the flashback he experiences, dying, is an earthly memory, of his swimming in the crystal waters of the Pacific with the boys from the island. The "other world" that Witt thinks he glimpses at certain moments in his life turns out to be not solitarily transcendent but, literally speaking, immersion and fellowship, imaged as beautiful movement through natural and, importantly, uninhabitable space, the camera looking upward from the submerged swimmers toward a shimmering sky. For Jones's intellectual accounts of spiritual ascent (best exemplified by the lengthy dialogue between Prewitt and his stockade guru Jack Malloy), Malick substitutes its phenomenological manifestation.

The image displaces the word, thereby recapitulating one characteristic element of the relationship between any literary source and its cinematic derivation. As throughout the film, striking images that prompt a revision of the human relationship to the physical world, their affect enhanced by a haunting score, carry the burden of a dominant theme implied in, but never directly expressed by, the narrative. Such images (with which the film begins and ends) attest to the undisplaceable primacy of beautiful, enigmatic nature, which redeems the ugliness of war from its anthropocentric self. As Michel Chion comments about this central aspect of Malick's film, "[T]he world does not cease to live because men are making war."[22] Hence what humans call "nature" does not forfeit its claim to be represented in any imagistic account of what is and what happens. Appropriately, then, the scene of Witt's death both exteriorizes his surrender to the undeniability of extinction (as he completes the spiritual evolution envisioned by Jones), and also establishes the natural world as the ground of existence, which is here represented metonymically by the ocean, the source of life to which human memory, at the moment that being is surrendered, peacefully returns. This understanding of the human connection to all else that, as the philosopher Martin Heidegger would say, "presences" itself and thus becomes the object of our consciousness, finds no reflex in the novel or in the Jonesian oeuvre more generally.

This climactic scene, intriguing in its own right, is also emblematic of the scheme Malick followed for adapting Jones's novel, whose ideas and representations are not only visualized, but contained and modified by that process, which thereby "restores" them to a hitherto occulted fullness of significance. The director's framing, however, is verbal as well as visual. Tellingly, the screenplay was completed before Malick decided on the extensive deployment of voiceovers of various kinds, a stylistic *tour* that plays a dominant role in his two earlier films and so, on one level, marks the incorporation of Jones's story within the Malickian oeuvre. Sometimes these voiceovers reveal the difference between the public and private selves, as when Colonel Tall, forced to adopt a humiliating servility to the younger man who is his general, meditates on the cost he has paid in his personal life for sticking with an unprofitable military career. Sometimes the voiceovers (including most of Witt's) make audible a character's thoughts, so that his actions may be explained, his spiritual evolution foregrounded.

The most striking of the film's voiceovers, however, have another purpose entirely: commentary in the Godardian manner. Although delivered by a homodiegetic narrator, these thoughts are coordinated neither with the advancing narrative nor with the silent images of the character on screen, but frequently play over images that frame rather than constitute plot elements. Fittingly, they are uttered by Private Train (John Dee Smith), another enlisted man who speaks with a southern accent rather similar to Witt's. Train plays a very minor role in the story as such, but his prayerful search for spiritual understanding speaks to the spiritual and philosophical issues raised by the experience of everyone in Charlie Company. The film's first image is of a crocodile slithering into a tropical pool rank with green slime. "What is this war at the heart of nature?" asks an unambiguously American but disembodied voice, only much later to be identified as Train's.

For Jones, more the moralist than the naturalist, the tropical jungle provides only the stage upon which an essentially psychological drama plays out. But from the outset Malick challenges that understanding, instead aligning the human with the natural and seeking an understanding of conflict not only in evil as such, but within the order of things. Is the violence that allows the crocodile to survive the same as men perpetrate on one another? No authority appears to provide an answer, though it is clear, as Chion remarks, that the director's point at least in part is that "war is not a thing invented by human beings," disputing the anthropocentrism at the heart of the Augustinian view of the just war (41). The significance of Train's question, in any event, lies in its asking, for it exceeds the customary self-imposed epistemological limitations of modern technological man, who is likely to see himself not as part of nature, but rather, in Heidegger's phrase, as "human material, which is disposed of with a view to proposed goals."[23]

A philosopher who abandoned an academic career in order to make films, Malick follows Heidegger in seeing modern Western society as a "destitute time," in which "mortals are hardly aware and capable even of their own mortality" and "have not yet come into ownership of their own nature." The result is that "death withdraws into the enigmatic," even as men are troubled by their understanding of themselves, which "lacks the unconcealedness of the nature of pain, death, and love" (96–97). The large-scale and sanctioned violence that is war, so the war film genre suggests, has its origin in some "fall" from the natural state of human society, imagined as peace, the condition of "real life" to which soldiers wish to return, a movement secured by the victory that comes from self-sacrifice. This fall, in the Augustinian view, is moral, an aggression against the innocent that forces them to defend themselves and restore the peace.

But modern war, fought in some sense, as Welsh observes, over "property," can also be viewed as the "context in which technological rationality and instrumentalisation reach an extreme."[24] Yet war, if exemplifying the crisis of self-understanding promoted by advanced civilization, paradoxically offers its solution, for it reveals our collective humanity, the sense in which we all share in the natural limit that is death – an essential element of spiritual growth, as Malick, following Heidegger, and Jones both agree. Our fate, to paraphrase Weil, is that nothing is sheltered, and this is a message of hope for the transcendentally inclined, if for the realist it is a cause for regret.

Poets in a destitute time

No adaptation, so Robert Stam suggests, can be true to its source because "a single novelistic text comprises a series of verbal signals that can generate a plethora of possible meanings." So "the literary text is not closed," but permits itself to be "reworked by a boundless context,"[25] a process evident not only in any reading, but also and most especially in that particular sort of iconic or imitative rewriting that is adaptation. When Jones's *The Thin Red Line* was brought to the screen a second time, that context was defined primarily by a reverential culture of remembrance, as American victory in World War II was celebrated and the service of the war's veterans honored. Although Jones attempted to obscure the fact, his novel offered the most notable of the many authentic accounts of an important campaign. It was true, as veterans such as Mailer recognized, not only to the facts of military history, but also to the psychological experiences of modern combat. Authentically transferred to the screen, such truth, however, proved less attractive to the filmgoing public than the time-honored conventions of the war film genre, which provides reassurance, as Spielberg's *Saving Private Ryan* evidenced, that the massive death and suffering of modern war were in this case morally justified, confirming the rightness of national purpose.

Malick's film is no antiwar tract, though it strongly disputes the modern understanding of war as an extreme form of "policy," a view that has a long history in Western culture from Virgil to von Clausewitz. Malick evokes the conflict not only historically (the film's representations are as "realistic" as anything in *Saving Private Ryan*), but also philosophically, following closely the model that Jones offered in the other two volumes of his war trilogy. In an important sense, the film is more Jonesian than the novel, a kind of extended *hommage* to a writer whose considerable accomplishments have yet to be properly recognized. But the return of a legendary director to commercial practice obscured the reception of Malick's film as an adaptation. *The Thin Red Line* was viewed instead as an antigeneric riposte to time-honored Hollywood conventions of representation, and it was thus read more for what it refused to do than for the disturbing and challenging version of history that it offered filmgoers.

Yet this is a film that does not exclude the notion of the heroic. At its thematic center is a somewhat different version of the same theme that dominates in *Saving Private Ryan*. Witt's moral and spiritual growth, his development of a "compassionate understanding" leads him to self-sacrifice, providing the fitting expression of his oft-expressed love for the men of Charlie Company. Yet Witt's movement toward the acceptance of his own extinction is framed within a greater, if complementary, revelation: that nature is the ground of human being, that man is not the measure of things, including and especially himself. For Jones and for Malick, war, however terrible, provokes those who wage it to acknowledge a central and indispensable truth: that death comes to all and marks the limit of human endeavor. The director's inflection of this theme, of course, is Heideggerian rather than transcendental or "Orientalist." For it is predicated on the view that modern life, especially when global war rages, is a "destitute time," characterized by the extreme instrumentalization of nature (its conversion into raw material) and of human beings (who become cannon fodder).

Destitute times, Heidegger says, call for poets, who "are under way on the track of the holy because they experience the unholy as such," a dual calling certainly evident in the contrasting scenes of degradation and haunting loveliness that Malick's camera captures (141). In disclosing the dark, yet beautiful secrets of human experience, even as they face squarely the facts of history, Jones and Malick prove to be such poets of a destitute time. As an adaptation, *The Thin Red Line* is not so much a transference of meaning from one form to another as a merging of visions in the construction of an unconventional monument to the national trial that was World War II. Like *Saving Private Ryan*, Malick's film portrays the sufferings of a generation that accepted the horrifying existential reality of global war, even celebrating (if more mutedly) victory over the enemy, and by implication the imposition of a righteous national will. This point is, of course, made without subtlety in Spielberg's film, which concludes with the ultimate patriotic image, a giant American flag waving in the breeze over the final resting place of the honored Allied dead. German cemeteries at Normandy, it goes without saying, find no place in this film.

Malick, however, goes beyond national self-congratulation to acknowledge, in gestures with which Jones would agree, the puzzlements of the human condition, as these are evoked in Train's final voiceover. After meditating on the shared adventure of his company (as the camera pans across a gallery of now-familiar faces), Train utters again the unanswerable question posed at the film's beginning: are darkness and light "the features of the same face"? But if the moral and metaphysical sources of human conflict resist probing, the best we can hope for is prayer, the expression, which can never be stifled, of the human desire for understanding. We have the power to voice a plea for unification, however temporary, with the divine, and for an acceptance of the world as it offers itself to us in its ineffaceable and multifarious beauty. Train speaks to an unquenchable yearning when he says, "Oh, my soul, let me be in You now! Look out through my eyes, look at the things You made, all things shining." The answer to Train's prayer (psalm?) is provided by the cinematic narrator's closing series of shots, which, abandoning the army to its continuing fate of island-hopping, returns us to the natural beauty of the island, apparently unchanged by the battle that has taken place there, with the primitive life of the natives continuing as it has presumably for eons. These things are, indeed, shown to be "all shining."

But then, moving to the beach where the landings took place, Malick's camera locates no signs of modern war, only a coconut, swept up by the tide. The coconut (carried there by chance? by design?) is just beginning to sprout, "presencing" itself in a manner that passes human understanding, as life, the incomprehensible force we share with it, emerges. The camera's unwavering, concluding focus tempts us to read the coconut as a message, as something there "for us." Yet it is just such an instrumentalizing temptation that the film cautions against, challenging as it does our conventional understanding of war as a purely political phenomenon and confirming our fascination with, but inability to penetrate, the secrets of the world that is mysteriously here with us, as we are here with it.

With this conclusion, Malick stands the meaning of Jones's novel on its head. For if the fiction ends with an account of introversion, as the experience of war becomes the memory that "one of our number" one day will use to produce an account of the battle, the film's last image offers a startling form of extroversion. The human perspective on things is turned out and against itself, as human actors are banished completely from the scene, leaving behind only the imperishable, provocative enigma of things as they are. The coconut, like the crocodile, for all its captivating strangeness and estrangement, is a sign of nothing but itself, and this is the truth, so Malick proposes, that frames all human experience. Recognizing this truth places us at last fully in the world at the very moment that the world marks our absence.

NOTES

1. Peter G. Jones, *War and the Novelist* (Columbia, MO: University of Missouri Press, 1978), p. 72.
2. Norman Mailer, *Cannibals and Christians* (New York: Dial Press, 1966), p. 112. Further quotations will be cited parenthetically in the text.
3. Jones, *War and the Novelist*, p. 172.
4. Paul Fussell, a writer who fought in the war, observes that "for most of the troops, the war might just as well have been about good looks, so evanescent at times did its meaning and purpose seem" (*Wartime: Understanding and Behavior in the Second World War* [New York: Oxford University Press, 1989], p. 129).
5. James Jones, *The Thin Red Line* (New York: Bantam, 1962), p. 510. Further quotations will be to this edition and will be cited parenthetically in the text.
6. James Jones, *WWII: A Chronicle of Soldiering* (New York: Ballantine, 1975), p. 37. Further quotations will be cited parenthetically in the text.
7. George Garrett, *James Jones* (New York: Harcourt Brace Jovanovich, 1984), p. 4.
8. Dudley J. Andrew, "The Well-Worn Muse: Adaptation in Film History and Theory," in S. M. Conger and J. R. Welsch, eds., *Narrative Strategies* (Macomb, IL: West Illinois University Press, 1980), p. 9.
9. John Orr, *The Contemporary Cinema* (Edinburgh: Edinburgh University Press, 1998), p. 173.
10. Tom Brokaw, *The Greatest Generation* (New York: Random House, 1998), p. xxx.
11. Costing about $70 million, *Saving Private Ryan* is reported to have grossed nearly $480 million worldwide. Figures from the Internet Movie Database; http://www.indlo.com.
12. Such spectacle in the film, much more graphic and disturbing than corresponding scenes in *The Thin Red Line*, violates one of the cardinal protocols of the war film. As the historian George H. Roeder, Jr. points out, "Modern warfare produces corpses in lavish abundance. Nonetheless, during World War II, the United States government rationed photographs of the American dead more stingily than scarce commodities" (*The Censored War: American Visual Experience During the Second World War* [New Haven, CT: Yale University Press, 1993], p. 7). The same can be said for the Hollywood film of

the period, for the studios and the government were fearful that, exposed to the harsh reality of the modern battlefield, the American public's resolve to win the war might waver. On one level, Spielberg violates a long-observed taboo and, by telling the truth, establishes the authentic nature of the sacrifice that "the greatest generation" made. On another level, the violent death spectacularized in the film is given an emotional tonality that is thoroughly traditional, with suffering and pain (and thus sympathy as well) displayed only in the death scenes of American soldiers.

13. John W. Dower, *War Without Mercy: Race & Power in the Pacific War* (New York: Pantheon, 1986), p. 17. For details of the cooperation between Hollywood and official Washington, see Clayton R. Koppes and Gregory D. Black, *Hollywood Goes to War: How Politics, Profits and Propaganda Shaped World War II Movies* (Berkeley: University of California Press, 1990).

14. Martin Flanagan, "'Everything a Lie': The Critical and Commercial Reception of Terrence Malick's *The Thin Red Line*," in Hannah Patterson, ed., *The Cinema of Terrence Malick: Poetic Visions of America* (London: Wallflower Press, 2004), p. 126.

15. See John Streamas, "The Greatest Generation Steps Over the Line," in Patterson, ed., *Cinema of Terrence Malick*, p. 143.

16. Simone Weil, "*The Iliad*, Poem of Might," in George A. Panichas, ed., *The Simone Weil Reader* (Mt. Kisco, NY: Moyer Bell, 1977), pp. 183, 163.

17. Tom Whalen, "'Maybe All Men Got One Big Soul'": The Hoax Within the Metaphysics of Terrence Malick's *The Thin Red Line*," *Literature/Film Quarterly* 27:3 (1999), p. 163.

18. Colin MacCabe, "Bayonets in Paradise," *Sight and Sound* 9:2 (1999), p. 13.

19. Even critics sympathetic to Jones have found his more overtly philosophical fiction heavy going. James R. Giles, for example, remarks that "In *Some Came Running*, the author and four of his main characters lecture the reader at great length on the sexual, proletarian, and other sources of artistic creativity. Some of this overt philosophizing is embarrassingly obvious, while some of it is so arcane that one wonders how seriously to take it" (*James Jones* [Boston: Twayne, 1981]), p. 70.

20. Steven R. Carter, *James Jones: An American Orientalist Master* (Urbana, IL: University of Illinois Press, 1998), pp. ix, 34, 7. Further quotations will be cited parenthetically in the text.

21. Quoted in Robert Silberman, "Terrence Malick, Landscape, and 'This War at the Heart of Nature,'" in Patterson, *Cinema of Terrence Malick*, p. 165.

22. Michel Chion, *The Thin Red Line* (London: BFI, 2004), p. 41. Further quotations will be cited parenthetically in the text.

23. Martin Heidegger, "What are Poets For?," in Heidegger, *Poetry, Language, Thought*, trans. Albert Hofstadter (New York: Harper & Row, 1971), p. 111. Further quotations will be cited parenthetically in the text.

24. Marc Fursteneau and Leslie MacAvoy, "Terrence Malick's Heideggerian Cinema: War and the Question of Being in *The Thin Red Line*," in Patterson, *Cinema of Terrence Malick*, p. 181.

25. Robert Stam, "Beyond Fidelity: The Dialogics of Adaptation", in James Naremore, ed., *Film Adaptation* (New Brunswick, NJ: Rutgers University Press, 2000), p. 57.

Filmography

Where there are several film versions of a single literary text, the filmography lists only those deemed significant.

Beloved (Harpo Films/Touchstone Pictures/Clinica Estetica, 1998)
Director: Jonathan Demme
Producers: Ron Bozman, Jonathan Demme, Kate Forte, Gary Goetzman
Screenplay: Toni Morrison (novel), Akosua Busia, Richard LaGravenese, Adam Brooks
Art director: Tim Galvin
Director of photography: Tak Fujimoto
Music: Diane McIntyre, Toni Morrison (songs), Rachel Portman (song)
Principal cast: Oprah Winfrey (Sethe), Danny Glover (Paul D. Garner), Thandie Newton (Beloved), Kessia Kordelle (Amy Denver), Kimberly Elise (Denver), Beah Richards (Baby Suggs), Lisa Gay Hamilton (Young Sethe), Albert Hall (Stamp Paid), Irma P. Hall (Ella), Carol Jean Lewis (Janey Wagon)

The Color Purple (Amblin Entertainment/Guber-Peters/Warner Brothers, 1985)
Director: Steven Spielberg
Producers: Peter Guber, Carole Isenberg, Quincy Jones, Kathleen Kennedy, Frank Marshall, Jon Peters, Steven Spielberg
Screenplay: Alice Walker (novel), Menno Meyjes
Art director: Bo Welch
Director of photography: Allen Daviau
Music: Quincy Jones, Andraé Crouch (songs), Jeremy Lubbock (songs), Caiphus Semenya (songs), Rod Temperton (songs)
Principal cast: Danny Glover (Albert), Whoopi Goldberg (Celie), Margaret Avery (Shug), Oprah Winfrey (Sofia), Willard E. Pugh (Harpo), Akosua Busia (Nettie), Desreta Jackson (Young Celie), Adolph Caesar (old Mister), Rae Dawn Chong (Squeak), Dana Ivey (Miss Millie), Leonard Jackson (Pa), Bennet Guillory (Grady)

The Day of the Locust (Long Road/Paramount Pictures, 1975)
Director: John Schlesinger
Producers: Jerome Hellman, Sheldon Schrager
Screenplay: Nathanael West (novel), Waldo Salt
Art director: John J. Lloyd

Director of photography: Conrad Hall
Music: John Barry, Robert O. Ragland, Ben Bernie (song), Al Goering (song),
   Walter Hirsch (song)
Principal cast: Donald Sutherland (Homer Simpson), Karen Black (Faye
   Greener), Burgess Meredith (Harry Greener), William Atherton (Tod
   Jackett), Geraldine Page (Big Sister), Richard A. Dysart (Claude Estee),
   Bo Hopkins (Earle Shoop), Pepe Serna (Miguel), Lelia Goldoni (Mary
   Dove), Billy Barty (Abe Kusich), Jackie Earle Haley (Adore)

Intruder in the Dust (Metro-Goldwyn-Mayer, 1949)
Director: Clarence Brown
Producer: Clarence Brown
Screenplay: William Faulkner (novel), Ben Maddow
Art director: Randall Duell, Cedric Gibbons
Director of photography: Robert Surtees
Music: Adolph Deutsch
Principal cast: David Brian (John Gavin Stevens), Claude Jarman, Jr. (Chick
   Mallison), Juano Hernandez (Lucas Beauchamp), Porter Hall (Nub
   Gowrie), Elizabeth Patterson (Miss Habersham), Charles Kemper
   (Crawford Gowrie), Will Geer (Sheriff Hampton), David Clarke (Vinson
   Gowrie), Elzie Emanuel (Aleck), Lela Bliss (Mrs. Mallison), Harry Hayden
   (Mr. Mallison), Harry Antrim (Mr. Tubbs)

The Killers (Mark Hellinger/Universal Pictures, 1946)
Director: Robert Siodmak
Producer: Mark Hellinger
Screenplay: Ernest Hemingway (novel), Anthony Veiller, Richard Brooks, John
   Huston
Art director: Martin Obzina
Director of photography: Woody Bredell
Music: Miklós Rózsa
Principal cast: Burt Lancaster (Ole Andersen/Pete Lund), Ava Gardner (Kitty
   Collins), Edmond O'Brien (Jim Reardon), Albert Dekker (Big Jim Colfax),
   Sam Levene (Lt. Sam Lubinsky), Vince Barnett (Charleston), Virginia
   Christine (Lilly Harmon Lubinsky), Charles D. Brown (Packy), Jack
   Lambert (Dum-Dum Clarke), Donald MacBride (R. S. Kenyon), Charles
   McGraw (Al), William Conrad (Max), Phil Brown (Nick Adams), Queenie
   Smith (Mary Ellen Daugherty), Jeff Corey (Blinkie Franklin)

The Killers (Revue Studios/Universal Pictures, 1964)
Director: Don Siegel
Producer: Don Siegel
Screenplay: Ernest Hemingway (story), Gene L. Coon
Art director: Frank Arrigo, George B. Chan
Director of photography: Richard L. Rawlings
Music: John Williams, Don Raye (song)
Principal cast: Lee Marvin (Charlie Strom), Angie Dickinson (Sheila Farr),
   John Cassavetes (Johnny North), Clu Gulager (Lee), Claude Akins (Earl
   Sylvester), Norman Fell (Mickey Farmer), Ronald Reagan (Jack

Browning), Virginia Christine (Miss Watson), Robert Phillips (George), Kathleen O'Malley (receptionist)

The Last Tycoon (Academy Productions/Paramount Pictures, 1976)
Director: Elia Kazan
Producer: Sam Spiegel
Screenplay: F. Scott Fitzgerald (novel), Harold Pinter
Art director: Jack T. Collis
Director of photography: Victor J. Kemper
Music: Maurice Jarré
Principal cast: Robert De Niro (Monroe Stahr), Tony Curtis (Rodriguez), Robert Mitchum (Pat Brady), Jeanne Moreau (Didi), Jack Nicholson (Brimmer), Donald Pleasence (Boxley), Ray Milland (Fleishacker), Dana Andrews (Red Ridingwood), Ingrid Boulting (Kathleen Moore), Peter Strauss (Wylie), Theresa Russell (Cecilia Brady), Tige Andrews (Popolos), Morgan Farley (Marcus), John Carradine (tour guide), Jeff Corey (Doctor), Diane Shalet (Stahr's secretary), Seymour Cassel (seal trainer), Angelica Huston (Edna)

Lolita (Anya/Harris-Kubrick/Seven Arts, 1962)
Director: Stanley Kubrick
Producers: James B. Harris, Eliot Hyman
Screenplay: Vladimir Nabokov (novel), Vladimir Nabokov, Stanley Kubrick
Art director: William C. Andrews
Director of photography: Oswald Morris
Music: Bob Harris
Principal cast: James Mason (Professor Humbert Humbert), Shelley Winters (Charlotte Haze), Sue Lyon (Lolita Haze), Gary Cockrell (Dick Schiller), Jerry Stovin (John Farlow), Peter Sellers (Clare Quilty), Diana Decker (Jean Farlow), Lois Maxwell (Nurse Mary Lore), Marianne Stone (Vivian Darkbloom)

Lolita (Guild/Pathé, 1997)
Director: Adrian Lyne
Producers: Mario Kassar, Joel B. Michaels
Screenplay: Vladimir Nabokov (novel), Stephen Schiff
Art director: Chris Shriver
Director of photography: Howard Atherton, Stephen Smith (France)
Music: Ennio Morricone
Principal cast: Jeremy Irons (Professor Humbert Humbert), Melanie Griffith (Charlotte Haze), Frank Langella (Clare Quilty), Dominque Swain (Lolita Haze), Suzanne Shepherd (Miss Pratt), Keith Reddin (Reverend Rigger), Erin J. Dean (Mona), Joan Glover (Miss LaBone), Pat Pierre Perkins (Louise), Ben Silverstone (Young Humbert), Emma Griffiths Malin (Annabelle Leigh)

The Member of the Wedding (Stanley Kramer Productions/Columbia Pictures, 1952)
Director: Fred Zinnemann

Producers: Stanley Kramer, Edna Anhalt, Edward Anhalt
Screenplay: Carson McCullers (novel, play), Edna Anhalt, Edward Anhalt
Art director: Cary Odell
Director of photography: Hal Mohr
Music: Alex North
Principal cast: Ethel Waters (Berenice Brown), Julie Harris (Frankie Addams),
    Brandon de Wilde (John Henry), Arthur Franz (Jarvis), William Hansen
    (Mr. Addams), James Edwards (Honey Camden Brown), Harry Golden
    (T. T. Williams)

Naked Lunch (Naked Lunch Productions and others, 1991)
Director: David Cronenberg
Producers: Gabriella Martinelli, Jeremy Thomas
Screenplay: William S. Burroughs (novel), David Cronenberg
Art director: James McAteer
Director of photography: Peter Suschitzky
Music: Ornette Coleman, Howard Shore
Principal cast: Peter Weller (Bill Lee), Judy Davis (Joan Frost/Joan Lee), Ian
    Holm (Tom Frost), Julian Sands (Yves Cloquet), Roy Scheider (Dr.
    Benway), Monique Mercure (Fadela), Nicholas Campbell (Hank), Michael
    Zelniker (Martin), Robert A. Silverman (Hans), Joseph Scoren (Kiki)

Ship of Fools (Columbia Pictures, 1965)
Director: Stanley Kramer
Producer: Stanley Kramer
Screenplay: Katherine Anne Porter (novel), Abby Mann
Art director: Robert Clatworthy
Director of photography: Ernest Laszlo
Music: Ernest Gold
Principal cast: Vivien Leigh (Mary Treadwell), Simone Signoret (La Condesa),
    José Ferrer (Siegfried Rieber), Lee Marvin (Billy Tenny), Oskar Werner
    (Willie Schumann), Elizabeth Ashley (Jenny Brown), George Segal
    (David), José Greco (Pepe), Michael Dunn (Carl Glocken), Charles
    Korvin (Captain Thiele), Heinz Rühmann (Julius Lowenthal), Lilia Skala
    (Frau Hutten), Barbara Luna (Amparo), Christiane Schmidtmer (Lizzi
    Spokentidler), Werner Klemperer (Lt. Huebner)

Short Cuts (Avenue Picture Productions and others, 1993)
Director: Robert Altman
Producers: Cary Brokaw, Scott Bushnell, Mike E. Kaplan. David Levy
Screenplay: Raymond Carver (writings), Robert Altman, Frank Barhydt
Art director: Jerry Fleming
Director of photography: Walt Lloyd
Music: Gavin Friday, Mark Isham
Principal cast: Andie MacDowell (Ann Finnigan), Bruce Davison (Howard
    Finnigan), Jack Lemmon (Paul Finnigan), Lane Cassidy (Casey Finnigan),
    Julianne Moore (Marian Wyman), Mathew Modine (Dr. Ralph Wyman),
    Anne Archer (Claire Kane), Fred Ward (Stuart Kane), Jennifer Jason Leigh
    (Lois Kaiser), Chris Penn (Jerry Kaiser), Joseph C. Hopkins (Joe Kaiser),

Josette Maccario (Josette Kaiser), Lili Taylor (Honey Bush), Robert
Downey, Jr. (Bill Bush), Madeleine Stowe (Sherri Shepard), Tim Robbins
(Gene Shepard), Lily Tomlin (Doreen Piggot), Tom Waits (Earl Piggot),
Peter Gallagher (Stormy Weathers)

Slaughterhouse-Five (Universal Pictures/Vanadas Productions, 1972)
Director: George Roy Hill
Producers: Jennings Lang, Paul Monash
Screenplay: Kurt Vonnegut (novel), Stephen Geller
Art directors: Alexander Golitzen, George C. Webb
Director of photography: Miroslav Ondricek
Music: Glenn Gould
Principal cast: Michael Sacks (Billy Pilgrim), Ron Leibman (Paul Lazzaro),
    Eugene Roche (Edgar Derby), Sharon Gans (Valencia Pilgrim), Valerie
    Perrine (Montana Wildhack), Holly Near (Barbara Pilgrim), Perry King
    (Robert Pilgrim), Kevin Conway (Roland Weary), Robert Blossom (Wild
    Bob Cody), John Dehner (Professor Rumfoord), Richard Schaal (Howard
    W. Campbell, Jr.)

The Thin Red Line (A. C. E. Films/Allied Artists, 1964)
Director: Andrew Marton
Producers: Bernard Glasser, Sidney Harmon, Lester A. Sansom, Philip Yordan
Screenplay: James Jones (novel), Bernard Gordon
Art director: José Algueró
Director of photography: Manuel Berenguer
Music: Malcolm Arnold
Principal cast: Keir Dullea (Pvt. Doll), Jack Warden (Sgt. Welsh), James
    Philbrook (Col. Tall), Bob Kanter (Fife), Ray Daley (Capt. Stone), Kieron
    Moore (Lt. Band), Jim Gillen (Capt. Gaff), Merlyn Yordan (lady).

The Thin Red Line (Fox 2000, 1998)
Director: Terrence Malick
Producers: Robert Michael Geisler, Grant Hill, Sheila Davis Lawrence, John
    Roberdeau, George Stevens, Jr., Michael Stevens
Screenplay: James Jones (novel), Terrence Malick
Art director: Ian Gracie
Director of photography: John Toll
Music: Hans Zimmer
Principal cast: Sean Penn (Sgt. Welsh), Adrien Brody (Cpl. Fife), Jim Caviezel
    (Pvt. Witt), Ben Chaplin (Pvt. Bell), George Clooney (Capt. Bosche), John
    Cusack (Capt. Gaff), Woody Harrelson (Sgt. Keck), Elias Koteas (Capt.
    Staros), Jared Leto (Lt. Whyte), Dash Mihok (Pvt. Doll), John D. Smith
    (Pvt. Train), Tim Blake Nelson (Pvt. Tills), Nick Nolte (Col. Tall), John
    C. Reilly (Sgt. Storm), Larry Romano (Pvt. Mazzi), John Savage (Sgt.
    McCron), John Travolta (Gen. Quintard), Arie Verveen (Pvt. Dale), Kirk
    Acevedo (Pvt. Tella)

Wise Blood (Anthea/Ithaca, 1979)
Director: John Huston

Producers: Hans Brockmann, Kathy Fitzgerald, Michael Fitzgerald, Wolfgang
   Limmer
Screenplay: Flannery O'Connor (novel), Benedict Fitzgerald, Michael
   Fitzgerald, John Huston (uncredeted)
Art director: Sally Fitzgerald
Director of photography: Gerry Fisher
Music: Alex North
Principal cast: Brad Dourif (Hazel Motes), John Huston (Grandfather), Dan
   Shor (Enoch Emory), Harry Dean Stanton (Asa Hawks), Amy Wright
   (Sabbath Lily), Mary Nell Santacroce (Mrs. Flood), Ned Beatty (Hoover
   Shoates), William Hickey (Solace Mayfield)

Index